THE ARTHRITIS
HELPBOOK

THE ARTHRITIS HELPBOOK

A Tested Self-Management Program for Coping with Your Arthritis

Third Edition

Kate Lorig, R.N., Dr.P.H.
Director, Patient Education Research
Stanford Arthritis Center

James F. Fries, M.D.
Associate Professor of Medicine
Stanford University School of Medicine

Contributors		
Maureen R. Gecht, O.T.R./L.	Occupational Therapist
Lynn A. Kaplan, O.T.R./L.	Occupational Therapist
Dennis M. Keane, M.P.H.	Health Educator
Marian Minor, R.P.T., Ph.D.	Physical Therapist
Ingrid Sausjord, M.P.H.	Nutritionist
Nancy L. Brannigan	Illustrator

ADDISON-WESLEY PUBLISHING COMPANY, INC.
Reading, Massachusetts • Menlo Park, California • New York
Don Mills, Ontario • Wokingham, England • Amsterdam • Bonn
Sydney • Singapore • Tokyo • Madrid • San Juan • Paris
Seoul • Milan • Mexico City • Taipei

Many of the designations used by manufacturers and sellers to distinguish their products are claimed as trademarks. Where those designations appear in this book and Addison-Wesley was aware of a trademark claim, the designations have been printed in initial capital letters (e.g., Tylenol, Water-Pik). Aspirin is a registered trademark in Canada.

This book is not meant to replace medical care. If you are under the care of a doctor and other health professionals, follow their advice first. Read medicine labels carefully because instructions may vary from year to year. If any problem persists beyond a reasonable time, see a doctor.

Library of Congress Cataloging-in-Publication Data
Lorig, Kate.
    The arthritis helpbook.

  Includes bibliographical references and index.
  1. Arthritis—Popular works.   I. Fries, James F.
II. Title.   III. Title: Arthritis help book.
RC933.L628   1990   616.7'22   90-1197
ISBN 0-201-52403-1

Cover design by Steve Snider
Set in 10-point Melior by Compset, Inc., Beverly, MA

7 8 9 10 11 12-AL-95949392
Seventh printing, February 1992

To our more than 1,500 leaders
and to over 100,000
Arthritis Self-Help class participants
around the world

Contents

Acknowledgments

We would like especially to thank the Stanford Arthritis Center folks: Pat Spitz, Gene Fauro Pratt, Dee Simpson, Beth Kant, Audrey Schomer, R. Guy Kraines, Jim Standish, Alison Harlow, Cathy Williams, Dr. Dennis McShane, Dr. Jeffrey Brown, Dr. Cody Wasner, Dr. Paul Feigenbaum, Dr. Halsted Holman, Dr. Andrei Calin, Dr. Melvin Britton, Dr. Tom Okarma, Dr. William Lages, Dr. David Schurman, Patricia Schweikert, Pam Shelby, Wade Gray, Rebecca Pronchick, Catherine Regan, Diana Laurent, Virginia González, Connie Hartnett, and Jane Howard-McKellar.

The Midpeninsula Health Service people: Dr. Joseph Hopkins, Judy Staples, Jeanne Ewy, Virginia de Lemos, and Sally Semans.

The University of California at Berkeley Health Education Faculty: Dr. Robert Miller, Dr. Andrew Fisher, Dr. William Griffiths, Dr. Meredith Minkler, Dr. Carol D'Onofrio, and Dr. John Ratcliffe.

Significant others: Dr. Robert Swezey, John Staples, Donna Holsten, Dr. Lawrence Green, Dr. Sarah Archer, Janice Pigg, Dr. Floyd Pennington, Dr. Stan Shoor, Dr. Peter Wood, Melinda Seeger, Dr. Larry Bradley, Michele Boutaugh, Roseanne Glick, Dr. Ann O'Leary, Dr. B. Shapiro, and Gail Schreiber.

Many people have kindly agreed to review sections of this edition. Their comments have made us rethink and rewrite. To all of you, many thanks.

In addition, there are many people in all four countries who have written us and reviewed our materials.

Australian Reviewers
  Pauline Brooks, Physiotherapist M.C.S.P., Adelaide
  Elizabeth Couche, Perth
  Jenny Davidson, R. N., Melbourne
  Valerie Sayce, B.A., D.I.P., Physiotherapist, Melbourne

Canadian Reviewers
  Paul Adams, M.S.W., Vancouver
  Sally Frost, R.P.T., Vancouver
  Sherry Lynch, B.S.W., Vancouver
  Patrick McGowan, M.S.W., Vancouver
  Greg Taylor, B.S.W., Vancouver

New Zealand Reviewers
  Chree Barker, Auckland
  Gwynneth Carter, Physiotherapist, Wellington
  Nerida Miller, Napier
  Billie Sepsy, Dunedin

United States Reviewers
  Barbara F. Banwell, P.T., Ann Arbor
  Bruce F. Campbell, Ph.D., Palo Alto
  Jane A. Friedrich, San Jose
  Victoria Gall, R.P.T., M.Ed., Boston
  Virginia González, M.P.H., Stanford
  Kathleen M. Haralson, P.T., St. Louis
  Diana Laurent, M.P.H., Stanford
  Carolee Moncur, P.T., Ph.D., Salt Lake City
  Linda G. Price, M.A., Columbia

Finally, thanks to the many people coping with arthritis who have posed for the photos.

Preface

Before we start, we would like to say a little about how this book came to be written and what we have learned in the process.

In 1979 the Stanford Arthritis Center began giving lessons to persons with arthritis. (From the very beginning our class members told us that they did not want to be called "patients.") The classes were taught by forty people from our community who have arthritis or who are interested in arthritis. With a few exceptions, the teachers were not health professionals. The Arthritis Center staff worked with the teachers, and the lay teachers led the classes.

Our arthritis education classes use the same principles we presented earlier in *Take Care of Yourself, Taking Care of Your Child, Arthritis: A Comprehensive Guide*, and, most recently, *Aging Well*. They have benefited greatly from the many thousands of encouraging letters and helpful suggestions we have received. In these classes we are not concerned solely with improving knowledge. We also seek to help persons with arthritis change their activities and abilities, decrease their pain, and most importantly, develop more confidence in themselves as caretakers for their bodies.

In our classes we emphasize three concepts:

1. Each person with arthritis is different. There is no one treatment that is right for everyone.

2. There are a number of things people can do to feel better. These things will not cure most kinds of arthritis, but they will help to relieve pain, maintain or increase mobility, and prevent deformity.

3. With knowledge, each individual is the best judge of which self-management techniques are best for him or her.

Therefore, this book was developed to give details about a variety of self-management treatments. We felt that it was not enough just to know that you should exercise. Instead, you must know about particular exercises, types of exercise, when to exercise, and how much to exercise. You need to understand the relationship between exercise and pain. The same considerations hold for what you need to know about relaxation, nutrition, problem solving, and all other self-management techniques. In *Arthritis: A Comprehensive Guide* we provided all the factual knowledge about arthritis. In this companion volume we try to help you use the information. This is a how-to-do-it book that has been developed with the help of many people very much like you.

When our class members first used this book they liked it but were quick to point out its faults: a neck exercise that caused too much pain, a nutrition section that was unclear, omission of a section on sleep disturbances, and so forth. Taking these suggestions we have added, revised, clarified, re-used, re-revised in a continuing cycle that has resulted in this present edition.

While only seven names appear on the title page as authors and contributors, this book was really written and guided by you, people with arthritis. As of late 1990, more than 100,000 people have attended these classes and used this book. From all of them we have gained insights that we hope will be helpful to you.

All these people helped us in other ways, too. We have been carefully studying the effect of our classes on the way people get along with their arthritis, and our class members have served as the subjects for these studies. In effect, we "drew straws" to see which of the subjects on the waiting list would attend the next set of classes and which would have to wait four months. Then we compared how the people who went to the classes did with how the people on the waiting list did. Data from long questionnaires went into the computer, and after elaborate analyses we found what we had suspected all along.

People who become good arthritis self-managers have less pain and are more active than those people who feel there is nothing they can do for themselves. These were among the first controlled studies that have ever been done relating education programs in arthritis to outcomes, and they are very encouraging. The bottom line is that arthritis self-managers feel better! We would like to help you become an arthritis self-manager.

Now a few words of caution. First, you did not get stiff, painful joints overnight. Therefore, relief will not come quickly. Self-management is in no way a quick cure; it is a way of life to be practiced every day for the rest of your life. However, it is never too late to start. Our oldest self-manager was 100 when she first came to class.

Second, not everything works for everyone. Experiment, but give each activity two weeks to a month for first results. Don't give up too soon. If one thing does not work for you, try another.

This book is not meant to replace medical care. Rather, it is a supplement to that care. Most doctors do not have or do not take the time to explain exercises or pain-management techniques in enough detail to help you very much. Therefore, we are hopeful that this book will assist both you and your physician. All of the advice and activities that we describe have been reviewed by many, many doctors, physical therapists, occupational therapists, nutritionists, and nurses, including the entire staff of the Stanford Arthritis Center. They represent a sound program essentially the same as that recommended by most health authorities today. If you have particular questions please talk them over with your doctor.

Finally, if you are reading this book after the year 2000, the information is probably somewhat out of date. Things do change. Check with your bookseller or library to find out if there is a more recent edition of this *Helpbook* available.

We would like you to feel that you are part of our cast of thousands. If you have comments or suggestions please send them to us by writing:

750 Welch Rd., Suite 315
Palo Alto, CA 94304
U.S.A.

Your suggestions will be reviewed and considered for our next edition. To all of you who helped in the past and whom we couldn't name, many thanks, and to those of you who are just joining, a hearty welcome.

Stanford, California   K. L.
May 1990   J. F. F.

1

Arthritis
What Is It?

Arthritis. The very word evokes a specter of fear and pain. People think of getting old, being unable to get around, and of becoming more dependent upon others. More so than with any other disease, the term *arthritis* carries with it a sense of hopelessness and futility. But the very opposite should be true. All arthritis can be helped.

In order to understand how to work with your arthritis, it is necessary to know a little about it. In fact, arthritis is not just a single disease. There are over 100 kinds of arthritis, all of which have something to do with one or more joints in the body. Even the word *arthritis* is misleading. The *arth* part comes from the Greek word meaning "joint," while *itis* means "inflammation or infection." Thus, the word *arthritis* means "inflammation of the joint." The problem is that in many kinds of arthritis, the joint is not inflamed. A better description might be "problems with the joint."

The next step is to understand what a joint looks like and what the various parts do.

A joint is a meeting of two bones for the purpose of allowing movement. It has the following six parts.

1. **Cartilage.** The end of each bone is covered with cartilage, a tough material that cushions and protects the ends of the bone. To get some idea

1

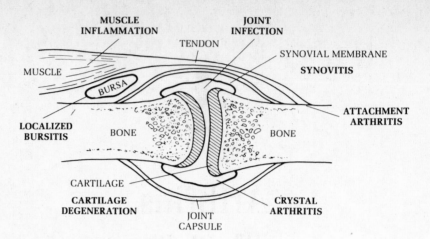

of what cartilage is like, feel the middle of your nose or your ears. These are also made of cartilage. Cartilage in meat is "gristle."

2. **Synovial membrane (synovial sac).** Around each joint is the synovial sac, which protects the joint and also secretes the synovial fluid, which oils the joint. In fact, this fluid has many times the lubricating power of oil.

3. **Bursa.** A bursa is a small sac that is not part of the joint but is near the joint. It contains a fluid that lubricates the movement of muscles: muscle across muscle and muscle across bones. In some ways it is similar to the synovial sac.

4. **Muscle.** The muscles are elastic tissues that, by becoming shorter and longer, move the bones and thus move you.

5. **Tendon.** The tendons are fibrous cords that attach the muscles to the bones. You can feel them on the back of your hand or in the back of your knee.

6. **Ligament.** The ligaments are much shorter fibrous cords that attach bone to bone and make up the joint capsules.

When someone says, "I have arthritis," it means that something is wrong with one or more of these parts. For example, when the synovial membrane becomes inflamed, this is true arthritis. That is, the joint is inflamed. However, if the muscle becomes stretched from overexercise or is injured, this is not arthritis. The joint itself is not affected.

In each major kind of arthritis, a different joint tissue is involved. In *rheumatoid arthritis*, the problem is chiefly "synovitis," that is, an inflammation of the synovial membrane. This inflammation must be reduced with medication in addition to your self-management program. In *ankylosing spondylitis*, the problem is an "enthesopathy," an inflammation where the ligaments attach to the bone. This inflammation also needs to be suppressed by medication, and the affected joints need to be regularly and vigorously stretched. In *osteoarthritis*, the problem is a breakdown of the joint cartilage, but it is helped by exercise and proper use of your joints. In *gout*, the problem is crystals which form in the joint space and cause inflammation and pain. Each kind of arthritis is different, and different treatment is needed.

Here is a quick overview of the two most common types of arthritis.

	Rheumatoid Arthritis	**Osteoarthritis**
Pathology: what happens	Inflammation of synovial membrane, bone destruction, damage to ligaments, tendons, cartilage, joint capsule	Cartilage degeneration; bone regeneration (spurs)
Joints Affected	Symmetrical: wrists, knees, knuckles (both sides)	Hands, spine, knees, hips. May be one-sided
Features and Symptoms	Swelling, redness, warmth, pain, tenderness, nodules, fatigue, stiffness, muscle aches, fever	Localized pain, stiffness; bony knobs of end joints of fingers; usually not much swelling
Long-term Prognosis	Less aggressive with time; deformity can often be prevented	Less pain for some, more pain and disability for others; few severely disabled
Age at Onset	Adults in 20s–50s, children approaching adolescence	Age 45–90. Most of us have some features with increasing age.
Sex	75% female, ½ of 1% of US population	Males and females equally.
Heredity	Familial tendency	The form with knobby fingers can be familial.
Tests	Rheumatoid factor (80%), blood tests, x-rays, examination of joint fluid	X-rays
Treatment	Reduce inflammation. Balanced exercise program, joint protection, weight control, relaxation, heat, sometimes medication and/or surgery	Maintain activity level. Exercise, joint protection, weight control, relaxation, heat, sometimes medication and/or surgery

While there are over 100 types of arthritis, we discuss in detail only the major types. If you are interested in knowing more about other types of arthritis, read *Arthritis: A Comprehensive Guide,* by Dr. James F. Fries (Reading, Mass.: Addison-Wesley, 1990).

References

Arthritis Foundation. *Understanding Arthritis: What It Is, How It's Treated, How to Cope With It.* ed. I. Kushner. New York: Scribner's, 1985.

Davidson, Paul. *Are You Sure It's Arthritis? A Guide to Soft-Tissue Rheumatism.* New York: New American Library, 1987.

Davidson, Paul. *Chronic Muscle Pain Syndrome.* New York: Villard, 1990.

Fries, James F. *Arthritis: A Comprehensive Guide to Understanding Your Arthritis.* 3rd ed. Reading, MA: Addison-Wesley, 1990.

2

Rheumatoid Arthritis
Inflamed Joints

Rheumatoid arthritis (RA) is more than just arthritis. Indeed, many doctors call it "rheumatoid disease" to emphasize its widespread nature. The name is trying awkwardly to say the same thing; *rheum* refers to the stiffness, body aching, and fatigue that often accompany rheumatoid arthritis. Persons with RA often describe feeling much like they have a virus, with fatigue and aching in the muscles, except that, unlike a usual viral illness, the condition may persist for months or even years.

About one-half of one percent of the population has rheumatoid arthritis, about twenty million people around the world. Most of these people (about three-quarters) are women. The condition usually appears in middle life, in the forties or fifties, although it can begin at any age. Rheumatoid arthritis in children is quite different. Rheumatoid arthritis has been medically identified for about 200 years, although bone changes in the skeletons of some Mexican Indian groups suggest that the disease may have been around for thousands of years.

Since RA is so common, and because it can sometimes be severe, it is a major international health problem. It can result in difficulties with employment, problems with daily activities, and can put a severe stress on family relationships. In its most severe forms, and without good treatment, it can result in deformities of the joints. Fortunately, most people with RA do better

5

than this, and most can lead normal lives. Fear of rheumatoid arthritis, sometimes greatly exaggerated, can be as harmful as the disease itself.

In RA, the synovial membrane lining in the joint becomes inflamed. We don't have a good explanation as to why this inflammation starts, but the cells in the membrane divide and grow, and inflammatory cells come into the joint. Because of the bulk of these inflammatory cells, the joint becomes swollen, and feels puffy or boggy to the touch. The increased blood flow that is a feature of the inflammation makes the joint warm. The cells release chemicals (called *enzymes*) into the joint space and the enzymes cause further irritation and pain. If the process continues for years, the enzymes may gradually digest the cartilage and bone of the joint, actually eating away parts of the bone.

This then is rheumatoid arthritis, a process in which inflammation of the joint membrane, over many years, can cause damage to the joint itself.

FEATURES

Swelling and pain in one or more joints, lasting at least six weeks, are required for a diagnosis of rheumatoid arthritis. Usually, both sides of the body are affected similarly, and the arthritis is said to be "symmetrical." Often there are slight differences between the two sides, usually the right side being slightly worse in right-handed people and vice versa. Occasionally the condition skips about in an erratic fashion. The wrists and knuckles are almost always involved. The knees and the joints of the ball of the foot are often involved as well, and any joint can be affected. Of the knuckles, those at the base of the fingers are most frequently painful, while the joints at the ends of the fingers are often normal.

Lumps, usually between the size of a pea and a mothball, may form beneath the skin. These *rheumatoid nodules* are most commonly located near the elbow at the place where you rest your arms on the table, but they can pop up anywhere. Each represents an inflammation of a small blood vessel. They come and go during the course of the illness and usually are not a big problem. They do tend to occur in people with the most severe kinds of RA. In rare cases, they become sore or infected, particularly if they are located around the ankle. Even more rarely, they form in the lungs or elsewhere in the body.

Laboratory tests can sometimes help a doctor recognize rheumatoid arthritis. The *rheumatoid factor* or *latex fixation* is the most commonly used blood test. Although this test may be negative in the first several months, it is eventually positive in about 80 percent of persons with RA. The rheumatoid factor is actually an antibody to certain body proteins and can sometimes be found in individuals with other diseases. Some doctors think that it is a way the body fights the disease; others think that it may play a role in causing the joint damage.

The *sed rate* is another frequently used blood test. This test is called in full an *erythrocyte sedimentation rate*, and the name sometimes is abbreviated ESR. It doesn't help in diagnosis, but it does help tell the severity of the disease. A high sed rate (over 30 or so) suggests that the disease is quite active. The joint fluid is sometimes examined in rheumatoid arthritis in order to look at the inflammatory cells or to make sure that the joint is not infected with bacteria.

X-rays are not very helpful in the initial diagnosis of rheumatoid arthritis. It is unusual for changes to be seen in the bones or cartilage in the first few months of the disease, even when it is most severe. X-rays can help the doctor determine if damage to the bones or cartilage has occurred as the disease progresses. Some doctors like to get baseline X-rays to compare with later X-rays. Simple hand X-rays probably should be done in the first year of disease and every two or three years thereafter.

Most people with RA notice problems in parts of their bodies other than the joints themselves. Usually, these are general problems such as muscle aches, fatigue, muscle stiffness (particularly in the morning), and even a low fever. Morning stiffness is often considered a hallmark of RA and is sometimes termed the *gel phenomenon*. After a rest period or even after just sitting motionless for a few minutes, the whole body feels stiff and is difficult to move. After a period of loosening up, motion becomes easier and less painful. People often have problems with fluid accumulation, particularly around the ankles. Occasionally, the rheumatoid disease may attack other body tissues, including the whites of the eyes, the nerves, the small arteries, and the lungs. Anemia (low red blood cell count) is quite common, although it is seldom severe enough to need any treatment. Some patients will develop *Sjögren's disease*, or sicca syndrome, in which the tear fluids and the saliva dry up, causing dry eyes and dry mouth. This happens because the lacrimal (tear) glands and the salivary glands become involved in the rheumatoid process.

There can be unusual features due to the inflammation of the joint membrane. A *Baker's cyst* can form behind the knees and may feel like a tumor. It is just the synovial sac full of fluid, but it can extend down into the back of the calf and may cause pain. Or, the fluid in the joint can become infected and require immediate treatment. Suspect this if a single joint, usually a knee, becomes suddenly and severely worse.

Rheumatoid arthritis is one of the most complicated and mysterious diseases known. It is a challenge to patient and physician alike. Fortunately, the course of RA can be dramatically changed in most individuals. More so than with any other form of arthritis, if you have RA you need to develop an effective partnership with your doctor, as discussed in Chapter 18.

PROGNOSIS (THE FUTURE OF THE DISEASE)

Rheumatoid arthritis is the condition that most people think of when they hear the word *arthritis*. An image that comes to mind is of a person in a wheelchair, with swollen knees and twisted hands. True, most such people have rheumatoid arthritis. On balance, rheumatoid arthritis is the most destructive kind of arthritis known. Erosion of the bone itself, rupture of tendons, and slippage of the joints can result in crippling. But most people with rheumatoid arthritis do very much better than this. And it is probable that many of the serious problems could have been prevented by good, early treatment.

Often it is hard for persons with RA and their relatives to appreciate that inflammation in even the worst forms of rheumatoid arthritis tends to lessen with time. The arthritis usually becomes less aggressive. The inflammation (synovitis) is less active and the fatigue and stiffness decrease. New joints are less likely to become involved after several years of disease. But even though the disease is less violent, any destruction of bones and ligaments that occurred in earlier years will persist. Thus deformities usually will not improve, even though no new damage is occurring. Hence, it is important to treat the disease correctly in the early years so that the joints will work well after the disease activity subsides.

TREATMENT

Treatment programs for rheumatoid arthritis are often complicated and can be very confusing. In this section we give the broad outlines for sound management. But you need to work out with your doctor the combination of measures that is best for you. It has been said that the person who has himself for a doctor has a fool for a patient. In many areas of medicine, and for some kinds of arthritis, this is not true—you can do just as well looking out for yourself. But with rheumatoid arthritis you do need a doctor. Indeed, if your rheumatoid arthritis is at all severe, you may want to be seen, at least occasionally, by a specialist in arthritis, a *rheumatologist.*

First, some common sense. Your rheumatoid arthritis may be with you, on and off, for months or years. The best treatments are those that will help you maintain a life that is as nearly normal as possible. Often the worst treatments are those that offer immediate relief. They may allow joint damage to progress or may cause delayed side effects that ultimately make you feel worse. So you must develop some patience with the disease and with its management. You have to adjust your thinking to operate in the same slow time scale that the disease uses. You and your doctor will want to be anticipating problems before they occur so that they may be avoided. The adjustment to a long-term illness, with the necessity to plan treatment programs that may take months to get results, is a difficult psychological task. It is easy to understand in principle but hard to put into daily action. This adjustment will be one of your hardest jobs in battling your arthritis.

Synovitis is the underlying problem. The inflammation of the joint membrane releases enzymes that very slowly damage the joint structures. Good treatment reduces this inflammation and stops the damage. Painkillers can increase comfort but do not decrease the arthritis. In fact, pain per se helps to protect the joints by discouraging too much use. Therefore, in RA it is important to treat pain by treating the inflammation that causes the pain. By and large, pain relievers such as codeine, Percodan, Darvon, or Demerol must be avoided. (To learn more, read Chapter 17.)

The proper balance between rest and exercise is hard to understand. Rest reduces the inflammation, and this is good. But rest also lets joints get stiff and muscles get weak. With too much rest, tendons become less strong and bones get softer. Obviously, this is bad. So moderation is the basic principle. It may help you to know that your body usually gives you the right signals about what to do and what not to do. If it hurts too much, don't do it. If you don't seem to have much problem with an activity, go ahead. As a general rule, if you continue to have exercise-caused pain for more than two hours after exercising, you have done too much.

A particularly painful joint may require a splint to help it rest. Still, you will want to exercise the joint by stretching it gently in different directions to keep it from getting stiff. You will not want to use a splint for too long, or you may want to use it just at night. As the joint gets better you will want to begin using the joint, gently at first but slowly progressing to more and more activity. In general, favor activities that build good muscle tone, not those that build great muscle strength. Walking and swimming are better than furniture moving and weight lifting, since tasks requiring a lot of strength put a lot of stress across the joint. And regular exercises done daily are better than occasional sprees of activity that unduly stress joints not ready for so much exertion.

Common sense and a regular, long-term program are the keys to success. Should you take a nap after lunch? Yes, if you're tired. Should you undertake some particular outing? Go on a trip? You know your regular daily activity level. Common sense will answer most such questions. Full normal activity should be approached gradually with a long-term conditioning program that includes rest when needed and gradual increases in activity during nonresting periods.

Physical therapists and occupational therapists can often help with specific advice and helpful hints. The best therapists will help you develop your own program for home exercise and will teach you the exercises and activities that will help your joints. However, don't expect the therapist to do your program for you. Your rest and exercise program cannot consist solely of formal sessions at a rehabilitation facility. You must take the responsibility to build the habits that will, on a daily basis, protect and strengthen your joints. It is important to start exercise and proper use of your joints before you have problems. These are good preventive measures.

Medications are required by most persons with rheumatoid arthritis and often must be continued for months or years. Every person with arthritis should know all about Aspirin. Aspirin is a strong anti-inflammatory drug with an acceptable level of side effects. It is very helpful when used correctly.

Drugs roughly similar to Aspirin are called *nonsteroidal anti-inflammatory drugs* and are very frequently used. Examples of such drugs are Motrin, Nalfon, Tolectin, Naprosyn, and Indocin. (For more information, see Chapter 17.) These drugs are important, but are not central to arthritis management since they do not affect the underlying course of the disease. They are symptomatic medications and serve as adjuncts to the more important medical treatments. Nonsteroidal drugs can have serious gastro-intestinal side effects.

There are now eight medications available (hydroxychloroquine, auranofin, sulfasalazine, gold salts, d-penicillamine, methotrexate, azathioprine, and cyclophosphamide) that are effective at modifying rheumatoid arthritis when used early in the course of the disease. In the past, these drugs were used only after damage had occurred, and they were less effective. It is now thought that treatment with these drugs is best begun in the first few months of active disease, though they can be beneficial at almost any point. This new thinking is incorporated throughout this edition of the *Helpbook*. While all drugs have side effects, these drugs (excepting cyclophosphamide) have reasonable safety profiles, and the ratio of effectiveness to toxicity is good. Usually, each is effective only for a period of months to a few years, so they are used sequentially and sometimes in combination. More such medications are under development. (For more information, see Chapter 17.)

Corticosteroids, most frequently prednisone, are strong hormones with dangerous long-term side effects. Their use in rheumatoid arthritis is controversial; some physicians feel they should almost never be used, and others use them, but only in very small doses. They are now again being used more frequently, but cautiously.

Surgery sometimes can restore the function of a damaged joint. Hip replacement, knee replacement, and synovectomy (removal of the joint membrane) are the most common operations. (See Chapter 18.)

3

Osteoarthritis

Osteoarthritis (osteoarthrosis, OA, degenerative joint disease, DJD) is the kind of arthritis that everybody gets. It is a practically universal problem, increasing with age, and one that, because of its relationship to the aging process, is not as responsive to medical treatment as we might like. However, there are many things you can do for yourself to alleviate this disease. Fortunately, osteoarthritis usually is a relatively mild condition. Osteoarthritis is a much less severe form of arthritis than rheumatoid arthritis. In other words, the changes in the skeleton that occur with age are inevitable, but they cause symptoms in a minority of people and severe symptoms in very few.

Osteoarthritis used to be thought of as the inevitable result of "wear and tear." In fact, most activities with a lot of "wear" don't seem to cause much "tear," and authorities now recognize the need for exercise to strengthen the joints, both before and after signs of arthritis have developed.

The tissue involved in osteoarthritis is the cartilage. This is the gristle material that faces the ends of the bones and forms the surface of the joint on both sides. Gristle is tough, somewhat elastic, and very durable. The cartilage or gristle does not have a blood supply, so it gets its oxygen and nutrition from the surrounding joint fluid. In this it is aided by being elastic and by being able to absorb fluid. When we use a joint, the pressure squeezes fluid and waste products out of the cartilage, and when the pressure is relieved, the fluid seeps back, together with oxygen and nutrients. Hence, the

11

health of the cartilage depends on use of the joint. Over many years, the cartilage may become frayed and may even wear away entirely. When this happens, the bone surface on one side of the joint grates against the bone on the other side of the joint, providing a much less elastic joint surface. With time, the opposing bony surfaces may become polished, a process called *eburnation*. As this happens, the joint may again move more smoothly and cause less discomfort. This is one of the reasons it is important to continue to use painful joints.

Osteoarthritis is sometimes called *osteoarthrosis*. The difference between these two terms has to do with the question of inflammation. The suffix *-itis* denotes inflammation, and with osteoarthritis very little inflammation is to be found. Hence, some experts prefer osteoarthrosis, which does not imply inflammation. Both words mean the same.

There are three common types of osteoarthritis. The first and mildest causes knobby enlargement of the finger joints. The end joints of the fingers become bony and the hands begin to assume the appearance we associate with old age. The other joints of the fingers may also be involved. This kind of arthritis (or arthrosis) usually causes little difficulty beyond the cosmetic. There may be some stiffness.

The second form of osteoarthritis involves the spine and is sometimes called *degenerative joint disease*. Bony growths (spurs) appear on the spine in the neck region or in the low back. Usually the bony growths are associated with some narrowing of the space between the vertebrae. This time the disc rather than cartilage is the material that becomes frayed. Changes in the spine begin early in life in almost all of us, but cause symptoms relatively seldom.

The third form of osteoarthritis involves the weight-bearing joints, almost always the hips and knees. These problems can be quite severe. It is possible to have all three kinds of osteoarthritis or any two of them, but often a person will have only one.

Individuals who have had fractures near a joint or have a congenital malformation at a joint seem to develop osteoarthritis in those joints at an earlier age. But, as noted, the usual description of this arthritis as "wear and tear" is not accurate. While excessive wear and tear on the joint can theoretically result in damage, activity helps the joint remain supple and lubricated, and this tends to cancel out the theoretically bad effects.

Careful studies of people who regularly put a lot of stress on joints (such as individuals who operate pneumatic drills or run long distances on hard paved surfaces) have been unable to show a relationship between these activities and the development of arthritis. Hence, intensive activity does not predispose you to arthritis any more than intensive activity predisposes you to heart disease. In fact, the very opposite may be true.

FEATURES

The bony knobs that form around the end joints of the fingers are called *Heberden's nodes* after the British doctor who first described them. In the middle joints of the fingers, similar knobs can be found. Usually, the bony enlargement occurs slowly over a period of years and is not even noticed. In most cases, all of the fingers are involved more or less equally.

Osteoarthritis of the spine does not cause symptoms unless there is pressure on one of the nerves or irritation of some of the other structures of the back. If someone tells you that you have arthritis in your spine, do not assume that the pain you feel is necessarily related to that arthritis. Most people with X-rays showing arthritis of the spine do not have any problem at all.

Osteoarthritis of the weight-bearing joints, particularly the hip and knee, develops slowly and often involves both sides of the body. Pain in the joint may remain fairly constant or may wax and wane over a period of years. In severe cases walking may be difficult or even impossible. Fluid may accumulate in the affected joint, giving it a swollen appearance, or a knee may wobble a bit when weight is placed on it. Usually, in the knee, the osteoarthritis will affect the inner or the outer half of the joint more than the other; this may result in the leg becoming bowed or splayed and may cause difficulty in walking.

X-rays can be helpful in evaluating osteoarthritis. The two major findings on the X-ray are narrowing of the joint space and the presence of bony spurs. X-rays pass right through cartilage. Hence, in a normal joint the X-ray looks as though the two bones are separated by a space. In reality, the apparent space is filled with cartilage. As the cartilage is frayed, the apparent joint space on the X-ray narrows until the two bones may touch each other. *Osteophytes*, or spurs, are little bone growths that appear alongside the places where the cartilage has degenerated. It is as though the body is trying to react to a cartilage problem by providing more surface area for the joint, so as to distribute the weight more evenly. The bony growth provides a larger joint surface, although the new bone is not covered by cartilage. In addition, X-rays can sometimes show the holes through which the nerves pass and indicate whether these holes are narrowed or not.

In contrast to X-rays, blood tests are not very helpful in diagnosing osteoarthritis. There is not anything wrong with the rest of the body, so all the tests are normal.

PROGNOSIS (THE FUTURE OF THE DISEASE)

Prognosis is good to excellent for all forms of osteoarthritis. When you think of an aging process, you tend to think of a progressive condition that will continue to get worse and worse. That is not necessarily the case. Osteoarthritis may get worse for a while and then become stable for a long time. A joint that has lost its cartilage may not function well at first, but with use the bone may be molded and polished so that a smooth and more functional joint is developed. Even in the worst cases, osteoarthritis progresses slowly. You have lots of time to think about what kinds of treatment are likely to help. If a surgical decision is needed, you can consider for some time whether you want an operation or not. Crippling from osteoarthritis is relatively rare, and most persons with osteoarthritis can remain essentially free of symptoms.

TREATMENT

The revolution in thinking here emphasizes the role of exercise. The consequence of osteoarthritis can be loss of physical functional ability. Because of pain, you tend to be less active, and this accelerates the loss of function. People used to be told to "take it easy." Now, it is recognized that even the first symptoms of osteoarthritis are a signal for a regular, dedicated exercise program to increase heart, muscle, ligament, tendon, and bone strength.

Joints should be exercised through their full range of motion several times a day. If weight-bearing joints are involved, body weight should be kept under control; obesity accelerates the rate of damage. The most helpful exercises seem to be swimming, walking, and bicycling, which are easy, can be gradually increased, and are smooth rather than jerky. Exercise should be regular. Thus, if you start getting some osteoarthritis, it is not a signal to begin to tune down your life, but rather to develop a sensible regular exercise program to strengthen the bones and ligaments surrounding the affected joints and to preserve mobility in joints that are developing spurs. (For details, see Chapter 7.)

Drug therapy is much less important. We use it to control the discomfort to a certain extent. Aspirin in moderate doses (or acetaminophen, such as Tylenol) is frequently helpful. Indomethacin and other anti-inflammatory drugs may be helpful for some people, particularly if the osteoarthritis is in the hip or the knee. We try to avoid codeine or other strong pain relievers because pain is a signal to the body that helps protect a diseased joint; it is important that this signal is received. (For details, see Chapter 17.)

Frequently some kinds of devices can assist. A cane may be helpful; less commonly, crutches are needed. Occasionally, special shoes or lifts on one side of the foot may be helpful.

Most physicians now believe that osteoarthritis may be substantially prevented by good health habits. If you are active, maintain a lean body weight, exercise your muscles and joints regularly to nourish cartilage, and let your common sense tell you when you have done too much and something hurts, your joints should last a lifetime. Like exercise of the heart muscle, exercise of the muscles and joints provides reserve for the occasional strenuous activities we all encounter. Exercise builds strong tissues that last a long time.

Injection of osteoarthritic joints with corticosteroids is occasionally helpful, and sometimes removal of some fluid from a joint may help. Unfortunately, injections usually do not help much since there is not much inflammation to be suppressed. Injections should not be frequently repeated, because the injection itself may damage the cartilage and the bone.

Surgery can be dramatically effective for persons with severe osteoarthritis of the weight-bearing joints. Total hip replacement is the most important operation yet devised for any form of arthritis. Practically all individuals are free of pain after the surgery and many walk normally and carry out normal activities. The total knee replacement is a more recent operation which gives far better results than the knee surgery available just a few years ago. Surgery is never urgent, and you and your doctor will want to decide when the discomfort or the limitation of your walking has become bad enough to warrant the discomfort, costs, and small risk associated with the operation. (For more information on surgery, see Chapter 18.)

4

Osteoporosis

Osteoporosis is a bone disease in which the bones lose calcium, become more brittle, and break more easily. While anyone can have osteoporosis, it is most common in elderly people, particularly women. Because of osteoporosis, one in five women breaks a hip before the age of seventy-five. Inactivity makes osteoporosis worse.

Thankfully, we now have treatments for osteoporosis and ideas about ways to prevent it. As with all kinds of arthritis, consistent good health practices are crucial. The following pages outline the healthy habits that are useful in preventing and dealing with osteoporosis.

DIETARY CALCIUM

Our bones cannot maintain their strength unless our bodies regularly receive an adequate supply of calcium. Most adults should consume at least 800 milligrams (mg) of calcium every day. Higher amounts (1,500 mg a day) may be even better, especially for young adults, pregnant and nursing women, women who are past menopause, and men over the age of sixty-five. Unfortunately, many of us take in considerably less than the recommended amount of calcium.

To bring your calcium intake up to 800 or 1,000 mg, eat two or three servings of milk products a day (nonfat milk is best) and regularly include other calcium-rich foods in your meals. Also, try to moderate the amount of salt and meat you eat. (Chapter 16 discusses how to do this.) Excessive amounts of sodium or meat can increase your need for calcium.

The accompanying chart gives you a good idea of the types of food that are relatively rich in calcium. Notice that you can get significant quantities of calcium without drinking milk. Yogurts, cheeses, and hot cereals made with milk all supply calcium. Canned salmon, mackerel, and sardines are excellent sources of calcium *if* you eat the soft bones.

FOOD SOURCES OF CALCIUM

Food	Amount	Calcium (approx)	Calories (approx)
Low-fat and Nonfat Milk Products*			
Nonfat milk	1 cup (235 mL)	300 mg	85
Low-fat milk (1% fat)	1 cup (235 mL)	300 mg	100
Low-fat milk (2% fat)	1 cup (235 mL)	295 mg	120
Nonfat dry milk powder	3 tbsp (45 mL)	280 mg	80
Nonfat yogurt (plain)	1 cup (235 mL)	450 mg	125
Low-fat yogurt (plain)	1 cup (235 mL)	415 mg	145
Low-fat cottage cheese (2% fat)	1 cup (235 mL)	155 mg	205
Part-skim ricotta cheese	½ cup (120 mL)	335 mg	170
Part-skim mozzarella	2 oz (56 g)	365 mg	145
Full-fat Milk Products			
Whole milk (3.5% fat)	1 cup (235 mL)	290 mg	150
Whole-milk yogurt (plain)	1 cup (235 mL)	275 mg	140
Swiss cheese	1 oz (28 g)	270 mg	105
Processed Swiss cheese	1 oz (28 g)	220 mg	95
Cheddar cheese	1 oz (28 g)	205 mg	115
Processed American cheese	1 oz (28 g)	125 mg	105
Ice milk (hard, not soft-serve)	1 cup (235 mL)	175 mg	185
Ice cream (regular, 10% fat)	1 cup (235 mL)	175 mg	270
Ice cream (rich, 16% fat)	1 cup (235 mL)	150 mg	350
Other Calcium-Rich Foods			
Almonds	1 oz (28 g)	75 mg	165
Broccoli (boiled)	1 cup (235 mL)	180 mg	45
Corn tortilla	1	40 mg	65
Great northern beans (boiled)	1 cup (235 mL)	120 mg	210
Kale (boiled)	1 cup (235 mL)	95 mg	40
Navy beans (boiled)	1 cup (235 mL)	130 mg	260
Pinto beans (boiled)	1 cup (235 mL)	80 mg	235
Tofu (soybean curd)	½ cup (120 mL)	130 mg	95
Canned jack mackerel (eaten with bones in)	½ cup (120 mL)	230 mg	150
Canned salmon (including bones)	3 oz (84 g)	190 mg	125
Canned sardines (including bones)	1 oz (28 g)	85 mg	55

*For most people, low-fat and nonfat dairy products are better choices than full-fat products. See Chapter 16.

SUPPLEMENTAL CALCIUM

It is better to get calcium from your foods than to rely on calcium supplements. But if you cannot eat two or more servings of dairy products every day, or if you want to take in more than 1,000 mg of calcium, supplements can provide practical help.

Chapter 16 explains how to choose a calcium supplement and some important precautions to observe. In general, choose a supplement that contains between 500 and 1,000 mg of "elemental calcium" (50 to 100 percent of the recommended daily allowance). Take one or two full doses a day, depending on your needs, not more.

As the charts illustrate, the elemental calcium in a supplement can come from any of several different calcium compounds. Less expensive "store-brand" supplements are usually fine; use the product that suits you best. Sometimes inexpensive calcium tablets won't dissolve in your stomach, however, so try this test. Put a tablet in half a glass of water for thirty minutes. It should become shaggy and partly dissolve. If not, fill the glass the rest of the way with vinegar, stir gently, and wait another half-hour. If the tablet is still not dissolved, it is not a good product for you.

Sources of Supplemental Calcium	Elemental Calcium Content
Calcium carbonate (in oyster shell calcium, BioCal, Caltrate 600, OsCal, Tums)	40%
Calcium citrate (in CitraCal)	21%
Calcium lactate (available in store-brand products)	13%

COST OF 500 MG CALCIUM FROM SUPPLEMENTS
(In the U.S. as of Fall 1989)

Brand or Type of Supplement	Calcium Content (per tablet)	Cost of 500 mg Calcium
Oyster shell calcium (store brand)	500 mg	2¢
Calcium carbonate (store brand)	600 mg	3¢
Life-Line Cal-600	600 mg	6¢
Life-Line Oyster Shell Calcium	250 mg	6¢
Tums	200 mg	6¢
Calcium lactate (store brand)	84 mg	10¢
Caltrate 600	600 mg	10¢
BioCal	500 mg	11¢
OsCal 500 Chewable	500 mg	11¢
OsCal 250 + D	250 mg	13¢
OsCal 500	500 mg	13¢
CitraCal 1500 + D	315 mg	22¢
CitraCal 950	200 mg	24¢

MYTHS ABOUT CALCIUM

1. "Calcium causes bone spurs." Maintaining a calcium intake of 800 to 1,500 mg a day (or even much higher) will not cause bone spurs.

2. "Calcium causes kidney stones." While it is prudent to avoid calcium intakes that exceed 2,000 to 2,500 mg a day, consuming a total of 800 to 1,500 mg a day is unlikely to lead to kidney stones. If you have had kidney stones in the past, you should check with your doctor before starting a calcium supplement. Otherwise, just be sure to drink plenty of fluids whenever you take a calcium tablet.

3. "Calcium causes constipation." Large doses of calcium can cause constipation in some people. But the problem generally can be avoided by drinking plenty of fluids and eating foods high in fiber. See Chapter 16 for more information.

HORMONES

Calcium by itself will not stop bone loss. The body needs a stimulus to absorb the calcium and to get it into the bone. The two best stimuli are estrogen therapy for postmenopausal women and adequate weight-bearing exercise for everybody. The use of hormones such as estrogen after menopause has long been a topic of controversy. This is a subject every woman should discuss with her physician. The following discussion is to help you understand some of the issues.

There are two female hormones, estrogen and progestin. These hormones are normally created during the menstrual cycle. After menopause, their levels fall greatly. Taking supplemental estrogen after menopause seems to protect against osteoporosis. However, it is believed by some to increase the likelihood of endometrial cancer (cancer of the lining of the uterus). When progesterone is taken with the estrogen, this risk is greatly reduced, and the prevention of osteoporosis is increased. The decision to take no hormone, one hormone (either estrogen or progestin), or a combination of the two is a personal one and should be discussed with a physician. The correct treatment is still in debate, but more and more physicians are recommending estrogens for postmenopausal women.

EXERCISE

Weight-bearing exercise is most important in maintaining strong bones. The body reacts to such exercise by increasing the calcium content and thus the strength of the bones. Walking is the best example. If at all possible, walk half a mile to a mile (1 to 1½ km) a day. Even if this is unrealistic for you, remember that even a little weight-bearing exercise is important. Do as much as you can. For suggestions on developing a walking program, see Chapters 7 and 9. Recent research has shown that women need to walk four miles (6 km) a week to get maximal exercise benefit for osteoporosis prevention. This includes all the walking we do in our daily lives. (Note: Swimming is *not* a weight-bearing exercise.)

ACCIDENT PREVENTION

Unfortunately, it is not always possible to prevent osteoporosis or undo damage already done. Thus, accident avoidance is very important to prevent broken bones. The following are a few hints:

- Avoid throw rugs—they are slippery and have a bad habit of tripping the unwary.

- Be sure all stairs have a secure railing that is easy to grasp.

- If advised to do so by a health professional, use a cane, stick, or walker. Don't be ashamed; these can be real bone savers.

- Even if you don't usually use a cane, consider using one for getting up at night. This is a time when most of us may be easily unbalanced and a cane can help prevent bad spills.

- Watch for uneven walks, curbs, floors, and so on.

- Move the phone to a convenient place so you won't trip over the cord.

- Wear shoes that give good support.

- Use step stools that are stable and in good repair.

- Use nonskid mats in the bathtub and shower, and on the bathroom floor. Permanently install grab bars to wall or edge of tub.

- If you are unsteady on your feet, sit on a stool with nonskid feet when showering or bathing.

- Have light switches at the top and bottom of all stairs.

- Be careful not to hold your breath when you are on the toilet. This can cause you to pass out and fall.

In summary, there are four things you can do to help prevent and treat osteoporosis:

1. Do some weight-bearing exercises daily.

2. Using diet or a combination of diet and supplements, take 1,000 to 1,500 mg of elemental calcium daily.

3. If advised by your physician, take estrogen, progestin, or a combination of these hormones.

4. Make your home and other surroundings accident-safe.

5

Those Nagging Pains

Most of the problems we tend to call arthritis don't involve the joints and really aren't even diseases. This is good news. Painful local conditions involving only one or two parts of the body are almost always just an irritation or injury of that part. After that part is rested or fixed, everything is all right again. There is no crippling, no threat to life, no need for dangerous medications. Remember the basic principle: for a local problem use a local treatment. Very seldom will you want to take a medication by mouth for a pain in, say, an elbow.

There are a lot of names for these conditions—bursitis, low back strain, sciatica, metatarsalgia, Achilles tendinitis, heel-spur syndrome, sprained ankle, cervical neck strain, frozen shoulder, tennis elbow, housemaid's knee, carpal-tunnel syndrome, and others. Many people call all of these "bursitis," while doctors have other and fancier names for them. But they are all local conditions and are approached the same way. At first you don't even need a doctor for them, but if they don't respond after six weeks of self-treatment or seem alarmingly severe, be sure to see the doctor.

BURSITIS

A bursa is a small sac of tissue similar to the synovial tissue which lines the joints. The bursa sac contains a lubricating fluid, and the bursa is designed to ease the movement of muscle across muscle or muscle across bone. A

23

bursa does not connect to the joint space of the nearby joint but is a separate sac. In the grand scheme of things the bursa is just an annoying little body area, but bursae can be very painful when they become inflamed. Usually, only one or two will be inflamed at a time, but bursitis of over twenty bursae can occur, and the problems can come and go over the years.

"Housemaid's knee" is an outdated term for *prepatellar bursitis*, in which the bursa in front and just below the kneecap is inflamed. *Olecranon bursitis* occurs over the point of the elbow, and sometimes a fluid-filled sac is visible at that point. *Subdeltoid bursitis* occurs at the shoulder, or more precisely, on the outer part of the upper arm just below the shoulder.

Features

Bursitis is inflammation of a bursa and results in localized pain. Sometimes the pain is on both sides of the body, as with both knees. There is pain when the inflamed area is pressed, and heat and redness are common. If the bursa is located close enough to the skin, swelling can be seen. Many bursae, however, are buried deep between muscles.

Bursitis comes on relatively suddenly, from within hours to days. It frequently follows injury to the area, repeated pressure on the area, or overuse. In the shoulders, particularly, it may be associated with inflammation of the tendon and can be part of a "frozen shoulder" problem.

Prognosis

Almost all episodes of bursitis will subside within several days to several weeks, but may recur. If the process causing the bursitis is continued, the bursitis may persist, otherwise it follows a normal healing course over a period of from one week to ten days. Some people seem more prone to bursitis than others and have recurrent problems throughout their lives. If the affected part is held rigid, some permanent stiffness may result; otherwise no crippling whatsoever should result from bursitis.

Treatment

If the problem is tolerable, treat it with "tincture of time." Wait for the body to control and heal the process. Avoid the precipitating cause. Use drugs very sparingly; the process is local, so systemic drugs like Aspirin are not very helpful. Resting the part will speed the healing, and you may want to use a sling or other device to increase the rest. Gentle warmth provided by a heating pad or warm bath frequently makes the bursitis feel better. Additional techniques described in Chapter 10 may also be helpful.

Patience and avoidance of reinjury are the major tactics, but you should remain active. The affected area should be worked through its full range of motion two to four times a day, even if it is a bit tender, to prevent stiffness from developing. Continue to exercise other parts of the body regularly.

If the discomfort persists for a number of weeks despite the measures outlined above, see the doctor. Often, the doctor will recommend that you continue the same general measures discussed here. Alternatively, an anti-inflammatory drug may be prescribed; these help few people and are generally just a way of buying a little more patience from the patient. Finally, the doctor may inject the bursa with corticosteroids (see Chapter 17). These injections are usually successful and not overly painful. They are relatively free of side effects and most physicians feel that they are appropriate treatment for a local condition that is severe and persistent.

FIBROSITIS

Features

Fibrositis is a condition of widespread aches and pains which is very common but has only been recognized recently. People with arthritis often have a "fibrositic component" to their arthritis, and this is often relatively easy to treat, although pain medication does not help.

Prognosis

Fibrositis involves minor injuries of the muscles and joints, together with tension and stress. The muscles stay tense throughout the day and often even when you are asleep. This puts extra strain on the ligaments and results in pain, often severe and persistent for many months. Sleep is often disturbed. Points in the muscle or over the ligaments can be very sore when pressure is applied.

Treatment

The key to management of fibrositis is increased physical activity, together with relaxation techniques. The self-management techniques described in the next chapter are designed to help with any fibrositis problems you may have, as well as with arthritis.

GETTING OLD

Local injuries, like bursitis, are often dismissed as "just getting old, I guess." It is true that more older people than younger people have these problems, and they do have something to do with the way our bodies age.

But they do not need to happen. These problems are sometimes due to abuse of a body part, as in the traditional prepatellar bursitis from scrubbing floors on your knees. Much more frequently, however, they are due to disuse. In our society, as you get older you are expected to be less active. And then you get the kinds of health problems that happen to inactive people of all ages. The relationship between local problems and age is mostly accidental; it is really an association of local problems with inactivity.

So you need to be active. If your muscles are trim and in good tone, your heart and lungs are conditioned, your body weight is normal and constant at that level, and you have a regular exercise program, you will have far fewer of these problems, and your body will not grow old as rapidly. These measures will keep calcium in your bones, your bursae free and well lubricated, your tendons firm and strong, and your joint cartilage well nourished.

You can control a lot of the aging of your body. The worst mistake you can make is to consider bursitis or another local problem to be a signal to slow down. It is a signal to speed up, because your body is drifting out of condition. In Chapters 7, 8, and 9 we go through some of the exercises that can help.

6

Becoming an Arthritis Self-Manager

Self-management seems like a simple enough term, yet it needs some explaining. Both at home and in the business world the managers direct the show. They don't do everything themselves; they work with others, including consultants, to get the job done. What makes them managers is that they are responsible for making the decisions and making sure that these decisions are carried through. As an *arthritis self-manager*, your job is much the same. You gather information from friends, family, the Arthritis Foundation or Society, and written materials. You hire a consultant or a team of consultants: your physician, physical therapist, pharmacists, and other health professionals. Once they have given you their best advice, it is up to you to follow through. Arthritis, like diabetes and other chronic diseases, needs to be managed. Cures are usually not possible. However, your quality of life, and how you are affected by the disease, is very much up to you. Have you noticed that some people with severe physical problems get on very well, while others with lesser problems seem to give up on life? The difference is management style.

Being a good manager means working with others, discussing problems, and, most importantly, understanding that the management is a day-to-day job. This doesn't mean that all your decisions will be correct. Managing arthritis, like managing a family, is a complex undertaking. There are many

27

twists, turns, and mid-course corrections. By learning self-management skills you can ease the problems of living with arthritis.

The key to success in any undertaking is first learning a set of skills and then practicing them until they have been mastered. Children cannot read without first learning to recognize the letters of the alphabet. They then learn the sounds of combinations of letters. Later, they learn the meanings of simple words and phrases. It is only after years of practice and mastery that one is able to read a novel. Think about it. The same is true with almost everything we do, from baking a cake to driving a car to planting a garden. These tasks are all based on learning skills and mastering them. Success in arthritis self-management is the same. One needs to learn a set of skills and then to practice them daily until success is reached.

This book is full of skills that can help relieve some of the problems caused by arthritis. However, we have learned that knowing the skills is not enough. Most of us need a way of incorporating these skills into our daily lives. Unfortunately, whenever we try a new skill, the first attempts are clumsy and slow, and show few results. It is easier to return to our old ways than to continue to try to master new and sometimes difficult skills. One of the best ways to master new skills is through goal setting. In the following pages, we will try to outline some of the principles of goal setting. If you use these principles, the success of an arthritis self-management program is almost assured.

In arthritis, you are your own manager. Like any manager of an organization or household, you must

1. Decide what you want to accomplish (your long-term **goal**).

2. Determine the necessary **steps** to accomplish this goal.

3. Start making short-term plans (**contracts** with yourself).

4. **Carry out** your contracts.

5. **Check** the results.

6. Make mid-course **corrections** as needed.

GOALS

Deciding what you want to accomplish may be the easiest part of being a manager. Think of all the things you would like to do. One of our self-managers wanted to climb twenty steps to her daughter's home so she could join her family for a holiday meal. Another wanted to lose weight so a hip replacement would be possible. Still another wanted to be more socially active. In each case the goal was one that would take several weeks or even months to accomplish. In fact, one of the problems with goals is they often seem more like dreams. They are so far off that we don't even try to accomplish them. However, a good management program starts (but does not end) with goals. Take a moment now and write your goals here.

Goals:

1. _____

2. _____

3. _____

STEPS

There are many different ways to reach any specific goal. For example, our self-manager who wanted to climb twenty steps could start off with a slow-walking program, knee-strengthening exercises, learning how to use a cane, or starting to climb a few stairs each day. The man who wanted to lose weight could decide not to eat between meals, to give up desserts, to cut down on fried foods, or to start an exercise program. The self-manager who wanted more social contact could find out about community college classes, church groups, or other organizations, or could call or write friends, or maybe find out about organized trips. As you can see, there are many options for reaching each goal. The job here is to list the options and then choose one or two on which you would like to work. Write the options for each of your goals here. Put a star next to those on which you would like to work:

Options:

1. _____

2. _____

3. _____

4. _____

5. _____

CONTRACTS

A short-term plan, which we will call a contract, calls for a specific action that you can realistically expect to accomplish within the next week. This is probably your most important self-management tool. Most of us can do things that would make us healthier but often fail to do them. For example, most people with arthritis can walk: some just across the room, others for half a block. Most can walk several blocks, and some can walk a mile (1½ km) or more. However, few people have a systematic exercise program, even though they know it would be good for them. A contract helps us to do the things we know we should. Let us go through all the steps for making a realistic contract. This is a very important skill and may well determine the success of your self-management program.

First, decide what you will do this week. For our step climber this might be climbing three steps on four days. The man trying to lose weight may decide not to eat between meals for three days. This action must be something that you want to do, that you feel you realistically can do, and that is a step on the way to your long-term goal.

Then make a specific plan. This is the most difficult and important part of making a contract. Deciding what you want to do is worthless without a plan to do it. The plan should contain all of the following steps.

1. Exactly what is it that you are going to do? For example, how far will you walk, how will you eat less, what pain-management technique will you practice?

2. How much will you do? For example, walk around the block, walk for fifteen minutes, climb three stairs, write letters to two friends.

3. When will you do this? Again, this must be specific: before lunch, in the shower, when I come home from work. Connecting a new activity with an old habit is a good way to be sure it gets done.

4. How often will you do the activity? This is a bit tricky. We would all like to do things every day. However, we are human and this is not always possible. It is usually best to contract to do something three or four times a week. If you do more, so much the better. However, if you are like most of us, you can do your activity three or four times and still succeed at your contract.

In writing your contract there are a couple of rules that may help you toward success. First, start where you are or start slowly. If you can walk around the block, start your walking program with walking around the block, not with walking a kilometer or mile. If you have never done any exercise for arthritis, start with just a few minutes of warm-up, endurance, and cool-down exercises. A total of five to ten minutes is enough. If you want to lose weight, set a goal based on your eating behaviors, such as not eating after dinner. See Chapter 7 for help in starting an exercise program and Chapter 16 for more information on diet and nutrition.

Also, give yourself some time off. All people have days when they don't feel like doing anything. Therefore, it is best to say that you will do something three to five times a week but not every day. That way, if you don't feel like walking one day, you can still meet your contract.

Once you've made your contract, ask yourself the following question: "On a scale of 0 to 100, with 0 being totally unsure and 100 being totally certain, how certain am I that I can complete all of this contract?"

If your answer is 70 or above, this is probably a realistic contract. Congratulate yourself, you have done the hard work. If your answer is below 70, then you should reassess your contract. Ask yourself what makes you uncertain. What problems do you foresee? Then see if you can either solve the problems or change your contract to make yourself more certain of success.

Once you have made a contract you are happy with, write it down on a contract form and post this sheet where you will see it every day. Keep track of how you are doing and the problems you encounter. Page 33 is an example of a contract sheet. You may want to make copies of this, since you will be making contracts weekly.

CARRYING OUT YOUR CONTRACT

If the contract is well-written and realistic, fulfilling it is generally pretty easy. Ask family or friends to check with you on how you are doing. Having to report your progress is good motivation. While carrying out your plan, keep track of your daily activities. All good managers have lists of what they want to accomplish, and check things off as they are completed. This will give you guidance on how realistic your planning was, and will also be useful in making future plans. Make daily notes, even of the things you don't understand at the time. Later, these notes may be useful in establishing a pattern which can be used for problem solving.

For example, our stair-climbing friend never did her climbing. Each day, she had a different problem: not enough time, being tired, the weather being too cold, and so on. When she looked back at this, she began to realize that the real problem was that she was afraid that she might fall with no one around to help her. She then decided to use a cane while climbing stairs and to do it when a friend or neighbor was around.

Checking the results

At the end of each week, see if you are any nearer to accomplishing your goal. Are you able to walk farther? Have you lost weight? Are you less fatigued? Taking stock is important. You may not see progress day by day, but you should see a little progress each week. If your contract involves exercise, you can use some of the self-tests in Chapters 8 and 9. Also, at the end of each week, check on how well you have fulfilled your contract. If you are having problems, this is a good time to use consultants. Depending on the problem, consultants may be friends, family, or members of your health-care team. Remember, consultants never solve your problems. They only help *you* accomplish your goal.

Corrections

In any business, the first plan is not always the workable plan. If something doesn't work, don't give up. Try something else. Modify your short-term plans so that your steps are easier. Give yourself more time to accomplish difficult tasks. Choose new steps to your goal. Or check with your consultants for their advice and aid.

If you run into problems, don't stop; get help. For example, one self-manager we know was going to walk with a coworker every day at lunch. The problem was that even though the coworker tried to slow down, she walked too fast. The solution was simple. The woman asked her coworker to always walk slightly behind her. Thus, the self-manager set the pace and was able to continue on her daily walk.

Another self-manager wanted to tell her grown children that hosting big holiday dinners had just become too much for her. However, she didn't know how to do this. By talking to friends, she first decided to offer to cook the turkey and have the children each bring a dish and clean up. Then, she rehearsed saying, "I know how much of a tradition holiday dinners are. However, I just can't do as much anymore. I'll cook the turkey, and will you each bring something?" This story had a happy ending, as the children had all wanted to help for years but had not offered for fear of offending their mother. Chapters 11, 12, and 15 can help you with problem solving.

For some problems, consultants can be most helpful. If medications are causing problems, ask the advice of your physician. If you just stop taking the drug, you are cheating yourself in two ways. First, you are not getting the benefits of medication. Second, you have not supplied your consultant with the vital information he or she needs to help you manage successfully.

If you really enjoy swimming, but have problems because you cannot comfortably turn your head, check with an occupational therapist. You probably don't need ongoing treatment, but one problem-solving visit with a professional may keep you in the water. (In this case the solution might be a face mask and snorkel.)

The best part of being a good self-manager is the rewards you will get in accomplishing your goals. However, don't wait until your goal is attained; reward yourself frequently. For example, decide that you won't read the paper until after you exercise. Thus, reading the paper becomes your reward. One self-manager (she is one of this book's authors) buys only one or two pieces of fruit at a time and walks the half-mile to the supermarket every day or two to get more fruit. Rewards don't have to be fancy or expensive, just something that is pleasant and meaningful in your life.

In review, a successful self-manager

1. sets goals,

2. determines what is necessary to carry out the goal,

3. makes short-term plans or contracts,

4. carries out the contract,

5. checks on progress weekly, and

6. makes mid-course corrections as necessary.

In writing a contract, be sure it includes:

1. *What* you are going to do.

2. *How much* you are going to do.

3. *When* you are going to do it (what time of day).

4. *How many* days a week you are going to do it.

For example: This week I will walk (what) around the block (how much) before lunch (when) three times (how many).

This week I will _____(what)

_____(how much)

_____(when)

_____(how many days)

How certain are you? _____%

For each day you accomplish your contract, put a checkmark: _____ Comments _____

Monday   _____   _____

Tuesday   _____   _____

Wednesday _____   _____

Thursday   _____   _____

Friday   _____   _____

Saturday   _____   _____

Sunday   _____   _____

7

Exercise for Fitness

The spirit of exercise and fitness is everywhere. Well, almost everywhere. It's easy to see why arthritis and an active life can be hard to combine. When you want to exercise but aren't sure what to do, arthritis pain, stiffness, and the fear of doing harm can be powerful forces to overcome. Until recently, many people with arthritis knew they should "exercise for arthritis"; however, they thought exercising for fun and fitness was only for others. Medical advice cautioned against strenuous activity, and prescribed rest and stretching or range-of-motion exercises only. These are still important parts of arthritis management. However, when your arthritis is under control, they shouldn't be your only exercise.

New research has changed how we think about exercise and arthritis. Thanks to many people with arthritis who have worked with many different kinds of health professionals, we can now advise exercise for fun and fitness. Exercising regularly lessens fatigue, builds stronger muscles and bones, increases your flexibility, gives you more stamina, and improves your general health and sense of well-being—all important for good arthritis care. Research shows that people with both osteoarthritis and rheumatoid arthritis have improved fitness by walking, bicycling, or aquatic exercise. After two or three months most exercisers also reported less pain, anxiety, and depression.

Traditional medical care of arthritis is based on helping people mainly when their arthritis flares. During a flare it's important to rest more and to protect the inflamed joints. But continuing to be inactive after the flare is over can be bad for your health and actually increase some arthritis problems. Unused joints, bones, and muscles deteriorate quickly. Long periods of inactivity can lead to weakness, stiffness, fatigue, poor appetite, constipation, high blood pressure, obesity, osteoporosis, and increased sensitivity to pain, anxiety, and depression. These are some of the same problems that occur when a person has arthritis. So it can become difficult to tell whether it is arthritis, inactivity, or some combination of the two that is to blame.

In this chapter you will learn how to improve your fitness and make wise exercise choices. This advice is not intended to take the place of therapeutic exercises. If you've had an exercise plan prescribed for you, take this book to your doctor or therapist and ask what he or she thinks about this program.

WHAT IS PHYSICAL FITNESS?

Physical fitness for people is much like good maintenance and proper use for an automobile. Both allow you to start when you want, enjoy a smooth and relaxed trip, get to your destination without a breakdown, and have some fuel in your tank when you arrive. How well an automobile works depends on its points and plugs, filters, hoses, tires, lubrication, and fuel systems. A person's physical fitness is a combination of

1. heart, lungs, and blood vessels (cardiovascular fitness),

2. muscle strength,

3. muscle endurance,

4. flexibility, and

5. percent of body fat.

Fitness is possible for people of all abilities, sizes, shapes, ages, and attitudes. Just as looking at a parked automobile won't tell you much about how it drives, appearance won't tell you much about a person's physical fitness. That new, shiny model may not perform as well as the well-maintained car that has a few dents or a little rust. There is another important similarity between keeping your body fit and your car running: both work best when used regularly and responsibly.

Regular exercise benefits everyone. By exercising you can reduce your risk for diabetes, cardiovascular disease, and osteoporosis. You increase your stamina and have more energy. Regular exercise helps control weight and avoid constipation. When you exercise, you feel better about yourself and your abilities.

If you have arthritis, regular exercise and fitness has special benefits. Strong muscles that do not tire quickly help protect joints by improving stability and absorbing shock. Good flexibility lessens pain and reduces the risk of sprains and strains. Maintaining a good weight helps take stress off weight-bearing joints. Regular exercise helps nourish joints and keeps cartilage and bone healthy. Higher energy levels, less anxiety and depression, and less discomfort are other advantages to exercise and fitness.

Thinking of your exercise as a physical fitness program helps you take a positive, mainstream approach to exercise. By understanding physical fitness and exercise, you'll be able to improve your health, feel better, and manage your arthritis, too. Feeling more in control and less at the mercy of arthritis is one of the biggest and best benefits of becoming an exercise self-manager.

A GOOD FITNESS PROGRAM

A fitness program has three parts: a warm-up, an aerobic exercise period, and a cool-down. It includes exercises for flexibility, strength, endurance, and cardiovascular fitness, and helps you maintain a good body weight. If you haven't exercised regularly in some time, or have pain, stiffness, or weakness that interferes with your daily activities, you should begin your fitness program with just the flexibility and strengthening warm-up, getting ready for more vigorous aerobic exercise at the next stage.

The Warm-Up

A warm-up routine consists of flexibility and strengthening exercises and a gradual increase in your activity level. It raises the temperature in your muscles and joints, nourishes joints, and safely prepares your heart to work harder for more vigorous exercise. Maintaining flexibility and strength is vital when you have arthritis, and therefore this routine is always an important part of your exercise program.

Always do flexibility and strengthening exercises before your aerobic exercise. On some days, however, you may want to do only the gentle warm-up exercises and not the aerobics. Doing some flexibility exercises at least three times a week or, better yet, every day helps you keep the exercise habit and maintain flexibility without aggravating your arthritis.

Choose a variety of flexibility and strengthening exercises from Chapter 8. Start with three to five repetitions of your chosen exercises to make five to ten minutes of exercise. Each week add a few exercises and increase repetitions until you are exercising for fifteen minutes. Depending on your needs, you could choose a combination of exercises that includes all joints. Another approach is to work on particular body areas, changing exercises as needed. If you're doing aerobic exercise, always loosen up and warm up the parts of the body you'll use next. Ask a physical therapist for specific suggestions if necessary.

You might enjoy creating a routine of warm-up exercises that flow together. Arrange them so that you don't have to get up and down often. Exercising to gentle, rhythmical music can also add to your enjoyment. When you can comfortably do fifteen minutes of strengthening and flexibility exercises, you're ready to add ten minutes of an aerobic activity and a cool-down.

Aerobic Exercise

Aerobic exercises use the large muscles of your body in a rhythmical, continuous activity. The most effective activities involve your whole body: walking, swimming, mowing the lawn, and so on. Aerobic exercise improves your cardiovascular fitness and lessens fatigue. It also helps with weight control. Aerobic exercise also promotes a sense of well-being, can help ease depression and anxiety, promotes restful sleep, and is an energizer.

Even with arthritis, almost everyone can do some kind of aerobic exercise. If you are over thirty-five, are at risk for heart disease, have been inactive for more than six months, or have questions about starting an aerobic exercise program, it is best to check with your doctor or therapist first. Take this book with you when you discuss your exercise ideas, or prepare a list of your specific questions.

Include aerobic exercise in your program when the joints you'll be using are not actively inflamed and your arthritis is stable and under control. Remember, you should be able to perform at least fifteen minutes of flexibility and strengthening exercises before starting aerobic activities. Don't exercise vigorously if you are ill.

There are many kinds of aerobic exercise. Walking, swimming, bicycling, and aquatic exercise are what most people with arthritis choose. These are all described in Chapter 9. Pick two or three activities you think you would enjoy and that wouldn't put undue stress on your joints. (Even if your arthritis is in your knees or feet, you can probably walk or bicycle if you build up to it slowly.) Choose activities that can be easily worked into your daily routine. If an activity is new to you, try it out before going to the expense of buying equipment or joining a health club. By having more than one exercise, you can keep active while adapting to vacations, seasons, and changing problems with your arthritis. Variety also helps keep you from getting bored.

There are other good aerobic activities that we don't have room to include in this book. Some people dance; folk, square, and even belly dancing all have their devotees. Gardening and housecleaning can qualify as endurance exercise if you use both arms and legs, move at a steady pace for at least twenty minutes, and feel some exertion. Mowing the lawn can certainly be counted as part of your aerobic exercise program.

The Cool-Down

A short five- to ten-minute cool-down period after you have finished a more vigorous activity is important to help your body gradually relax again. The cool-down allows your heart to slow gradually, lets your body lose some of the heat you generated during exercise, and gives your muscles a chance to relax and stretch out. Cooling down helps reduce the muscle soreness that sometimes follows vigorous activity.

To cool down, continue your aerobic exercise in "slow motion" for three to five minutes. For example, after a brisk walk, cool down with a casual stroll. End a bicycle ride with slow, easy pedaling. It is also good to do some flexibility exercises (see Chapter 8) because your muscles and joints are now warm. If you have been walking or bicycling, be sure to include the Achilles Stretch (p. 63).

You can also do your cool-down routine on days when your arthritis flares or days when you aren't doing aerobic exercise.

PREPARING TO EXERCISE

Figuring out how to make the commitment of time and energy to regular exercise is a challenge for everyone. If you have arthritis, you have even more challenges. You must take precautions and find a program that is safe and comfortable. You also have to understand how to adapt your exercise to changes in your arthritis and joint problems. Learning how much is enough before you've done "too much" is especially important. We hope that this chapter will help you gain knowledge to meet these challenges and enjoy the benefits of physical fitness.

Start by learning your arthritis needs. If possible, talk with your doctor and other professionals who understand your kind of arthritis. Get their ideas about special exercise needs and precautions. Read the section "Exercise Ideas for Specific Diseases" at the end of this chapter. Learn to be aware of your own body, and plan your activities accordingly. Your personal exercise program should be based on *your* current level of health and fitness, *your* goals and desires, *your* abilities and special needs, and *your* likes and dislikes. Deciding to improve your fitness, and feeling the satisfaction of success, has nothing to do with competition or comparing yourself to others.

Opportunities in Your Community

Most people who exercise regularly do so with at least one other person. Two or more people can keep each other motivated, and a whole class can build a feeling of camaraderie. On the other hand, exercising alone gives you the most freedom. You may feel that there are no classes that would work for you or no buddy to exercise with. If so, start your own program: as you progress, you may find that these feelings change.

The Arthritis Foundation and the Arthritis Society sponsor exercise programs taught by trained instructors and developed specifically for people with arthritis. Consult your local chapter or branch office.

Most communities now offer a variety of exercise classes, including special programs for people over fifty, adaptive exercises, mall walking, fitness trails, and others. Check with the local Y, community and senior centers, parks and recreation programs, adult education, and community colleges. There is a great deal of variation in the content of these programs, as well as in the professional experience of the exercise staff. By and large, the classes are inexpensive, and those in charge of planning are responsive to people's needs.

Hospitals with cardiac rehabilitation programs often offer exercise classes. These programs tend to be more expensive than other community classes, but there is the advantage of medical supervision if that's important to you.

Health and fitness clubs usually offer aerobic studios, weight training, cardiovascular equipment, and sometimes a heated pool. For all these services they charge membership fees, which can be high. Ask about low impact, beginners, and over fifty exercise classes, both in the aerobic studio and in the pool. Gyms that emphasize weight lifting generally don't have the programs or personnel to help you with a flexible, all-around fitness program. These are some qualities you should look for:

1. **Classes** that are designed for moderate- and low-intensity exercise. You should be able to observe classes and participate in at least one class before signing up and paying.

2. **Instructors** who have qualifications and experience. Knowledgeable instructors are more likely to understand special needs and be willing and able to work with you.

3. **Membership policies** that allow you to pay only for a session of classes, or let you "freeze" membership at times when you can't participate. Some fitness facilities offer different rates depending on how many services you use.

4. **Facilities** that are easy to get to, park near, and enter. Dressing rooms and exercise sites should be accessible and safe, with professional staff on site.

5. **A pool** that allows "free swim" times when the water isn't crowded. Also, find out the policy about children in the pool; small children playing and making noise may not be compatible with your program.

6. **Staff and other members** with whom you feel comfortable.

PUTTING YOUR PROGRAM TOGETHER

The best way to enjoy and stick with your exercise program is to suit yourself! Choose what you want to do, a place where you feel comfortable, and an exercise time that fits your schedule. A young mother with school-age children will find it difficult to stick with an exercise program that requires her to leave home for a five o'clock class. A retired man who enjoys lunch with friends and an afternoon nap is wise to choose an early or mid-morning exercise time.

Having fun and enjoying yourself are benefits of exercise that often go unmentioned. Too often we think of exercise as serious business. However, most people who stick with a program do so because they enjoy it. They think of their exercise as recreation rather than a chore. Start off with success in mind. Allow yourself time to get used to new experiences, and you'll probably find that you look forward to exercise.

Some well-meaning health professionals can make it hard for a person with arthritis to stick to an exercise program. You may have been prescribed exercises to do on your own at home (sometimes four times a day) for the rest of your life! What a lonely sounding chore! No wonder so many people never start, or give up quickly. Not many of us make lifelong commitments to unknown projects. Experience, practice, and success are necessary to establish a habit. Follow the self-management steps in Chapter 6 to make beginning your program easier.

First fill out the Fitness Planner on page 42. This will help you plan a 6 to 8 week program. Then, using the self-management steps in Chapter 6, decide what you will do *this week*. Use the Exercise Diary on page 00 to keep track of your daily exercise.

1. **Choose exercises you want to do.** Combine any activities your doctor or another professional recommends, with exercises from the next two chapters, and/or some of your favorites. Write them down.

2. **Choose the time and place to exercise.** Tell your family and friends your plan.

3. **Make a contract with yourself.** Decide how long you'll stick with these particular exercises. Six to twelve weeks is a reasonable time commitment for a new program.

4. **Make an Exercise Diary or calendar.** Leave space to write down your exercises, how long you do them, your heart rate, and your reactions. We've shown an example of a diary on page 43. Put your diary where you can see it and fill it out every day.

5. **Do some self-tests.** You will find these at the end of the next two chapters. Record the date and results on the fitness planner.

6. **Start your program.** Remember to begin gradually if you haven't exercised in a while.

7. **Repeat the self-tests.** At the end of your time period, repeat the self-tests, record the results, and check the changes. Record your daily and weekly progress in your Exercise Diary. Repeat the self-tests every 3 to 4 weeks and record the results on your Fitness Planner.

8. **Revise your program. Look over your planner and diary for ideas.** Decide what you liked, what worked, and what made exercising difficult. Modify your program and contract for another few weeks. You may decide to change some exercises, the place or time you exercise, or your exercise partners.

9. **Reward yourself for a job well done.**

FITNESS PLANNER
(6–8 Week Program)

DATES: _____ TO _____

EXERCISE GOALS:

1. _____

2. _____

3. _____

EXERCISE ACTIVITIES

WARM UP (Strengthening/   Self Test Score
Flexibility)   Time 1   Time 2   Time 3

1. _____   _____   _____   _____

2. _____   _____   _____   _____

3. _____   _____   _____   _____

4. _____   _____   _____   _____

5. _____   _____   _____   _____

6. _____   _____   _____   _____

AEROBIC EXERCISE   Time 1   Time 2   Time 3

Activity: _____   _____   _____

Frequency: _____   _____   _____

Duration: _____   _____   _____

Exercise Heart Rate: _____   _____   _____

Perceived Exertion: _____   _____   _____

COOL DOWN

1. _____

2. _____

3. _____

4. _____

COMMENTS/REVISIONS:

WEEK # _____ WEEKLY GOAL: _____

DATE	EXERCISES	FREQUENCY/ DURATION	EHR/ RPE	FEELINGS
____	_____	_____	_____	_____
____	_____	_____	_____	_____
____	_____	_____	_____	_____
____	_____	_____	_____	_____
____	_____	_____	_____	_____
____	_____	_____	_____	_____
____	_____	_____	_____	_____

COMMENTS:

WEEK # _____ WEEKLY GOAL: _____

DATE	EXERCISES	FREQUENCY/ DURATION	EHR/ RPE	FEELINGS
____	_____	_____	_____	_____
____	_____	_____	_____	_____
____	_____	_____	_____	_____
____	_____	_____	_____	_____
____	_____	_____	_____	_____
____	_____	_____	_____	_____
____	_____	_____	_____	_____

COMMENTS:

KEEPING IT UP

If you haven't exercised recently, you'll undoubtedly experience some new feelings and discomfort in the early days. It's normal to feel muscle tension and possibly tenderness around joints, and to be a little more tired in the evenings. Muscle or joint pain that lasts more than two hours after the exercise, or feeling tired into the next day, means that you probably did too much too fast. Don't stop; just exercise less vigorously or for a shorter time the next day.

When you do aerobic exercise, it's natural to feel your heart beat faster, your breathing speed up, and your body get warmer. Feeling short of breath, nauseous, or dizzy, however, is not what you want. If this happens to you, stop exercising and discontinue your program until you check with your doctor.

People who have arthritis have additional sensations to sort out. It can be difficult at first to figure out which come from arthritis and which come from exercise. Talking to someone else with arthritis who has had experience starting a new exercise program can be a big help. Once you've sorted out the new sensations, you'll be able to exercise with confidence.

Think of your head as the coach and your body as your team. For success, all parts of the team need attention. Be a good coach. Encourage and praise yourself. Design "plays" you feel your team can execute successfully. Choose places that are safe and hospitable. A good coach knows his or her team, sets good goals, and helps the team succeed. A good coach is loyal. A good coach does not belittle, nag, or make anyone feel guilty. Be a good coach to your team.

Besides a good coach, everyone needs an enthusiastic cheerleader or two. Of course, you can be your own cheerleader, but being both coach and cheerleader is a lot to do. Successful exercisers usually have at least one family member or close friend who actively supports their exercise habit. Your cheerleader can exercise with you, help you get other chores done, praise your accomplishments, or just consider your exercise time when making plans. Sometimes cheerleaders pop up by themselves, but don't be bashful about asking for a hand.

With exercise experience you develop a sense of control over yourself and your arthritis. You learn how to alternate your activities to fit your day-to-day needs. You know when to do less and when to do more. You know that a flare, or a period of inactivity in taking care of the arthritis, doesn't have to be devastating. You know how to get back on track again.

Give your exercise plan a chance to succeed. Set reasonable goals and enjoy your success. Stay motivated. When it comes to your personal fitness program, sticking with it and doing it your way makes you a definite winner.

EXERCISE IDEAS FOR SPECIFIC DISEASES

Everything we've suggested up to now applies to everyone with arthritis. Here are some additional exercise ideas and tips for people with specific diseases.

Osteoarthritis

Since osteoarthritis is primarily a problem with joint cartilage, an exercise program should include taking care of cartilage. Cartilage needs joint motion to stay healthy. In much the same way that a sponge soaks up and squeezes out water, joint cartilage soaks up nutrients and fluid, and gets rid of waste products by being squeezed when you move the joint. If the joint is not moved regularly, cartilage deteriorates. If the joint is continually compressed, as the hips and knees are by long periods of standing, the cartilage can't expand and soak up nutrients and fluid.

Any joint with osteoarthritis should be moved through its full range of motion several times daily to maintain flexibility and to take care of the cartilage. Judge your activity level so that pain is not increased. If hips and knees are involved, walking and standing should be limited to no more than two to four hours at a time, followed by at least an hour off your feet to give cartilage time to decompress. Good posture, strong muscles with good endurance, and shoes that absorb the shocks of walking are important ways to protect cartilage and reduce joint pain.

Rheumatoid Arthritis

People with rheumatoid arthritis should pay special attention to flexibility, strengthening, and appropriate use of their joints. Maintaining good posture and joint motion will help joints, ease pain, and avoid tightness. Arthritis pain and long periods spent sitting or lying down can quickly lead to poor posture and limited motion, even in the joints not affected by the arthritis. Be sure to include hand and wrist exercises in your daily program (see pp. 51–52). A good time to do these is after washing dishes or during a bath when hands are warm and more limber.

Rheumatoid arthritis sometimes affects the bones in the neck. It is best to avoid extreme neck movements and not to put pressure on the back of the neck or head.

Stiffness in the morning can be a big problem. Flexibility exercises before getting up or during a hot bath or shower seem to help. A favorite way to get loosened up is to "stretch like a cat and shake like a dog." Also, doing gentle flexibility exercises in the evening before bed has been shown to reduce morning stiffness.

Ankylosing Spondylitis and Psoriatic Arthritis

Ankylosing spondylitis and psoriatic arthritis can result in loss of motion in the neck, back, and hips. Flexibility exercises, including breathing and chest expansion, are important parts of the exercise program. Muscle strengthening exercises for back and hips are also needed to maintain erect posture. Correct head and neck posture is also extremely important to maintain good alignment.

Inflammation of muscles, tendons, and ligaments also occurs in these diseases, making them vulnerable to injuries and sprains. Repeated inflammation can result in shortening and thickening of tissue around joints and lead to loss of motion. Therefore, it is extremely important to do regular flexibility exercises. Exercise gently, with slow controlled holding movements. Bouncing or jerking is dangerous.

The Achilles tendon or heel cord is especially at risk. Use the Achilles Stretch (page 63) to keep the heel cord and tissue covering the sole of the foot elastic. This helps reduce the chance of tendon tears, plantar fasciitis, heel pain, and heel spurs. Sleeping on your stomach with your feet over the end of the bed is another way to encourage good posture.

Stiffness in the neck and spine doesn't mean you can't be physically fit. Swimming is an excellent exercise. Swimming strengthens back, shoulders, and hips and provides a good cardiovascular workout. Use a snorkel and mask to allow you to swim without turning your head to breathe.

Systemic Lupus Erythematosus (SLE)

The fatigue and joint pains that so many people with SLE experience can be a major stumbling block. These problems can be improved with a regular program of moderate exercise undertaken when the disease process is under control. A program that includes flexibility, strengthening, and aerobic exercise is appropriate. It is wise to avoid high-impact activities such as jumping or bouncing, especially if you're taking oral corticosteroids. Combining walking, bicycling, and swimming or pool exercise will give you a well-balanced program with maximum safety. Nighttime flexibility exercises may help reduce morning stiffness.

Raynaud's Phenomenon

If cold sensitivity or Raynaud's phenomenon is a problem, avoid extreme temperature changes when you plan your exercise. If you live where there are cold winters, develop a good interior exercise program. Some people have found that wearing disposable latex surgical gloves underneath a pair of regular gloves or mittens is useful. If you like water exercise but the water temperature is too cold for your hands, try putting on latex gloves before getting in the water.

Osteoporosis

Regular exercise plays an important part in preventing osteoporosis and in strengthening bones that already show signs of the disease. Endurance exercises such as walking are the most effective for strengthening bone. Exercises for back and stomach muscles are necessary for maintaining good posture. You can help yourself with a regular exercise program that includes some walking and general flexibility and strengthening of your back and stomach muscles.

If you have osteoporosis or think that you may be at risk for this condition, here are some exercise precautions for you to remember:

- No heavy lifting.

- Avoid falls. Be careful on pool decks, waxed floors, icy sidewalks, or cluttered surfaces.

- Don't bend down to touch your toes when standing. This puts unnecessary pressure on your back. If you want to stretch your legs or back, lie on your back and bring your knees up toward your chest.

- Sit up straight, and don't slouch. Good sitting posture puts less pressure on the back.

- If your balance is poor or you feel clumsy, consider using a cane or walking stick when you're in a crowd or on unfamiliar ground.

Fibrositis/Fibromyalgia

This condition can occur by itself or appear in people who also have other forms of arthritis. The symptoms are stiffness, fatigue, general aching, and extremely tender spots around the shoulders, upper back, hips, and knees. There are no signs of inflammation or joint involvement. Exercise for this condition is still being investigated. So far it seems that a general program of flexibility, strengthening, and moderate aerobic exercise is the best approach. People with fibrositis often get worse after doing very vigorous exercise, but low- to moderate-intensity exercise can help reduce muscle tension and aid relaxation.

References

Francis, Peter, Ph.D., and Lorna Francis, Ph.D. *If It Hurts, Don't Do It*. Prima Publishing and Communications: Rocklin, CA, 1988. An easy to read book about getting started with an enjoyable and sensible fitness exercise program.

Sayce, Valerie and Ian Fraser. *Exercise Can Beat Your Arthritis*. In North America, from Avery Publishing Group: Garden City Park, NY, 1989. In Australia and New Zealand, from Fraser Publications, Melbourne, Victoria, 1987. Well-illustrated and explained exercises for the whole body.

Exercise Tips

8

Flexibility and Strengthening Exercises

You can use the exercises in this chapter in several ways: to get in shape for more vigorous aerobic exercise, on days when you don't do aerobic exercise, and as part of your warm-up and cool-down routines. Choose exercises to build a strengthening and flexibility program for the whole body.

The exercises are arranged in order from the head and neck down to the toes. Most of the upper body exercises may be done either sitting or standing. Exercises done lying down can be performed on the floor or on a firm mattress. We've labeled the exercises that are particularly important for good posture "VIP" (Very Important for Posture).

These helpful hints apply to all the exercises that follow:

- Move slowly and gently. Do not bounce or jerk.

- To loosen tight muscles and limber up stiff joints, stretch just until you feel tension and then hold briefly.

- Start with no more than five repetitions of any exercise. Take at least two weeks to increase to ten.

- Arrange your exercises so you don't have to get up and down a lot.

- Always do the same number of exercises for your left side as for your right.

- Breathe naturally. Do not hold your breath. Count out loud to make sure you are breathing easily.

- If you feel increased pain that lasts more than two hours after exercising, next time do fewer repetitions or eliminate an exercise that seems to be causing the pain. Don't quit exercising.

NECK EXERCISES

1. Heads Up (VIP)

This exercise relieves jaw, neck, and upper back pain and is the start of good posture. You can do it while driving, sitting at a desk, sewing, reading, or exercising. Just sit or stand straight and gently slide your chin back. Keep looking forward as your chin moves backward. You'll feel the back of your neck lengthen and straighten. To help, put your finger on your nose and then draw straight back from your finger. (Don't worry about a little double chin—you really look much better with your neck straight!)

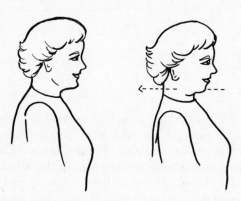

2. Two-Way Neck Stretch

In heads-up position (Exercise 1), and with your shoulders relaxed,

a. Turn slowly to look over your right shoulder. Then turn slowly to look over your left shoulder.
b. Tilt your head to the right and then to the left. Move your ear toward your shoulder. Do *not* move your shoulder up to your ear.

If these exercises make you dizzy, close your eyes. If you are still dizzy, skip it. Don't do these exercises if they cause neck pain, or pain or numbness in your arms or hands.

HAND AND WRIST EXERCISES

A good place to do these hand exercises is at a table that supports your forearms. Do them after washing dishes, after bathing, or when taking a break from handwork. Your hands are warmer at those times and more limber.

3. One-Two-Three Finger Exercises

For the best hand function, you should be able to touch the tips of your fingers to the palm and straighten the fingers completely. Use the one-two-three approach to stretch and strengthen fingers. To bend fingers, begin bending the joint closest to the tip of the finger (1), then bend the middle joint (2). When your fingertips are touching the palm, or are as close as possible, bend the knuckle joint (3). To straighten your fingers, just do the movements in reverse: first straighten the knuckles (3), then the middle joint (2), and last the fingertips (1). You can exercise your fingers individually or together, using your other hand to help if necessary.

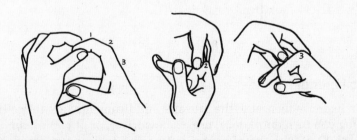

4. Thumb Walk

Holding your wrist straight, form the letter "O" by lightly touching your thumb to each fingertip. After each "O" straighten and spread your fingers. Use the other hand to help if needed.

 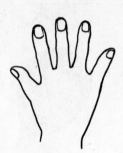

5. Hi and Bye

a. To strengthen and limber your wrist, rest your forearm on a table with your hand over the edge. Keep fingers relaxed and bend your wrist up and down.
b. To strengthen the small muscles of the hand, slide your arm back until your fingers hang over with your knuckles at the table edge. Keeping your fingers straight and together and your palm flat, move your fingers up and down.

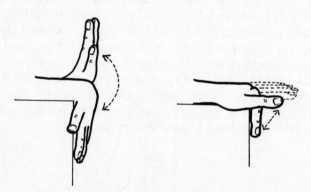

6. Door Opener

This is an exercise to stretch the muscles and ligaments that rotate the forearm, letting you turn doorknobs, use a screwdriver, or put your hand in your back pocket. Start with your forearm resting on a table, palm down. Keeping

your little finger on the table, turn your hand so the palm faces up. If you
use your other hand to help, grip your forearm, not the wrist or hand.

SHOULDER EXERCISES

7. Pendulum

This is a good way to begin exercise for a painful or limited shoulder. It helps
relax shoulder muscles and moves the joint in all directions. Either standing
or sitting, lean slightly forward. Let your arm hang freely in front of you.
Relax and feel the weight of your arm. Keeping the arm relaxed, begin to
make small circles. Gradually increase to larger circles. Exercise just past the
point of discomfort, but don't push yourself too hard.

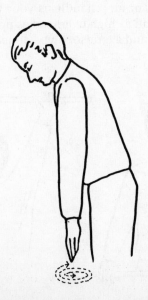

8. Shoulder Cradle

Grasp one arm near the elbow with your other hand and raise the arm up over your head. Holding your arm as high as it will go, bend and straighten your elbow. If your shoulder is painful or tight, you may prefer to do this exercise lying down.

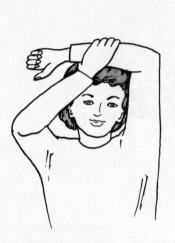
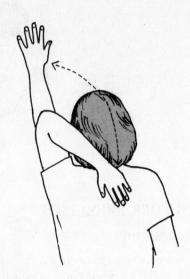

9. Wand Exercise

If one or both of your shoulders are particularly tight or weak, you may want to give yourself a "helping hand." This shoulder exercise and the next allow the arms to help each other.

Use a cane, yardstick, or mop handle as your wand. Place one hand on each end and raise the wand as high overhead as possible. You might try this in front of a mirror. This wand exercise can be done standing, sitting, or lying down.

10. Shoulder Pulley

Fasten a hook or pulley in a beam or on the top of a door frame. Place a piece of rope or clothesline through the hook, as shown. Start with enough rope to let you sit while exercising. Hold one end of the rope in each hand. If gripping the rope is uncomfortable, add padding or handles. Tying on pastry cutters with wooden handles or metal loops works well. As you pull down with one arm, the other arm will be raised. Move your arms up and down in front of you and also out to the side.

 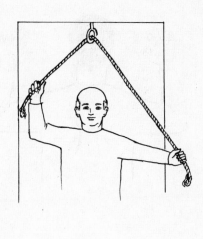

11. Pat and Reach

This double-duty exercise helps increase flexibility and strength for both shoulders. Raise one arm up over your head and bend your elbow to pat yourself on the back. Move your other arm to your back, bend your elbow, and reach up toward the other hand. Can your fingertips touch? Relax and switch arm positions. Can you touch on that side? For most people, one position will work better than the other.

12. Shoulder Blade Pinch (VIP)

This is a good exercise to strengthen the middle and upper back and to stretch the chest. Sit or stand with your head in heads-up position (Exercise 1) and your shoulders relaxed. Raise your arms out to the sides with elbows bent. Pinch your shoulder blades together by moving your elbows as far back as you can. Hold briefly, then slowly move your arms forward to touch elbows. If this position is uncomfortable, lower your hands to touch your shoulders.

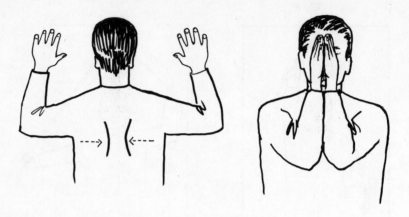

BACK AND ABDOMINAL EXERCISES

13. Knee-to-Chest Stretch

For a low back stretch, lie on the floor with knees bent and feet flat. Bring one knee toward your chest, using your hands to help. Hold your knee near your chest for ten seconds and lower the leg slowly. Repeat with the other knee. You can also tuck both legs at the same time if you wish. Relax and enjoy the stretch.

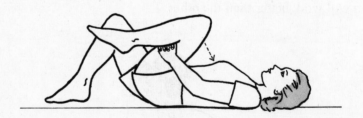

14. Pelvic Tilt (VIP)

This is an excellent exercise for low back pain. Lie on your back with knees bent, feet flat. Place your hands on your abdomen. Flatten the small of your back against the floor by tightening your stomach muscles and your buttocks. It helps to imagine bringing your pubic bone to your chin, or trying to pull your tummy in enough to zip a tight pair of trousers. Hold the tilt for five to ten seconds. Relax. Arch your back slightly. Relax and repeat the Pelvic Tilt. Keep breathing. Count the seconds out loud. Once you've mastered the Pelvic Tilt lying down, practice it sitting, standing, and walking.

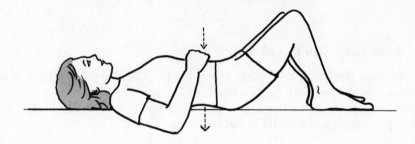

15. Back Lift (VIP)

a. This exercise improves flexibility along your spine. Lie on your stomach and rise up onto your forearms. If this is comfortable, straighten your elbows. Breathe naturally and relax. If you have moderate to severe low back pain, do not do this exercise unless it has been specifically prescribed for you.

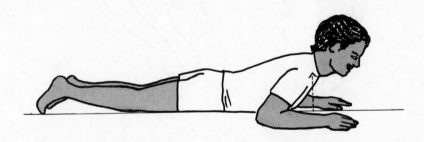

b. To strengthen back muscles, lie on your stomach with your arms at your side or overhead. Lift your head, shoulders, and arms. Do *not* look up. Keep looking down with your chin tucked in. Count out loud as you hold for a count of ten. Relax. You can also lift your legs off the floor instead of your head and shoulders.

Lifting both ends of your body at once as shown in the illustration is a fairly strenuous exercise. It may not be helpful for a person with back pain, but is a good exercise for someone with ankylosing spondylitis.

16. Low Back Rock and Roll

Lie on your back and pull your knees up to your chest with your hands behind the thighs. Rest in this position for ten seconds, then gently roll knees from one side to the other, rocking your hips back and forth. Keep your upper back and shoulders flat on the ground.

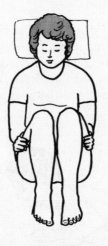 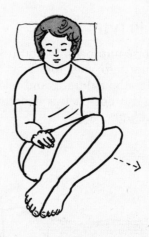

17. Curl Up (VIP)

A Curl Up, as shown here, will strengthen abdominal muscles. Lie on your back, knees bent, feet flat. Do the Pelvic Tilt (Exercise 14). Slowly curl up to raise your head and shoulders. Uncurl back down, or hold for ten seconds and slowly lower. Breathe out as you curl up, and breathe in as you go back down. Do *not* hold your breath. If you have neck problems, or if your neck hurts when you do this exercise, try the next one instead. Never tuck your feet under a chair or have someone hold your feet!

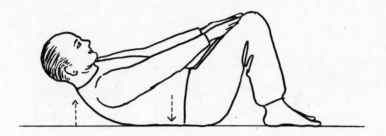

18. Roll Out

This is another good abdominal strengthener and easy on the neck. Use it instead of the Curl Up, or, if neck pain is not a problem, do them both.

a. Lie on your back with knees bent and feet flat. Bring one knee up to your chest. Do the Pelvic Tilt (Exercise 14) and hold your lower back firmly against the floor.
b. Slowly and carefully, move one leg away from your chest as you straighten your knee. Move your leg out until you feel your lower back start to arch. When this happens, tuck your knee back to your chest. Reset your pelvic tilt and roll your leg out again. Breathe out as your leg rolls out. Do *not* hold your breath. Repeat with the other leg.

  You are strengthening your abdominal muscles by holding your pelvic tilt against the weight of your leg. As you get stronger, you'll be able to straighten your legs out farther and move both legs together.

HIP AND LEG EXERCISES

19. Straight Leg Raise

This exercise strengthens the muscles that bend the hip and straighten the knee. Lie on your back, knees bent, feet flat. Straighten one leg. Tighten the muscle on the top of that thigh and straighten the knee as much as possible. Keeping the knee straight, raise your leg one to two feet (about 50 cm) off the ground. Do not arch your back. Hold your leg up and count out loud for ten seconds. Relax. Repeat with the other leg.

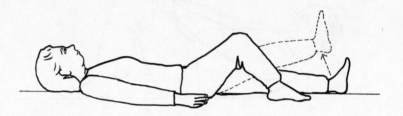

20. Hip Hooray

This exercise can be done standing or lying on your back. If you lie down, spread your legs as far apart as possible. Roll your legs and feet out like a duck and then in, pigeon-toed. If you are standing, move one leg out to your side as far as you can. Lead out and in with the heel. Hold onto a counter for support.

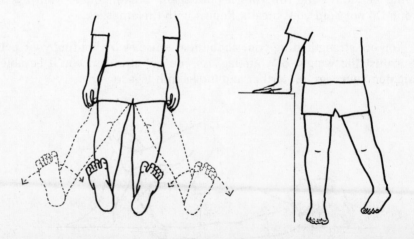

21. Back Kick (VIP)

This exercise increases the backward mobility and strength of your hip. Hold onto a counter for support. Move the leg up and back, knee straight. Stand tall and do not arch your back.

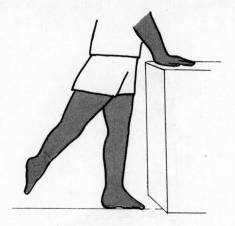

22. Knee Strengthener (VIP)

Strong knees are important for walking and standing comfortably. This exercise strengthens the knee. Sitting in a chair, straighten the knee by tightening up the muscle on top of your thigh. Place your hand on your thigh and feel the muscle work. Holding your knee as straight as possible, push out with your heel and then point your toes. Make circles with your toes. As your knee strengthens, see if you can build up to holding your leg out for thirty seconds. Count out loud. Do *not* hold your breath.

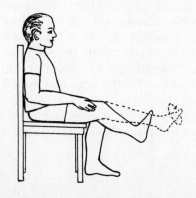

23. Power Knees

This exercise strengthens the muscles that bend and straighten your knee. Sit in a straight-backed chair and cross your legs above the ankles. Your legs can be almost straight, or you can bend your knees as much as you like. Try several positions. Push forward with your back leg and press backward with your front leg. Exert pressure evenly so that your legs do not move. Hold and count out loud for ten seconds. Relax. Change leg positions. Be sure to keep breathing.

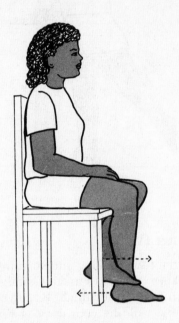

24. Hamstring Stretch

Do the self-test for hamstring tightness (page 67) to see if you need to do this exercise. It is also a good exercise to do if you get muscle cramps in the back of your thigh. If you have unstable knees, or "back knee" (a knee that curves backward when you stand up), do not do this exercise.

If you do have tight hamstrings, lie on your back, knees bent, feet flat. Grasp one leg at a time just above the knee and hold the leg at a right angle with the body. Holding the leg out at arm's length, slowly straighten the knee. Hold the leg as straight as you can as you count to ten.

Be careful with this exercise. It's easy to overstretch and be sore.

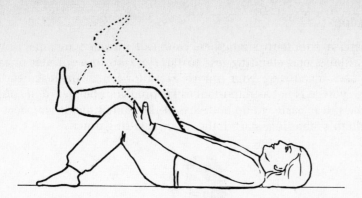

25. Achilles Stretch

This exercise helps maintain flexibility in the Achilles tendon, the large tendon you feel at the back of your ankle. Good flexibility helps reduce the risk of injury, calf discomfort, and heel pain. The Achilles Stretch is especially helpful for cooling down after walking or cycling, and for people with ankylosing spondylitis or psoriatic arthritis. Also do this exercise if you get calf cramps.

Stand at a counter or against a wall. Place one foot in front of the other, toes pointing forward and heels on the ground. Lean forward, bend the knee of the forward leg and keep the back knee straight, heel down. You will feel a good stretch in the calf. Hold the stretch for ten seconds. Do *not* bounce. Move gently.

It's easy to get sore doing this exercise. If you've worn shoes with high heels for a long time, be particularly careful.

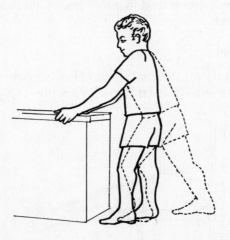

26. Tiptoes

This exercise will help strengthen your calf muscles and make walking, climbing stairs, and standing less tiring. Hold on to a counter or table for support and raise up on your tiptoes. Hold for ten seconds. Lower slowly. How high you go is not as important as keeping your balance and controlling your ankles. It is easier to do both legs at the same time. If your feet are too sore to do this standing, start doing it while sitting down.

ANKLE AND FEET EXERCISES

Do these exercises sitting in a straight-backed chair with your feet bare. Have a bath towel and ten marbles next to you. These exercises are for flexibility, strength, and comfort.

27. Ankle Circles

Hold your feet slightly off the ground and slowly circle your ankles to the right and then to the left. Go as far in each direction as you can.

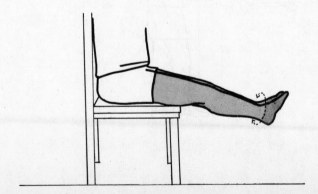

28. Towel Grabber

Spread a towel out in front of your chair. Place your feet on the towel with your heels on the edge closest to you. Keep your heels down. Scoot the towel back underneath your feet by pulling it with your toes as you arch your feet. When you have done as much as you can, reverse the toe motion and scoot the towel out again.

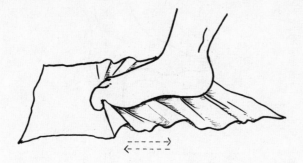

29. Marble Pickup

Do this exercise one foot at a time. Place several marbles on the floor between your feet. Keep your heel down and pivot your toes toward the marbles. Pick up a marble in your toes and pivot your foot to drop the marble as far as possible from where you picked it up. Repeat until all the marbles have been moved. Reverse the process and return all the marbles to the starting position. If marbles are difficult, try other objects like jacks, dice, or wads of paper.

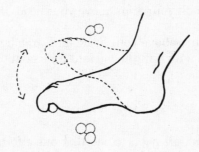

30. Foot Roll

Place a rolling pin (or a large dowel or closet rod) under the arch of your foot and roll it back and forth. It feels great and stretches the ligaments in the arch of the foot.

THE WHOLE BODY

31. The Stretcher

This exercise is a whole-body stretch to do lying on your back. Start the motion at your ankles as explained here, or reverse the process if you want to start with your arms first.

a. Point your toes, and then pull your toes toward your nose. Relax.
b. Bend your knees. Then flatten your knees and let them relax.
c. Arch your back. Do the Pelvic Tilt. Relax.
d. Breathe in and stretch your arms above your head. Breathe out and lower your arms. Relax.
e. Stretch your right arm above your head, and stretch your left leg by pushing away from you with your heel. Hold for a count of ten. Switch to the other side and repeat.

SELF-TESTS

Whatever our goals, we all need to see that our efforts make a difference. Since an exercise program produces gradual change, it's often hard to tell if the program is working and to recognize improvement. Choose several of these flexibility and strength tests to measure your progress. Not everyone will be able to do all the tests. Choose those that work best for you. Perform each test before you start your exercise program, and record the results in your Fitness Planner (see pg 42). After every four weeks, do the tests again and check your improvement.

1. Arm Flexibility

Do Exercise 11, Pat and Reach, for both sides of the body. Ask someone to measure the distance between your fingertips.

Goal: Less distance between your fingertips.

2. Shoulder Flexibility

Stand facing a wall with your toes touching the wall. One arm at a time, reach up the wall in front of you. Hold a pencil, or have someone mark how far you reached. Also do this sideways, standing about three inches (8 cm) away from the wall.

Goal: To reach higher.

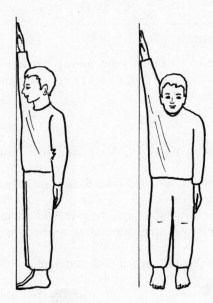

3. Hamstring Flexibility

Do the Hamstring Stretch, Exercise 24, one leg at a time. Keep your thigh perpendicular to your body. How much does your knee bend? How tight does the back of your leg feel?

Goal: Straighter knee and less tension in the back of the leg.

4. Ankle Flexibility

Sit in a chair with your bare feet flat on the floor and your knees bent at a 90-degree angle. Keep your heels on the floor. Raise your toes and the front of your foot. Ask someone to measure the distance between the ball of your foot and the floor.

Goal: One to two inches (3 to 5 cm) between your foot and the floor.

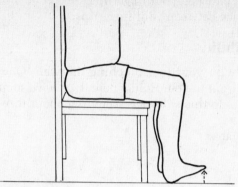

5. Abdominal Strength

Use the Curl Up, Exercise 17. Count how many repetitions you can do before you get too tired to do more, or count how many you can do in one minute.

Goal: More repetitions.

6. Ankle Strength

This test has two parts. Stand at a table or counter for support.

a. Do Exercise 26, Tiptoes, as quickly and as often as you can. How many can you do before you tire?
b. Stand with your feet flat. Put most of your weight on one foot, and quickly tap the front part of your other foot. How many taps can you do before you tire?

Goal: Ten to fifteen repetitions of each movement.

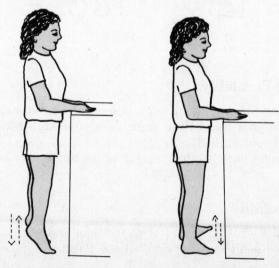

9

Aerobic Activities

HOW MUCH IS ENOUGH?

One of the biggest problems with aerobic exercise is that you may overdo it. Inexperienced exercisers think they have to work very hard for exercise to do any good. Exhaustion, sore muscles, and painful joints are the result of jumping in too hard and too fast. Finding out how much is enough doesn't need to be a guessing game. Use the following guidelines for frequency, duration, and intensity as you plan your aerobic exercise.

Three or four times a week is the best *frequency* for aerobic exercise. Taking every other day off gives your body a chance to rest.

Gradually increase the *duration* of your aerobic activity to about thirty minutes a session. You can safely increase the time by alternating intervals of brisk exercise with intervals of rest or easy exercise. For example, after three to five minutes of brisk walking, do one to two minutes of easy strolling, then another three to five minutes of brisk walking. Eventually you can build up to thirty minutes of activity. Then gradually eliminate rest intervals until you can maintain twenty to thirty minutes of brisk exercise.

Safe and effective aerobic exercise should be done at no more than moderate *intensity*. High-intensity exercise increases the risk of injury and causes discomfort, so not many people stick with it. Exercise intensity is measured by how hard you work. For a trained runner, completing a mile in twelve minutes is probably low-intensity exercise. For a person who hasn't exercised in a long time, a brisk ten-minute walk may be of moderate to high intensity. The trick, of course, is to figure out what is moderate intensity for you. There are several easy ways to do this.

Heart Rate

Unless you're taking heart-regulating medication, monitoring your heart rate while exercising is a good way to measure exercise intensity. The faster the heart beats, the harder you're working. (Your heart also beats fast when you are frightened or nervous, but here we're talking about how your heart responds to physical activity.) Aerobic exercise at moderate intensity raises your heart rate into a range between 60 and 80 percent of your maximum heart rate. Maximum heart rate declines with age, so your safe exercise heart rate gets lower as you get older. You can follow the general guidelines of the Age-Exercise Heart Rate Chart, or calculate your individual exercise heart rate. Either way, you need to know how to take your pulse.

Take your pulse by placing the pads of your middle three fingers at your wrist below the base of your thumb. Don't use the tips of your fingers, and don't use your thumb. You should be able to feel your blood pumping. Count how many beats you feel in fifteen seconds. Multiply this number by 4 to find out how fast your heart is beating in one minute. Start by taking your pulse whenever you think of it, and you'll soon learn the difference between your resting and exercise heart rates.

AGE-EXERCISE HEART RATE CHART

Age Range	Exercise Pulse (Beats in 15 seconds)
20–30	30–38
30–40	28–36
40–50	26–34
50–60	24–32
60–70	22–30
70–80	20–28
80 +	18–24

How to calculate your own exercise heart rate range:

1. Subtract your age from **220.**

    Example: You:

        $220 - 60 = 160$ $220 - \underline{\hspace{1cm}} = \underline{\hspace{1cm}}$

2. To find the lower end of your exercise heart rate range, multiply your
   answer in step 1 by **.6.**

   Example: You:
   $160 \times .6 = 96$ _____ $\times .6 =$ _____

3. To find the upper end of your exercise heart rate range, which you
   should not exceed, multiply your answer in step 1 by **.8.**

   Example: You:
   $160 \times .8 = 128$ _____ $\times .8 =$ _____

The exercise heart rate range in our example is from 96 to 128 beats per
minute. What is yours?

Most people count their pulse for fifteen seconds, not a whole minute.
To find your fifteen-second pulse, divide both numbers by 4. The person in
our example should be able to count between 24 and 32 beats in fifteen
seconds while exercising.

The most important reason for knowing your exercise heart rate range
is so that you can learn not to exercise too vigorously. After you've done
your warm-up and five minutes of aerobic exercise, take your pulse. If it's
higher than the upper rate, slow down. Don't work so hard.

At first some people have trouble getting their heart rate up to the lower
rate. Don't worry about that. Keep exercising at a comfortable level. As you
get more experienced and stronger your heart rate will rise, because you can
exercise more vigorously.

If you are taking medicine that regulates your heart rate, have trouble
feeling your pulse, or think that keeping track of your heart rate is a bother,
use one of the following methods to monitor your exercise intensity.

Talk Test

Talk to another person or yourself, sing, or recite poems while you exercise.
Moderate intensity exercise allows you to speak comfortably. If you can't
carry on a conversation or sing to yourself because you are breathing too
hard or are short of breath, you're working too hard. Slow down. The talk
test is an easy way to regulate exercise intensity.

Perceived Exertion

Another way to monitor intensity is to rate how hard you're working on a
scale of 0 to 10. Zero, at the low end of the scale, is lying down, doing no
work at all. Ten is equivalent to working as hard as possible—very hard work
that you couldn't do longer than a few seconds. Of course, you never want
to exercise that hard. A good level for aerobic exercise is between 3 and 6
on this scale.

Remember to follow the guidelines on frequency, duration, and intensity. Sometimes you need to tell yourself (and maybe others) that enough is
enough. More exercise is not necessarily better, especially if it gives you pain

or discomfort. As *The Walking Magazine* has said, "Go for the smiles, not the miles."

WALKING

You can walk to condition your heart and lungs, strengthen bones and muscles, relieve tension, control weight, and generally feel good. Walking is easy, inexpensive, safe, and accessible. You can walk by yourself or with company, and you can take your exercise with you wherever you go. Walking is safer and puts less stress on the body than jogging or running. It's an especially good choice if you are older, have been sedentary, or have joint problems.

Most people with arthritis can walk as a fitness exercise. If you walk to shop, visit friends, and do household chores, then you'll probably be able to walk for exercise. Using a cane or walker need not stop you from getting into a walking routine. If you are in a wheelchair, use crutches, or experience more than mild discomfort when you walk a short distance, you should consider some other type of aerobic exercise, or consult a physician or therapist for help.

Be cautious the first two weeks of walking. If you haven't been doing much for a while, ten minutes of walking may be enough. Build up your time with intervals of strolling. Each week increase the brisk walking interval by no more than five minutes until you are up to twenty or thirty minutes. Follow the frequency, duration, and intensity guidelines, and read these tips on walking before you start.

Walking Tips

1. **Choose your ground.** Walk on a flat, level surface. Walking on hills, uneven ground, soft earth, sand, or gravel is hard work and often leads to hip, knee, or foot pain. Fitness trails, shopping malls, school tracks, streets with sidewalks, and quiet neighborhoods are good places to get started.

2. **Always warm up and cool down with a stroll.** It's important to walk slowly for three to five minutes to prepare your circulation and muscles for a brisk walk, and to finish up with the same slow walk to let your body slow down gradually. Experienced walkers know they can avoid shin and foot discomfort when they begin and end with a stroll.

3. **Set your own pace.** It takes practice to find the right walking speed. To find your speed, start walking slowly for a few minutes, then increase your speed to a pace that is slightly faster than normal for you. After five minutes take your pulse and see if you are within your exercise heart rate range. If you are above the range or feel out of breath, slow down. If you are below the range, try walking a little faster. Walk another five minutes and take your pulse again. If you are still below your exercise range, don't try to raise your heart rate by walking uncomfort-

ably fast. Keep walking at a comfortable speed and take your pulse in the middle and at the end of each walk.

4. **Increase your arm work.** You can also raise your heart rate into exercise range by bending your elbows a bit and swinging your arms more vigorously. Alternatively, carry a one- (.5 kg) or two-pound (1 kg) weight (.75 kg) in each hand. You can purchase hand weights for walking, hold a can of food in each hand, or put sand, dried beans, or pennies in two small plastic beverage bottles or socks. The extra work you do with your arms increases your heart rate without forcing you to walk faster than you find comfortable.

Shoes

It's not necessary to spend a lot of money on shoes. Wear shoes of the correct length and width with shock-absorbing soles and insoles. Make sure they're big enough in the toe area: the "rule of thumb" is a thumb width between the end of your longest toe and the end of the shoe. You shouldn't feel pressure on the sides or tops of your toes. The heel counter should hold your heel firmly in the shoe when you walk.

Wear shoes with a continuous crepe or composite sole in good repair. Shoes with leather soles and a separate heel don't absorb shock as well as the newer athletic and casual shoes. Shoes with laces or Velcro let you adjust width as needed and give more support than slip-ons. If you have problems tying laces, consider Velcro closures or elastic shoelaces.

Many people like shoes with removable insoles which can be exchanged for ones that are more shock absorbing. Insoles are available in sporting goods stores and shoe stores. When you shop for insoles, take your walking shoes with you. Try on the shoe with the insole to make sure that there's still enough room inside for your foot to be comfortable. Insoles come in sizes and can be trimmed with scissors for a final fit. If your toes take up extra room, try the three-quarter insoles that stop just short of your toes. If you have prescribed inserts in your shoes already, ask your doctor or orthotist about insoles.

Possible Problems

1. If you have pain around your shins when you walk, you may not be spending enough time warming up. Do the ankle exercises before you start walking. Start your walk at a slow pace for at least five minutes. Keep your feet and toes relaxed.

2. Another common problem is sore knees. Fast walking puts more stress on knee joints. To slow your speed and keep your heart rate up, try doing more work with your arms (see above). Do the Knee Strengthener (Exercise 22 in Chapter 8) in your warm-up to help reduce knee pain.

3. Cramps in the calf and heel pain can often be eliminated by doing the Achilles Stretch (Exercise 25 in Chapter 8) before and after walking. A

slow walk to warm up also is helpful. If you have circulatory problems in your legs and experience cramps while walking, alternate intervals of brisk and slow walking. If this doesn't help, check with your physician or therapist for suggestions.

4.   Maintain good posture. Remember the Heads Up position (Exercise 1 in Chapter 8) and keep your shoulders relaxed to help reduce neck and upper back discomfort.

SWIMMING

Swimming is another good aerobic exercise. The buoyancy of the water lets you move your joints through their full range of motion and strengthen your muscles and cardiovascular system with less joint stress than on land. Swimming uses the whole body. If you haven't been swimming for a while, consider a refresher course.

To make swimming an aerobic exercise, you will eventually need to swim continuously for twenty minutes. Use the frequency, duration, and intensity guidelines to build up your endurance. Try different strokes, modifying them or changing strokes after each lap or two. This lets you exercise all joints and muscles without overtiring any one area.

Swimming Tips

1.   **Use a mask and snorkel for breathing.** The breast stroke and crawl require a lot of neck motion and may be uncomfortable if you have neck pain. To solve this problem, use a mask and snorkel to breathe without twisting your neck.

2.   **Swim goggles protect eyes.** Chlorine can be irritating to eyes. A good pair of goggles will protect your eyes and let you keep your eyes open while you're swimming.

3.   **Take a hot shower or soak in a hot tub after your workout.** The warmth helps reduce stiffness and muscle soreness. Remember not to work too hard or get too tired. If you're sore for more than two hours, you should go easier next time.

4.   **Always swim where there are qualified lifeguards.**

If you don't like to swim or are uncomfortable learning strokes, you can walk laps in the pool, or join the millions who are aquacizing.

AQUACIZE

Exercising in the water is comfortable, fun, and effective as a flexibility, strengthening, and aerobic activity. The buoyancy of the water takes weight off hips, knees, feet, and back. People who have trouble walking for endurance can usually aquacize. The pool is a good place to do your own routine, because no one can see you much below shoulder level.

Getting Started

Joining a water exercise class with a good instructor is an excellent way to get started. The Arthritis Foundation and Arthritis Society sponsor water exercise classes and train instructors. Contact your local chapter or branch office to see what is available. Many communities and private health clubs offer water exercise classes, with some geared to older adults.

If you have access to a pool and want to exercise on your own, there are many water exercise books available. One we recommend is *Hydrorobics*, by Joseph A. Krasevec and Diane C. Grimes (Leisure Press, 1985). It contains a lot of good ideas for exercise in the water.

Water temperature is always a topic when people talk about water exercise. The U.S. Arthritis Foundation recommends a pool temperature of 84°F (29°C) with the surrounding air temperature in the same range. Except in warm climates, this means a heated pool. If you're just starting to aquacize, find a pool with these temperatures. If you can exercise more vigorously and don't have Raynaud's phenomenon or other cold sensitivity, you can probably aquacize in cooler water. Many pools where people swim laps are about 80 to 83°F (27 to 28°C). It feels quite cool when you first get in, but starting off with water walking, jogging, or another whole-body exercise helps you warm up quickly.

The deeper the water you stand in, the less stress there is on joints; however, water above mid-chest can make it hard to keep your balance. You can let the water cover more of your body just by spreading your legs apart or bending your knees a bit.

Aquacize Tips

1. **Protect your feet.** Wear something on your feet to protect them from rough pool floors and to provide traction in the pool and on the deck. Choices vary from terry cloth slippers with rubber soles (they stretch in water, so buy a size smaller than your shoe size) to footgear especially designed for water exercise. Some styles have Velcro tape to make them easier to put on. Beach shoes with rubber soles and mesh tops also work well.

2. **Keep warm.** If you are sensitive to cold or have Raynaud's phenomenon, wear a pair of disposable latex surgical gloves. Boxes of gloves are available at most pharmacies. The water trapped and warmed inside the glove seems to insulate the hand. If your body gets cold in the water, wear a T-shirt and/or the full-leg Lycra exercise tights for warmth.

3. **Try a step stool for easier access.** If the pool does not have steps, and it is difficult for you to climb up and down a ladder, suggest positioning a three-step kitchen stool in the pool by the ladder rails. This is an inexpensive way to provide steps for easier entry and exit, and it is easy to remove and store when not needed.

4. **Add more buoyancy.** Wearing a flotation belt or life vest adds extra buoyancy, to take weight off hips, knees, and feet. That makes exercising more comfortable for these joints.

5. **Regulate exercise intensity.** You can regulate how hard you work in the water by how you move. To make the work easier, move more slowly. Another way to regulate exercise intensity is to change how much water you push when you move. For example, when you move your arms back and forth in front of you under water, it is hard work if you hold your palms facing each other and clap. It is easier if you turn your palms down and slice your arms back and forth with only the narrow edge of your hands pushing against the water.

OUTDOOR BICYCLING

Cyclists who travel outdoors can socialize while riding, enjoy the scenery, and get out into the fresh air and sunshine. But they also face the risks of the streets and bike paths, especially the danger of falling. Falls from bicycles can be serious. If you have problems with balance, vision, or hearing, or if you have osteoporosis, outdoor bicycling may not be for you. Consider a stationary bicycle instead (see the next section).

If you live in a flat area, consider an adult tricycle. Though heavy and a little harder to pedal than a bicycle, they are very stable. The large cargo area between the two back wheels makes it easy to run errands and carry packages.

Finding the Right Bicycle

Reading, talking to other bicyclists, and taking an exploratory trip to a bike shop will help you decide on your kind of bike. Once you know the features you want, and have read the next section about bicycle fit, you may be able to find what you want at a yard sale or through a classified ad. There are usually excellent buys in used bikes. Just get a professional safety check and tune up before you ride.

Racing and touring bicycles, the models with the dropped handlebars, are lightweight and fast. Mountain, all-terrain, and "city" models have upright handlebars and are heavier and slower. New cyclists are often uncomfortable with dropped handlebars, and arthritis may make it more difficult to use this style. Some people get the best of both styles by replacing the dropped handlebars on a lightweight bicycle with upright handlebars.

Arthritis in your hands may limit your bicycle choice. Most bikes use hand brakes. Try the different styles to see if one is better for you than another. If you feel you do not have enough strength to squeeze the brakes, look for a one-speed bicycle. These bicycles use the back pedal brake system. One-speed bikes are heavy, have no gears, and are limited to flat ground.

If you have knee problems, ask about a "granny gear" for your bicycle.

The granny gear allows you to pedal more easily and takes strain off your knees.

Whatever style you choose, remember that bicycling uses different muscles than walking. Don't be surprised if a five- or ten-minute ride is enough at first. Follow the guidelines of frequency, duration, and intensity to progress gradually to twenty or thirty minutes of safe and enjoyable bicycling.

The Right Fit

Proper fit of the bicycle to your body is essential. Incorrect seat height is the most common cause of discomfort. It is also the easiest adjustment to make. To check seat height, have someone hold the bike while you sit on the seat. With your *heel* on the pedal, straighten your leg to the bottom of the pedal stroke. If your knee is still bent, the seat is too low. Keeping your knees bent while pedaling can cause pain at your kneecap and in the muscle above your knee. (People whose knees bend backward should leave just a little bend.) If you can't keep your heel on the pedal when the pedal is at its lowest point, you need to lower the seat. A seat that is too high can result in back pain.

The distance between the seat post and the handlebar stem (the "top tube length") should be correct for you. To test this measurement, sit on the bicycle and place your hands on the handlebar grips. Your elbows should be comfortably bent. If your elbows are straight or you have to stretch forward, the "top tube length" is too long. A bike shop can change this distance by adjusting the horizontal seat placement, the handlebars, or the stem. If none of these work, look for another bike that fits you better.

It's also important for there to be enough space on the pedal and within the toe clip to let your foot shift as you ride. Being able to change foot position as you pedal makes the ride easier on your knees and ankles.

Riding Tips

1. **Always wear a helmet.** The most important piece of equipment for bicycle riding is a helmet. Any fall can cause serious head injury. Don't risk it. There are ventilated helmets that weigh less than eight ounces (224 g). Look for a sticker showing that the helmet has been approved by a safety board, such as SNELL or ANSI in the United States.

2. **Follow the rules.** Learn and obey the bicycle road rules for your community. Take advantage of roads with a designated bicycle lane.

3. **Pedal with the *ball* of your foot, and always wear shoes.**

4. **Use gears correctly for safety and comfort.** Learn to use your gears so that you don't "grind." If you work hard to pedal and start to feel pain around your kneecap, you're probably grinding. To stop, shift down to a lower gear until you feel only slight resistance as you pedal. If you start to feel that the pedals are going faster than your feet, you are in too low a gear. Shift up slightly.

STATIONARY BICYCLES

Stationary bicycles offer the fitness benefits of outdoor bicycling without the outdoor hazards. They're preferable for people who don't have the flexibility or strength to be comfortable pedaling and steering on the road. If you live in a cold or hilly area, you may want to avoid the extra exertion of cycling outdoors.

Choosing a Bicycle

There are many models of stationary bicycles, and many options that come with them. Most models have a speedometer and odometer to show the speed and distance you would have traveled outdoors. One optional feature takes your pulse through an ear clip or finger rings and gives a digital read-out. Models at health clubs may have computer programs and video displays to take you over hills and dales. There are also recumbent bicycles that place hips and knees at about the same height. Some people find these the most comfortable.

The most important model differences are:

1. **Seat.** Regular bicycle and bench-style seats are both available. Seats can be adjusted vertically or both vertically and horizontally. Adjust the seat so that your knee is straight with your *heel* on the pedal when the pedal is at its lowest point. If your knees are unstable or loose, or bend backward, adjust the seat height so that there is a little bend left in your knee, rather than having your legs be completely straight. If your knees don't straighten all the way, adjust the seat so that they are as straight as they will go.

2. **Handlebars.** Stationary handlebars are for balance and for supporting your arms. Movable handlebars let you exercise the upper body. Using your arms as you exercise helps you spread the work out, instead of depending on your legs to do it all. You should be able to grip the handlebars with a slight bend in your elbows. If you can only reach with straight elbows or by stretching forward, adjustment is needed. If this adjustment is impossible, shop for another model that fits you better.

3. **Resistance.** How hard you have to push to turn the pedals can be adjusted with a dial or screw. On some models a fan wheel increases resistance as you pedal faster. If the resistance is manual, make sure you can easily reach and turn the control.

A loan or rental is a good way to start using a stationary bicycle. The classified ads are a great place to shop for your own. Not all models fit everyone so try out any bicycle you are considering. Make sure it adjusts to your

comfort and safety. Check all the points below.
Checklist:

- The bicycle is steady when you get on and off.

- The resistance is easy to set, and can be set to zero.

- The seat is comfortable.

- The seat can be adjusted for full knee extension when the pedal is at its lowest point.

- Large pedals and loose pedal straps allow feet to move slightly while pedaling.

- There is ample clearance from the frame for knees and ankles.

- The handlebars allow good posture and comfortable arm position.

Make It Interesting

The most common complaint about riding a stationary bike is that it's boring. If you ride while watching television, reading, or listening to music, you can become fit without becoming bored. One woman keeps interested by mapping out tours of places she would like to visit and then charts her progress on the map as she rolls off the miles. Other people set their bicycle time for the half hour of soap opera or news that they watch every day. There are videocassettes of exotic bike tours that put you in the rider's perspective. Book racks that clip on to the handlebars make reading easy.

Riding Tips

1. **Don't use too much resistance.** Bicycling uses different muscles than walking. Until your leg muscles get used to pedaling, you may only be able to ride a few minutes. Start off with no resistance. If you wish, increase resistance slightly every two weeks. Increasing resistance has the same effect as bicycling up hills. If you use too much resistance, your knees are likely to hurt, and you'll have to stop before you get the benefit of an endurance exercise.

2. **Pedal at a comfortable speed.** For most people, 60 revolutions per minute (rpm) is a good place to start. Some bicycles tell you the rpm, or you can count the number of times your right foot reaches its lowest point in a minute. As you get used to bicycling, you can increase your speed. However, faster is not necessarily better. Listening to music at the right tempo makes it easier to pedal at a consistent speed. Experience will tell you the best combination of speed and resistance.

3. **Progress gradually at moderate intensity.** Set your goal for twenty to thirty minutes of pedaling at a comfortable speed. Build up your time by alternating intervals of brisk pedaling with less exertion. Use your

heart rate, perceived exertion, or the talk test to make sure you aren't working too hard. If you're alone, try singing songs as you pedal. If you get out of breath, slow down.

4. **Chart progress.** Keep a record of the times and distances of your "bike trips." You'll be amazed at how much you can do.

5. **Keep the exercise habit.** On bad days, or if you have a painful knee, keep your exercise habit going by pedaling with no resistance, at fewer rpm, or for a shorter period of time.

The stationary bicycle is a particularly good alternative exercise. It does not put weight on your hips, knees, and feet, you can easily adjust how hard you work, and weather doesn't matter. Use the bicycle on days when you don't want to walk or do more vigorous exercise, or can't exercise outside.

OTHER EXERCISE EQUIPMENT

If you have trouble getting on or off a stationary bicycle, or don't have room for a bicycle where you live, you might try a restorator or arm crank. Ask your therapist or doctor, or call a medical supply house.

A restorator is a small piece of equipment with foot pedals which can be attached to the foot of a bed or a chair. It allows you to exercise by pedaling. Resistance can be varied, and placement of the restorator lets you adjust for leg length and knee bend. The restorator can be the first step in getting an exercise program started.

Arm cranks are bicycles for the arms. They are mounted on a table. People who are unable to use their legs for active exercise can improve their cardiovascular fitness by using the arm crank. It's important to work closely with a therapist to set up your program, because using only your arms for aerobic exercise requires different intensity monitoring than using the bigger leg muscles.

There is a wide variety of exercise equipment in addition to what we've mentioned so far. These include treadmills (self-powered and motor-driven), rowing machines, cross-country skiing machines, mini-trampolines, and stair-climbing machines. Most are available in both commercial and home models. If you're thinking about exercise equipment, have your objectives clearly in mind. For cardiovascular fitness and endurance, you want equipment that will help you exercise as much of your body at one time as possible. The motion should be rhythmical, repetitive, and continuous. The equipment should be comfortable, safe, and not stressful on joints. If you're interested in a new piece of equipment, try it out for a week or two before buying it.

Exercise equipment that requires you to use weights usually does not improve cardiovascular fitness. A weight-lifting program builds strength, but it can put excessive stress on joints, muscles, tendons, and ligaments. It is extremely important that you confer with your doctor or therapist when planning any program that uses weights or weight machines.

LOW IMPACT AEROBICS

Most people find low impact aerobic dance a safe and acceptable form of exercise. "Low impact" means that one foot is always on the floor and there is no jumping. However, low impact does not necessarily mean low intensity, nor do the low impact routines protect all joints. If you participate in a low impact aerobic class, you'll probably need to make some modifications for your arthritis.

Getting Started

Start off by letting the instructor know who you are, that you may modify some movements to meet your needs, and that you may need to ask for advice. It's easier to start off with a newly formed class than it is to join an ongoing class. If you don't know people, try to get acquainted. Be open about why you may sometimes do things a little differently. You'll be more comfortable and may find others who also have special needs.

Most instructors use music or count to a specific beat, and do a set number of repetitions. You may find that the movement is too fast or that you don't want to do as many repetitions. Modify the routine by slowing down to half-time, or keep up with the beat until you start to tire and then slow down or stop. If the class is doing an exercise that involves arms and legs and you get tired, try resting your arms and only doing the leg movements, or just walk in place until you are ready to go again. Most instructors will be able to instruct you in "chair aerobics" if you need some time off your feet.

Many low impact routines use lots of arm movements done at or above shoulder level to raise heart rates. For people who have shoulder problems or high blood pressure, too much arm exercise above shoulder level can cause problems. Modify the exercise by lowering your arms or taking a rest break.

Being different from the group in a room walled with mirrors takes courage, conviction, and a sense of humor. The most important thing you can do for yourself is to choose an instructor who encourages everyone to exercise at his or her own pace and a class where people are friendly and having fun. Observe classes, speak with instructors, and participate in at least one class session before making any financial commitment.

Aerobic Studio Tips

1. **Wear shoes.** Many studios have cushioned floors and soft carpet that might tempt you to go barefoot. Don't! Shoes help protect the small joints and muscles in your feet and ankles by providing a firm, flat surface on which to stand.

2. **Protect your knees.** Stand with knees straight but relaxed. Many low impact routines are done with bent, tensed knees and a lot of bobbing up and down. This can be painful and is unnecessarily stressful. Avoid

this by remembering to keep your knees relaxed (aerobics instructors call this "soft" knees). Watch in the mirror to see that you keep the top of your head steady as you exercise. Don't bob up and down.

3. **Don't overstretch.** The beginning (warm-up) and end (cool-down) of the session will have stretching and strengthening exercises. Remember to stretch only as far as you comfortably can. Hold the position and don't bounce. If the stretch hurts, don't do it. Ask your instructor for a less stressful substitute, or choose one of your own.

4. **Change movements.** Do this often enough so that you don't get sore muscles or joints. It's normal to feel some new sensations in your muscles and around your joints when you start a new exercise program. However, if you feel discomfort doing the same movement for some time, change movements or stop for a while and rest.

5. **Alternate kinds of exercise.** Many exercise facilities have a variety of exercise opportunities: equipment rooms with cardiovascular machines, pools, and aerobic studios. If you have trouble with an hour-long aerobic class, see if you can join the class for the warm-up and cool-down and use a stationary bicycle or treadmill for your aerobic portion. Many people have found that this routine gives them the benefits of both an individualized program and group exercise.

SELF-TESTS FOR AEROBIC FITNESS

It's important to see that your exercise program is making a measurable difference. Choose one of these aerobic fitness tests to perform before you start your exercise program. Pick the test that works best for you. Record your results. After four weeks of exercise, do the test again and check your improvement. Measure yourself again after four more weeks.

1. Distance Test

Find a place to walk or bicycle where you can measure distance. A running track works well. On a street you can measure distance with a car. A stationary bicycle with an odometer provides the equivalent measurement. If you plan on swimming, you can count lengths of the pool.

After a warm up, note your starting point and either bicycle, swim, or walk as briskly as you comfortably can for five minutes. Try to move at a steady pace for the full time. At the end of five minutes, mark your spot and immediately take your pulse and rate your perceived exertion from 0 to 10. Continue at a slow pace for three to five more minutes to cool down. Measure and record the distance, your heart rate, and your perceived exertion at the end of the five minutes of brisk exercise.

Repeat the test after several weeks of exercise. There may be a change in as little as four weeks. However, it often takes eight to twelve weeks to see improvement.

Goal: To cover more distance or to lower your heart rate or to lower your perceived exertion.

2. Time Test

Measure a given distance to walk, bike, or swim. Estimate how far you think you can go in about five minutes. You can pick a number of blocks, actual distance, or lengths in a pool.

Spend three to five minutes warming up. Start timing and start moving steadily, briskly, and comfortably. At the finish, record how long it took you to cover your course, your heart rate, and your perceived exertion.

Repeat after several weeks of exercise. You may see changes in as soon as four weeks. However, it often takes eight to twelve weeks for improvement.

Goal: To complete the course in less time or to lower your heart rate or to lower your perceived exertion.

References

Krasevec, Joseph A., and Diane C. Grimes. *Hydrorobics*. Champaign, IL: Leisure Press, 1985.

10

Pain Management

Pain is a problem shared by most people with arthritis. In fact, for many people, it is their number one concern. Unfortunately, pain is a very personal symptom. It cannot be seen by others, and we do not even have good words to describe most pain. Because it is so individual, pain is hard to treat, so it is important for you to know a little about pain.

The pain caused by arthritis really comes from at least three sources. Of course, the disease itself causes pain, from damaged and inflamed joints. A second type of pain comes from weak, tense muscles. When a joint is damaged, the natural response of the body is to tense the muscles in the area in an effort to protect the joint. Unfortunately, these muscles are often weak from not being used. In addition, tense muscles themselves cause pain by building up lactic acid. Try making a fist and holding it for five minutes to confirm the pain that comes from muscle tension. A final source of pain is fear and depression. When we are afraid and depressed, everything, including pain, seems worse.

Because pain comes from many sources, pain management must be aimed at all of these sources. The use of heat, medication, and even cold can help reduce the pain caused by the disease. Exercise strengthens muscles and, strangely enough, helps them relax. Learning about the disease and becoming an active arthritis self-manager can help with the fear and depression.

In addition, there are a whole set of pain-management techniques that are seldom taught. In one way or another all of these techniques use the mind to help relax muscles, reduce anxiety, and decrease pain. Like all activities, they require some skill, but mastering them has brought relief to many people. In the following pages, we will describe several pain-management techniques.

To use these techniques to the best advantage, we suggest you do the following:

1. Read the whole chapter.

2. Try several different techniques. You will probably like some and not others. Be sure you give your chosen technique a fair trial. This means at least two weeks of practice before you decide if it is going to be helpful.

3. Once you have found two or three techniques you like, think how you will use each one. For example, some exercises can be done anywhere while others require a quiet place. The best pain managers use a variety of techniques that can be mixed and matched to the situations in daily life. Include your choices in your weekly contract.

4. Finally, place some clues in your environment to remind you to practice your pain-management skills. You have to be regular with your program for it to work. For example, place some stars or other stickers where you will see them, and they will remind you to practice your skills. You can put a star on your mirror, your office or home telephone, or the dashboard of your car. Change the stickers every month or so. This will help you notice them.

RELAXATION TECHNIQUES

So much has been said and written about relaxation that most of us are completely confused. It is not a cure-all, but neither is it a hoax. Rather, like most treatment methods, it has specific uses. The advantage of relaxation in the management of arthritis is that muscles become less tense and thus it is easier and less painful to move the joints. In addition to releasing tension throughout the body, relaxation exercises help you sleep, and they are particularly helpful in relieving pain.

Like all exercise, the following techniques take practice. Thus, if you feel you are not accomplishing anything, be patient and keep trying. Try another method if the one you choose does not seem to work for you, but first give it two full weeks trial. Relaxation techniques should be practiced at least twice a day. With many forms of arthritis, it is wise to take short rest periods during the day, to avoid undue fatigue and to relieve stress on the joints. This is an excellent time to practice relaxation techniques.

The following are examples of relaxation techniques. Once you choose the one that works best for you, tape-record the technique. This is not necessary but is sometimes helpful if you find it hard to concentrate. With an inexpensive cassette recorder you can tape a routine to follow so you won't have to think hard or look at this book while you are trying to relax.

Here are some guidelines that will help you practice the relaxation techniques described in this chapter:

1. Pick a quiet time and place where you will not be disturbed for fifteen to twenty minutes.

2. Try to practice twice daily, but not less than four times a week.

3. Don't expect miracles. It will probably take three to four weeks of practice before you really start to notice benefits.

4. Relaxation should be helpful. At worst, you may find it boring, but if it is unpleasant or makes you nervous, then you might do better with other pain-management techniques.

JACOBSON'S PROGRESSIVE RELAXATION*

Many years ago a physiologist, Edmund Jacobson, discovered that in order to relax one must know what it feels like to be relaxed and to be tense. He believed that if one could recognize tension, one could then let it go and relax. Thus, he designed a very simple set of exercises to assist with the learning process.

To relax muscles, you need to know how to scan your body, recognize where you are holding tension, and release that tension. The first step is to become familiar with the difference between the feeling of tension and the feeling of relaxation. This brief exercise will allow you to compare those feelings and, with practice, to spot and release tension anywhere in your body.

Give yourself permission to take the next few minutes for yourself. For just a little while, let go of all outside concerns. Progressive relaxation is best done lying on your back either on a rug or in bed. However, it can be done seated in a comfortable chair. Choose a quiet time and place where you will not be disturbed for at least fifteen minutes. Make yourself as comfortable as possible. Loosen any tight clothing. Uncross your legs and ankles. Allow your body to feel supported by the surface on which you are sitting or lying.

Close your eyes. Take a deep breath, breathing all the way down to the abdomen. And as you breathe out, let as much tension as possible flow out with your breath.

As you tense and relax different muscle groups, notice if you have pain in a particular area. Do not tense those muscles, just try to relax them.

Become aware of the muscles in your *feet and calves*. Pull your toes

---

*Much of this section has been adapted from Gordon Paul, *Insight vs. Desensitization in Psychotherapy: An Experiment in Anxiety Reduction* (Stanford, Calif.: Stanford University Press, 1966).

back up toward your knees. Notice the tension in your feet and calves. Hold for a moment. Release and relax. Notice the discomfort leaving and the relief and warmth replacing it.

Now tighten the muscles of your *thighs and buttocks*. Hold and feel the tension. Let go and allow the muscles to relax. The relaxed muscles feel heavy and supported by the surface upon which you are resting.

Tense the muscles in your *abdomen and chest*. Notice a tendency to hold your breath as you tense. Relax, and notice that it is natural to want to take a deep breath now, breathing all the way down to the abdomen. As you breathe out, allow all the tension to flow out with your breath.

Since many people carry tension in this area, you may still have some remaining tension. Tighten the muscles of your abdomen and chest again, not quite so much this time. And take another deep breath, releasing all of the tension as you breathe out.

Now stretch out your *fingers and arm muscles*. Relax. Feel the tension flowing out and the circulation returning.

Lift your shoulders, tightening the muscles in your *shoulders and neck*. You may find you are exaggerating an already-existing tension, since this is another place where many of us carry a great deal of tension. Let go. Notice how the muscles feel warmer and more alive.

To further release tension in this area, press your shoulder blades together, than make circular motions with your shoulders. Notice how good it feels as the warmth and circulation return to your neck and shoulders.

Tighten all the muscles of your *face and head*. Notice the tension, especially around your eyes and in your jaw. Now relax, allowing your jaw to become slack and your mouth to remain slightly open.

If you detect any remaining tension in your face or head, tighten that area again and let go, being sure to allow the small muscles around your eyes to relax and your jaw to become slack and your mouth to remain slightly open.

Now take a deep breath and become aware of *any* remaining tension in your body. As you breathe out, allow all the muscles of your body to become limp and heavy.

Scan your body for any remaining pockets of tension. If you find any, deepen your relaxation further by imagining that the tension is a knot. Picture the knot gradually loosening until the muscle is limp and heavy.

Now take another deep breath, breathing all the way down to the abdomen. And as you breathe out, allow your body to sink heavily into the surface beneath you, becoming even more deeply relaxed.

Enjoy this comfortable feeling of relaxation. Remember it. With practice, you will become skilled at recognizing muscle tension and releasing it.

Prepare to come back into the here and now. Sit quietly for a moment before resuming your usual activities. And when you are ready, open your eyes.

Jacobson emphasizes that the purpose of voluntarily tensing the muscles is to learn to recognize and locate tension in your body. You will then become aware of tension and will use the same procedure of letting go. Once you learn the technique it will be unnecessary to tense voluntarily, just locate the tension and let it go.

For people with very painful joints, the Jacobson technique may not be the best exercise for relaxation. If it causes any pain, the pain may distract from the relaxation. If this is the case for you, try the following techniques.

THE RELAXATION RESPONSE

During the early 1970s Dr. Herbert Benson did extensive work on what he calls the relaxation response. He says that our bodies have several natural states. For example, if you meet a lion on the street, you will probably become quite tense—your response will be a "fight or flight" response. After extreme tension, the body's natural response is to relax. This is what happens after a sexual climax. As life becomes more and more complex, our bodies tend to stay in a constant state of tension. Thus, to elicit the relaxation response, many people will consciously need to practice the following exercise.

Four Basic Elements

1. **A quiet environment.** Turn off internal stimuli and external distractions.

2. **An object to dwell upon, or a mental device.** For example, repeat a word or sound like the word *one*, gaze at a symbol like a flower, or concentrate on a feeling such as peace.

3. **A passive attitude.** This is the most essential factor. It is an emptying of all thoughts and distractions from your mind. Thoughts, imagery, and feelings may drift into awareness—don't concentrate on them, just allow them to pass on.

4. **A comfortable position.** You should be comfortable enough to remain in the same position for twenty minutes.

Technique for Eliciting the Relaxation Response

1. Sit quietly in a comfortable position.

2. Close your eyes.

3. Deeply relax all your muscles, beginning at your feet and progressing up to your face. Keep them relaxed.

4. Breathe in through your nose. Become aware of your breathing. As you breathe out through your mouth, say the word *one* silently to yourself. Try to empty all thoughts from your mind; concentrate on *one*.

5. Continue for ten to twenty minutes—you may open your eyes to check the time, but do not use an alarm. When you finish, sit quietly for

several minutes, at first with your eyes closed. Do not stand up for a few minutes.

6. Do not worry about whether you are successful in achieving a deep level of relaxation. Maintain a passive attitude and permit relaxation to occur at its own pace. When distracting thoughts occur, try to ignore them by not dwelling upon them, and return to repeating *one*.

7. Practice once or twice daily, but ideally not within two hours after any meal, since digestive processes seem to interfere with elicitation of relaxation responses.

You may have noticed that this exercise is very much like meditation. In fact, meditation has provided the principles of the relaxation response. There is no need to spend several hundred dollars to learn to meditate. You now know all the steps.

GUIDED IMAGERY

A third relaxation technique is called "guided imagery." This is like a guided daydream where you transport yourself to another time and place. It is as though you were taking a mental stroll. The two guided imagery scripts presented here can be used in several different ways, depending on what technique works best for you. Consider each of the following:

1. Read a script over several times to familiarize yourself with it. Then sit or lie in a quiet place and try to reconstruct the scene in your mind. Each script should take ten to fifteen minutes to complete.

2. Have a family member or friend slowly read you the script. Wherever there is a series of dots (...) he or she should pause for five to ten seconds.

3. Make a tape of the script and play it to yourself.

Guided Imagery 1: A Happy Time

Before imagining or listening to this scene, close your eyes and take three deep breaths . . . breathe slowly and easily, in through your nose, out through your mouth . . .

Now picture a happy, pleasant time in your life . . . a time when you had little or no problems with your arthritis . . .

Fill in the details of that time . . . look at the surroundings—indoors? . . . outdoors? . . . who was there? . . . what were you doing? . . . listen to the noises . . . even those in the background . . . are there any pleasant smells? . . . feel the temperature . . . now just enjoy your surroundings . . . you are happy . . . your body feels good . . . enjoy your surroundings . . . fix this feeling in your mind . . . you can return any time you wish by just picturing this happy time . . .

When you are ready, take three deep breaths . . . with each breath say the word "relax" . . . imagine the word written in warm sand . . . open your eyes—remain quiet for a few moments before slowly returning to your activities.

Guided Imagery 2: A Flower Garden

Make yourself as comfortable as possible, sitting or lying down. Loosen any constricting clothing. Do not cross your legs or ankles. Allow your body to feel supported by the surface on which you are sitting or lying.

Close your eyes. . . . Take a deep breath, breathing all the way down to the abdomen.

Notice your *feet and calves, thighs and buttocks*. If you detect any tension, tighten those muscles a little more and then release the tension.

Is there any tension in your *abdomen or chest*? Take another deep breath and allow your stomach and chest to relax.

Notice your *hands and arms*. Gently exaggerate any tension you discover by tightening those muscles and then relax.

Are your *shoulders and neck* tense? Shrug your shoulders. Let go. Notice how the muscles feel warmer and more alive.

Notice any tension in your *face and head*, especially around your eyes or in your jaw. Tighten the muscles of your face and head. Now relax, allowing your jaw to become slack and your mouth to remain slightly open.

Now take a deep breath and become aware of any remaining tension in your body. As you breathe out, allow all the muscles of your body to sink into the surface beneath you, becoming even more deeply relaxed.

Imagine yourself on a country road. . . . You come to an old gate. . . . The gate creaks as you open it and enter.

You are surrounded by an overgrown garden . . . flowers growing where they have seeded themselves . . . vines climbing over a fallen tree . . . green grass, shade trees.

Smell the flowers . . . listen to the birds . . .

As you walk a little farther, the trees become denser . . . almost blotting out the sun. Feel the cool air . . . notice the moss . . .

You come upon a brook. . . . As you follow the path along the brook, you hear a waterfall in the distance. . . . Just where the path takes you out into a sunlit clearing you see a cascade of water . . . There is a rainbow in the mist . . .

You feel good, enjoying the warmth and solitude of this peaceful place . . .

It is now time to return, back down the path, . . . one last smell of the flowers and out the creaky gate. This secret garden is awaiting your return. You may return to it whenever you wish.

Now, take three deep breaths and, when you're ready, open your eyes.

VIVID IMAGERY

This is a little like guided imagery but can be used for longer periods or while you are engaged in other activities.

One way to use imagery is to recall pleasant scenes from your past. For example, try to remember every detail of a special holiday or party that made you happy. Who was there? What happened? What did you talk about? Of course, you can do the same sort of thing with a vacation. Another way to use imagery is to fill in the details of a pleasant fantasy. How would you spend a million dollars? What would be your ideal romantic encounter? What would your ideal home or garden be like?

Sometimes warm imagery can be especially helpful, such as thinking of yourself on a warm beach or visiting a tropical island.

Another form of vivid imagery is to think of symbols that represent painful parts of your body. For example, a painful joint might be red or might have a tight band around it or even a lion biting it.

Now try to change the image. Make the red fade until there is no color left, or imagine the band stretching and stretching until it falls off. Change the lion into a purring kitten.

A final way to use vivid imagery is to help you with goal setting (see Chapter 6). After you set your weekly contract, take a few minutes to imagine yourself taking a walk, doing your exercises, or taking your medications. Studies have shown that these few minutes of imagery will help you accomplish your goal. Many people become very skilled at vivid imagery. They find that as they change their pain images, the pain decreases.

BREATHING EXERCISES

These are really a special form of relaxation. You should concentrate on your breathing, taking a long slow breath through your nose, holding it for a few seconds, and breathing out through your mouth. As you do this, say "relax" to yourself. You can try to focus the breath either at the back of your chest or, if you wish, on your painful joint. The most important thing is to concentrate on your breathing and keep it slow and easy. To check this, you might place a lit candle in front of you. When blowing out a breath, you should make the candle flicker but not go out.

One problem with breathing exercises is that sometimes people hyperventilate. That is, they have a hard time catching their breath. Hyperventilation is scary but not dangerous. Strangely enough, it is caused by having too much oxygen and not enough carbon dioxide. An easy way to restore the balance is to breathe into a closed paper bag for a *short* time. Better yet, don't hyperventilate. By keeping your breathing slow and easy, you can completely avoid this problem.

DISSOCIATION

This technique involves mentally separating yourself from the painful part of your body. It is especially effective when pain is so severe that it is impossible to distract yourself.

To use dissociation, picture that the painful part of your body is separate from the rest of your body. Imagine that this body part is completely insensitive and therefore does not feel any pain. For example, tell yourself that your joint does not belong to you; it is completely separate from you. You cannot feel anything that happens to it. Whatever happens to your joint does not affect you at all. You can even imagine that you have floated away from your body and are looking at it from across the room.

DISTRACTION

Because our minds have trouble focusing on more than one thing at a time, you can lessen pain by focusing on something else. This technique can be especially helpful if you are going to do some short activity you know to be painful, such as climbing stairs or opening a jar. Following are some suggestions for practicing distraction, also called "attention refocusing."

1. While climbing stairs, plan exactly what you will be doing when you get to the top. Be as detailed as possible. Or you might name a different bird or flower for each step. You can even try to visualize a bird or flower for every letter of the alphabet.

2. During any painful activity, try to think of a person's name, a bird, a food, or whatever, for every letter of the alphabet. If you get stuck on one letter, go on to the next. (This is also a good exercise if you have problems sleeping.)

3. While sweeping, vacuuming, or mopping, imagine that the floor is a map of North America. Try to name all the states and provinces going from east to west or north to south. You can also do this with the map of Europe or, if you are really good in geography, Africa. If geography is not your strong suit, think of your favorite store and where each department is located.

4. When getting up from a chair or out of a car, imagine that you are in a spaceship where you are almost weightless, floating effortlessly upward. Or, try counting backward from 1,000 by threes, each time getting as far as you can until you are standing. Try to break your old record.

5. While opening a jar, try to think of as many uses as you can for the jar. Or, try to remember the words of a song and imagine the story taking place inside the jar. There are, of course, a million variations, now that you have the refocusing idea.

So far we have discussed short-term refocusing strategies. However, the distraction technique works for long-term projects as well. Find an activity that really interests you and you will find yourself distracted from your pain. This activity can be almost anything, from cooking or stamp collecting to watching a movie or doing volunteer work. One of the marks of a successful arthritis manager is that he or she has a variety of interests and always seems to be doing something.

RELABELING

This technique is the opposite of distraction or attention refocusing. Rather than thinking of something else, you will think about your pain. However, you will do more than that. You will try to analyze the pain. Is it sharp, dull, hot, cold? Exactly what are the sensations that you are feeling? Now, concentrate on your pulse, or the muscle tension in or around your joint, but don't think of "pain." Think of the various sensations. These sensations may increase, decrease, or level off. Just go along with them. See if you can begin to think of the sensations as mere dullness, as if the joint had become completely numb.

PRAYER

Over the years, we have had many people tell us that prayer has been very helpful in managing their pain. In many ways, prayer is similar to some relaxation techniques, and in other ways, it may be a dissociation technique. However, one does not need to have a scientific rationale for everything. As the oldest of all pain-management techniques, prayer is very important for many successful arthritis pain managers.

SELF-TALK—"I KNOW I CAN"

All of us talk to ourselves all the time. We wake up in the morning and think, "I really don't want to get out of bed. I'm stiff, and it's cold, and besides, I don't want to go to work." Or we leave an enjoyable evening with a friend and think, "That was really fun; I should get out more often. Once I'm someplace, I really have a good time."

Both of these are examples of self-talk. To a great extent our actions are determined by how we talk to ourselves. Unfortunately, much of our self-talk is negative. Such negativity can lead to increased pain. Changing self-talk takes practice but is not impossible. To make such a change, follow these steps:

1. Write down your negative self-talk statements.

2. Then write down a way of changing each statement to make it positive. For example, "I don't want to get out of bed, but a hot shower and cup of coffee sure would be nice. Guess I'd better get on with it."

3. Practice positive self-talk. At first it may seem artificial. However, you will be surprised at what a difference this can make.

HEAT AND COLD

Sometimes pain can be decreased by stimulating the skin over the painful area. This stimulation can be done with heat, such as a hot pad or a warm bath or shower (directed at the sore area). Some people prefer cold for soothing pain. A bag of frozen peas or corn makes an inexpensive, reusable ice pack. Whether using heat or cold, do it for fifteen to twenty minutes.

Another way to stimulate the skin is by using a counterirritant such as any of the mentholated creams, which give a cooling effect.

MASSAGE

Many people find that massage or rubbing the painful area can be very helpful. Massage is actually one of the oldest forms of pain management for arthritis. Hippocrates (c. 460–380 B.C.) said that "physicians must be experienced in many things, but assuredly also in rubbing that can bind a joint that is loose and loosen a joint that is too hard." Self-massage is a simple procedure that can be performed with little practice or preparation. It stimulates the skin, underlying tissues, and muscles by means of applied pressure and stretching.

Massage is not appropriate on a "hot joint," an infected joint, or one that is suffering from phlebitis, thrombophlebitis, or skin eruptions. Following are some basic massage techniques. A little experience will help you decide which works best for you.

After any kind of self-massage, allow yourself a minute to relax and let the tension subside. Breath deeply.

Stroking

Fit your hand to the contour of the muscle you want to massage and move it over the skin. By slightly cupping the hand, the palm and fingers will glide firmly over the muscle. A slow rhythmic movement repeated over the tense or sore area works best. Experiment with different pressures.

Kneading

If you have ever reached up and squeezed your tense neck or shoulder muscles, you were kneading. As if you are kneading dough, grasp the muscle between the palm and fingers or between the thumb and fingers, then slightly lift and squeeze it. Don't pinch the skin, but work more deeply into the muscle itself. A slow, rhythmic squeeze and release works best. Don't knead one spot for more than fifteen or twenty seconds.

Deep Circular Movement or Friction

To create friction that penetrates into the muscle, make small circular movements with the tips of the fingers, the thumb, or the heel of the hand, depending on how large an area you want to massage. Keeping the fingers, thumb, or palm in one place, begin lightly making small circles and slowly increase the pressure. Don't overdo it. After ten seconds or so, move to another spot and repeat.

A WORD OF CAUTION

The pain-management techniques taught in this chapter, along with such other techniques as self-hypnosis, biofeedback, and acupressure, are not "scientifically proven" treatments for arthritis, and we make no special claims for them. Many people in our classes report substantial benefits from these practices, however, and we feel that they have merit if used as an adjunct to and not a substitute for a basic, sound program that is medically directed.

Hypnosis is generally not recommended for people with arthritis. Like certain narcotics, it can mask pain and may thereby cause you to damage your joints. Some of the techniques discussed in this chapter are similar to those used in *self*-hypnosis, however.

Unfortunately, various pain-management techniques are sold in expensive packages as cure-alls for almost everything. Such expensive courses and treatments are *not* necessary. If you want to further explore these techniques, check the following points first to avoid unnecessary expense and disappointment.

1. Is the course or treatment offered by a reputable institution?

2. Is the cost reasonable? (Five to ten dollars for each hour of small group instruction is about average.)

3. Are claims or promises made for a cure? If so, look elsewhere.

References

Benson, Herbert, and Miriam Klipper. *The Relaxation Response.* New York: Avon, 1987.

Lipton, Samuel. *Conquering Pain: How to Overcome the Discomfort of Arthritis, Backache, Heart Disease, Childbirth, Period Pain, and Many Other Common Conditions.* New York: Arco, 1985.

Relaxation **tapes** for people with arthritis are available from the Stanford Arthritis Center. Write to: Stanford Arthritis Center — Tapes, 750 Welch Road, Suite 315, Palo Alto, CA 94304.

11

Outsmarting Arthritis
Solving Problems

Pain, fatigue, and stiffness are effects of arthritis that can limit you in a variety of ways. They may prevent you from completing a specific task, hinder the progress of your daily activities, or even leave you feeling completely overwhelmed. From simple physical tasks—unlocking doors, opening jars, getting on buses—to social activities, arthritis can interfere with your life. For example, you may find yourself avoiding new places because you do not know if there will be an accessible bathroom; or fear of fatigue may prevent you from entertaining.

As you will discover in this book, exercise, pain-management techniques, and medications can help to alleviate the symptoms of arthritis. In this chapter you will find a number of problem-solving approaches for overcoming various obstacles you may encounter in everyday life. Included are strategies for using your joints appropriately and labor-saving ideas and products that can make your daily activities easier and more pleasant. But before discussing strategies for outsmarting arthritis, it might help to talk more about pain, fatigue, and stiffness.

1. **Pain.** As you have learned, for the person with arthritis pain can occur for different reasons. Performing a stressful activity for long periods of time will increase the likelihood of pain. For example, writing a letter for five minutes may cause stress in the fingers but no pain. Continuing to write

for an hour might cause pain that lasts for two or three days. Too much body weight increases the load on joints, as does carrying heavy objects or performing activities that require you to work against gravity, such as climbing stairs, getting up from a chair, and carrying heavy grocery bags.

It is important to respect pain. Pain is the best indication of excess joint stress and serves as a warning sign for you to modify your activities.

2. **Fatigue.**   Fatigue is a common human experience. It occurs when certain basic needs are not met. For example, not getting proper food, enough sleep, or enough exercise. It can result from inflamed joints or from depression.

Too much activity will also cause fatigue. What is too much? For some people, running five miles (8 km) a day is not enough to tire them out, but for others, doing three loads of laundry, standing on the bus during rush hour, or climbing a full flight of stairs may cause fatigue. It's important to know your limits and work within them. In this way, they will gradually increase. Knowing limits is crucial for someone with arthritis. For example, you must be particularly careful not to overdo it when you're beginning to feel good again after an episode of pain. This can cause fatigue or more pain. If you feel fatigued often, consider your diet (see Chapter 16), your sleeping habits (see Chapter 13), and make sure you are getting enough, but not too much, exercise (see Chapter 7). Also, consider the possibility you may be depressed (see Chapter 14).

3. **Stiffness.**   Stiffness is the inability to move your joints and muscles easily. Arthritis contributes to stiffness. Arthritis-induced stiffness can be aggravated by maintaining one position for too long while writing, reading, chopping food, or participating in other repetitive activities. Sitting in a movie theater, traveling long distances in a car or plane, and sleeping will also make your body feel stiff.

Other factors contributing to stiffness are pain and the lack of strengthening exercise. When you experience pain, the natural reaction is to try to eliminate it. Protecting a joint by keeping it bent may offer temporary relief, but in the long run, it will cause more stiffness, and possible contractures, or permanent limitation of joint motion, resulting in the inability to fully bend or straighten a joint.

Pain, fatigue, and stiffness may occur separately or in combination. A good arthritis self-manager will be able to keep them all in check. However, left untreated, they can result in a cycle in which pain, fatigue, and stiffness lead to an unwillingness to move, increased stiffness, and shortening of muscles and joint tissues, resulting in more pain and limited movement. Don't contribute to your problems by ignoring them. Also take care not to overprotect joints because this too can lead to increased problems.

Now that you know about pain, fatigue, and stiffness, the next step is to identify how they factor in to your daily activities.

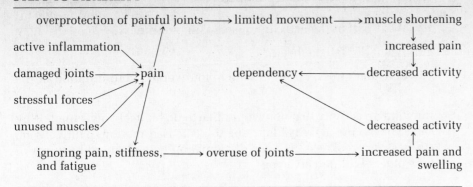

PROBLEM-SOLVING METHOD

Many of the problems caused by arthritis can be solved with the eight-step plan: *identify, pinpoint, list, select, assess, substitute, utilize resources,* and *accept.*

1. **Identify** the source of difficulty. This is the most important step and probably the most difficult. This step needs to be broken down to help you zero in on the true source of the problem. Identify specific activities that cause you pain, stiffness, or fatigue. If you are having trouble identifying activities that cause problems, review the past twenty-four hours, using the following method:

   • List your activities.

   • Check off activities that caused pain in the past.

   • Circle new activities.

   • Look at the checked and circled activities. Repeat those you checked off so you can see if you reproduce the symptoms. (Do not overdo the repetition.)

   Ask yourself if this is more or less activity than you usually do in a day.

   • Did your activities keep your joints in one position for long periods?

   • If none of the above help you identify the problem, ask yourself: "Are my joints red, hot, and swollen? Could my arthritis be in an active state? Are my basic needs being met? Am I under extra stress or tension? Have I been taking my medication as prescribed?"

2. **Pinpoint** the source of the problem.

   - What part of the activity caused pain or stiffness?

   - When did fatigue begin?

   - Consider stress, speed at which you worked, and duration of the task.

   Pinpoint an activity that you would like to do but feel you cannot. Why can't you do the activity? Is it due to decreased motion, pain, fatigue, stiffness, or weakness? Is your participation being limited by a fear of how others will perceive you?

3. **List** ideas that might solve your problem. If you are short of ideas, ask family or friends for suggestions.

4. **Select** an idea that you think will work, and try it out.

5. **Assess** the results. Did you feel that the problem was completely solved or was it a partial solution? If you still have problems, try the next step.

6. **Substitute** another idea from your list if the first one did not work. Continue to substitute until you exhaust all your ideas.

7. **Utilize resources.** If you exhaust your own ideas without solving the problem, use the following resources: health professionals, books, and the Arthritis Foundation or Arthritis Society.

8. **Accept** that the problem may not be solved at this time. Your present investigation may help you solve the problem or modify the activity in the future.

The following sections discuss techniques that will broaden your list of ideas and provide you with greater ability to select likely solutions. They may also play a role in preventing future problems by showing you how to get the task done with the least amount of effort. In the final section you will find examples of common problems and how to solve them using the method described above.

Body Mechanics

The principle of body mechanics is to use your muscles and joints efficiently in order to reduce stress, pain, and fatigue. Proper attention to these principles can solve many potential problems ahead of time.

1. DISTRIBUTE THE LOAD OVER STRONGER JOINT(S) AND/OR LARGER SURFACE AREA

Purpose

- To reduce joint stress and prevent joint pain by spreading the weight of objects you are carrying, pushing, or pulling.

- To eliminate tight grasping and pinching since these actions may stress your knuckles or cause hand stiffness. If you notice deformities developing in your hand(s), ask your doctor about consultation with an occupational therapist. A management program can be developed to meet your specific needs.

Examples

- Instead of using your fingers, use the palms of your hand, your forearms, or your elbows.

- Instead of your arms, use your whole body. Instead of your back, use your legs.

Wrong

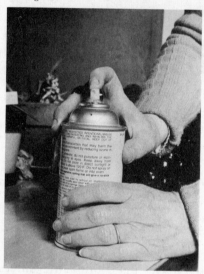

Right

*When using spray
cans or bottles, push
down with the palm of
the hand instead of
the finger tip.*

Close plastic
containers with your
elbow.

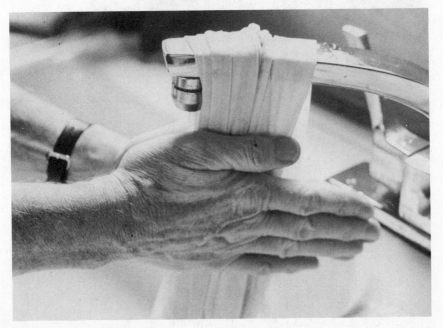

Wring out wet
washcloths or laundry
by wrapping the item
over the faucet and
squeezing excess water
out between the palms
of your hands. An
alternative is to wrap
the item in a thick
towel and let the towel
soak up the excess
moisture.

Spare your hands from
difficult-to-open
refrigerator doors or
cupboards by placing
a strap on the handle.
To open, simply place
your forearm through
the strap and pull.

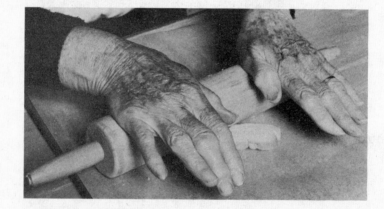

Instead of holding
onto the handles of a
rolling pin, place
hands flat on top and
roll beneath your
hands.

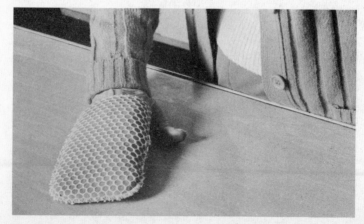

To wash dishes, there
is a scrubber that fits
over your hand
available in
supermarkets and
hardware stores. Since
you don't need to
grasp it, you can keep
your fingers in a
straightened position.

- Use a sponge instead of a dishrag to mop up tables and counters. The water can be squeezed out of the sponge more easily by putting it in the sink and pressing down with your flattened hand.

Wrong

Right

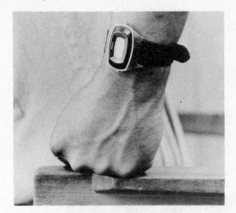

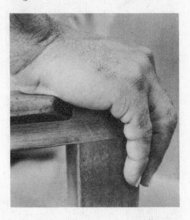

When pushing up from a chair, keep your hands facing palm down.

Use your hip to close kitchen or dresser drawers.

Use both arms to take
down or hang clothes
in the closet.

Instead of placing
your fingers through
the handle, encircle a
coffee cup with both
hands. Mugs are
especially good for
this.

Carry your plate back
to the kitchen by
"scooping" it up with
the palms of both
hands.

2. USE BODY LEVERAGE

Purpose

Holding objects close to your body will reduce the load, which will in turn reduce fatigue and joint stress. Objects feel heavier if held farther away from your body, and lighter when held closer.

Examples

Carrying a briefcase, use a shoulder strap—avoid using the handles. Carry a purse on your forearm or use a shoulder bag to avoid clutching in your hand.

Right

*Holding a brown
paper grocery bag
close to body with
both arms*

Wrong

*Holding a plastic
grocery bag with hand
down at the side of the
body*

3. AVOID MAINTAINING THE SAME JOINT POSITION FOR PROLONGED PERIODS

Purpose

- To reduce joint stiffness
- To prevent joint contractures

Examples

Hips and Knees

Alternate between sitting and standing positions. Although the sitting position is generally recommended to reduce stress on the lower joints and prevent fatigue, it is important to get up and stretch frequently.

A book holder or pillows on your lap will serve as a means to support a book and will free your hands.

Knees

When sitting, change the position of your legs so that your knees are often stretched out, feet supported by a footstool.

Ankles

Bend and point your toes while watching television or talking with a friend. You don't have to wait for a specific exercise time to do your stretching exercises (see Chapter 8).

Hands

Avoid sustained grasps on objects. For example, instead of writing with a pen, use a typewriter or a computer.

4. REDUCE EXCESS BODY WEIGHT
Purpose

To reduce stress on joints and fatigue. See Chapter 16.

5. USE GOOD POSTURE

Purpose

Proper body alignment when standing, sitting, lifting, and changing positions uses your muscles and joints more efficiently.

Examples

Pelvic Tilt

This exercise, which is a key component of posture, was described in Chapter 8. The degree that the pelvis is tilted in relation to the spine helps determine how straight the spine is aligned. The better the alignment, the less strain on both muscles and joints.

To feel this position, please refer to Exercise 14 on page 57. While doing these exercises, focus your awareness on the trunk and hips and try to maintain the pelvic tilt position later during the day.

To practice the Pelvic Tilt while standing, pretend you have a long tail. Bring the tail between your legs and hold it at belt level. Now pull straight up. Feel your pelvis tilt.

Standing

When standing for prolonged periods of time is necessary, alternate your position between the examples that follow.

Sitting

Position your body as follows:

- upper back straight
- knees slightly higher than hips
- forearms resting on work surface or arm rest
- shoulders relaxed, not elevated
- lower back flattened with a pelvic tilt
- buttocks flat on seat
- feet flat on floor or some surface

At right: Stand with weight distributed equally between both feet. For a back problem, to assist with maintaining a pelvic tilt, avoid locking your knees. Don't do this if you also have a knee problem.

 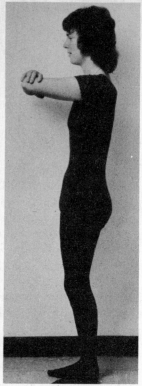

Wrong   Right

Place one foot on a footstool. This helps to maintain a pelvic tilt and thus alleviate low back strain. Wear flat or low-heeled shoes, not only for the greater stability and safety they afford, but also because they help to keep the pelvis tilted.

Select a chair that

- has a firm seat,

- has a fairly straight back, and

- is the right height for the work surface, in order to allow you to position your body as stated above.

When writing at a desk, do not lean forward, but sit tall and bend the neck only slightly. Persons with neck problems may want to consider a drafting table with an adjustable slant.

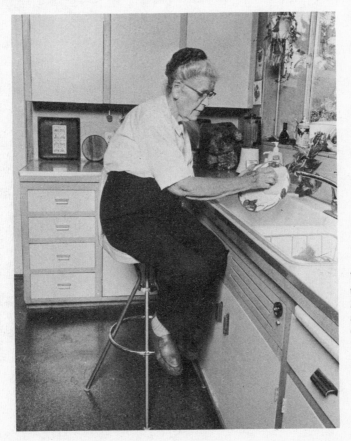

When working at your workbench or in the kitchen, a bar-height stool with footrest allows you to half sit, half stand. This helps to prevent fatigue, as well as provide a suitable height for working on projects, washing dishes, or preparing meals.

Working at a computer
terminal requires the
terminal to be at a
correct height and a
chair with good back
support. If a proper
chair is not available,
try a small pillow for
the lower back.

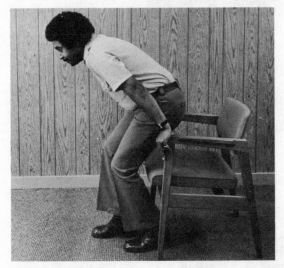

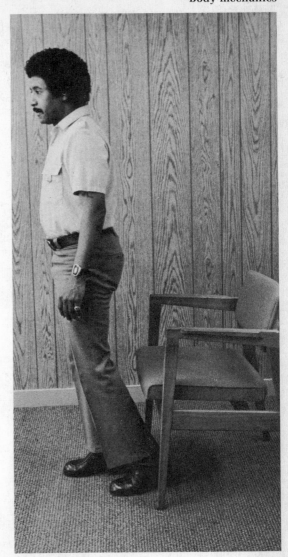

First, scoot forward in your chair so that you are near the edge. Second, place one foot slightly in front of the other so that it is directly under the knee. The other foot is behind the knee. Then lean foward until your hips automatically start to come off the chair.

Chairs that are several inches higher than normal, either through the use of pillows or chair leg extenders, make it easier to stand up.

Wrong

To lift objects from the
ground or low shelves,
bend your legs instead
of your back; pick up
the object, holding it
as close to your body
as possible, and rise,
letting your leg
muscles do the work.

Right

Persons with knee
problems may want to
let someone else lift
heavy objects, since
the knees will be
strained from the
weight of the object as
well as from their own
body weight.

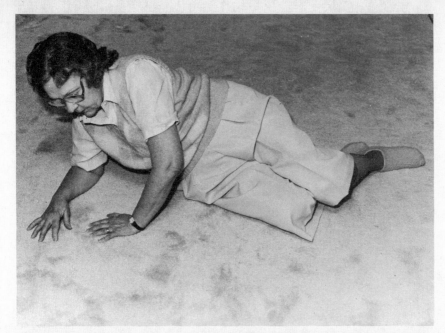

1. Roll onto one side.

2. With the upper hand, push yourself up enough to get your lower elbow under you.

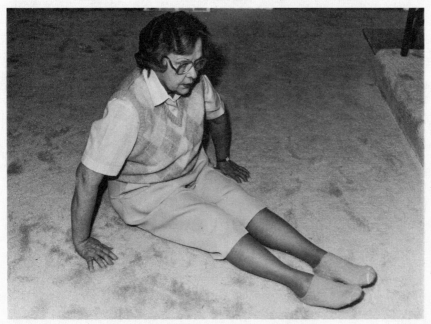

3. Gradually rise until you are sitting up.

4. Reach across your body until both hands are on the floor at one side.

5. Shift your weight
sideways; tuck your
knees under and get
up onto all fours.

6. Crawl to the nearest
steady chair and place
your hands on the seat
for support.

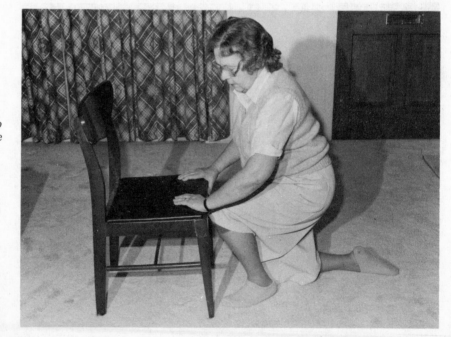

7. Putting weight onto
your hands, bring one
knee up and put that
foot flat. (If you have
one leg stronger than
the other, the strong
leg should be in the
position of "foot
flat"—ready to push
up.)

8. Push up with that
leg, bearing much of
your weight on your
hands as they rest on
the chair.

9. When you have straightened your legs, stop, keep your head down and let your circulation catch up with the change of positions.

10. Now, stand up fully straight. But again, stop a moment before you start to walk to let your circulation adjust; many people become dizzy if they get up too fast.

Efficiency Principles

If you plan and organize your tasks and workspaces you will eliminate unnecessary steps and save time and energy. This helps reduce fatigue. Hasty movements are no more quickly accomplished than organized movements, and they often end in extra work. As the saying goes, "Haste makes waste." Both tension and fatigue are increased when we feel rushed.

1. PLAN

Determine the Following:

- Is the task necessary?
- Can the task be simplified?
- Who should perform the task?
- What steps are involved in completing the task?

- In what order will these steps be most efficient?
- What is the best time of day or week to perform the task?
- Do you need rest periods to complete the task?
- What is the best body position to use to complete the task?

Examples

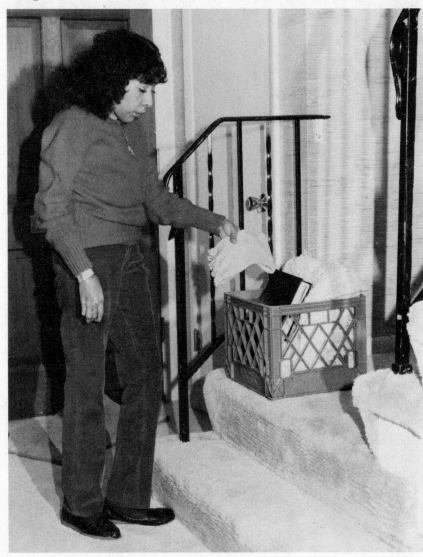

Combine several errands in one trip whenever possible. If you have to go downstairs or to another part of the house or place of work, try to accomplish several things at a time.

Work on an assembly-line basis. First gather all items you need to complete the task and place them at your workspace. Choose a comfortable position to work, then work in the order most efficient.

2. ORGANIZE

Organize in the Following Way

- Store equipment and supplies that are regularly used between eye and hip level to minimize bending, stooping, and needless searching. Store the heavier items in easy reach, such as on countertops.

- Eliminate clutter. Remove unnecessary or infrequently used items from shelves.

- Put duplicates of inexpensive items in all the places where they are most frequently used.

Examples

A hint to remove clutter: put items you do not use in a bin. If you do not look for these in a month, get rid of them.

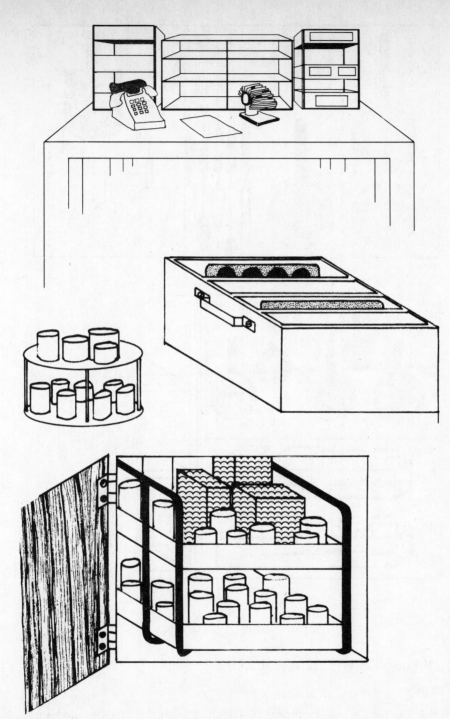

Organize storage areas with dividers, special racks, turntables, and pull-out shelves. Many of these items are available in local stores or can be easily made by a carpenter.

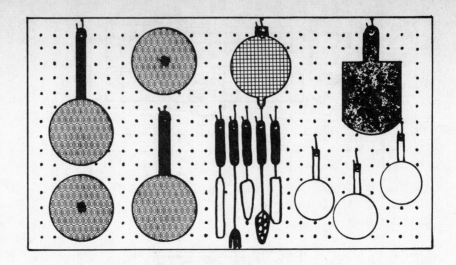

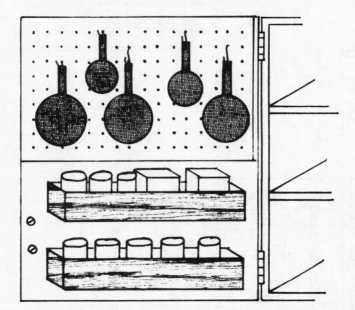

Use pegboards and hooks to hang objects.

3. BALANCE WORK WITH REST

Purpose

One of the most effective means of avoiding fatigue is to schedule short but frequent rest periods throughout the day. Forcing ourselves to rest before we get tired is often difficult because we all want to get our work done. If we can prevent fatigue, even if it means stopping in the middle of a job, our endurance over the long run will be increased. While stopping to rest is difficult, remember that long work periods require longer recovery periods.

Examples

- Schedule frequent rest periods throughout the day. These will vary for each individual, but an example might be to rest ten minutes out of every hour, instead of working for three hours straight. Even a momentary break is better than nothing.

- Alternate heavy and light work tasks during each day. In addition, plan the more difficult or lengthy tasks when you know you have the endurance to do them.

- Sitting to work is a form of rest since it uses less energy than standing. However, if you spend your workday behind a desk, you will find that moving around at regular intervals will help to keep you more alert and energetic.

Product Selection Principles

Using products with the features described in this section will help reduce joint stress, pain, and fatigue by allowing you to complete a task with the least amount of effort. These principles will help you choose new products and evaluate those you already own.

If you need information about finding any of these items call your Arthritis Foundation or Arthritis Society chapter or contact the occupational therapy department at your local hospital.

1. USE WHEELS

Purpose

- To reduce friction, lessening the resistance between surfaces

- To avoid lifting and carrying

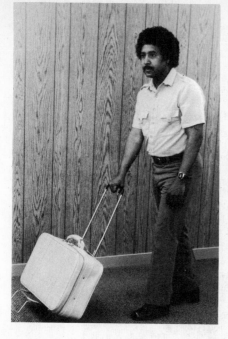

At left: Use a luggage carrier or suitcase on wheels when traveling. This allows you to take most of the strain off your arms as you push or pull the suitcase.

At right: "Deluxe" trash cans are now available that come equipped with wheels and a push handle. In addition, trash toters also have wheels in front and generally hold two regular-size trash cans.

Use wheels to transport. Utility carts, tea tables, and shopping carts are just a few examples of readily available items on wheels.

2. USE LEVERS

Purpose

Products with long handles or long attachments will let you manipulate objects using less force. These products help conserve strength.

Examples

A piece of wood, metal, or firm plastic can be attached to many types of objects to increase the area of gripping.

A doorknob extender allows you to open the door with the palm of the hand instead of with the fingers.

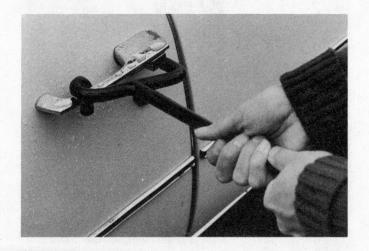

Open a car door with an aid in the palm of your hand.

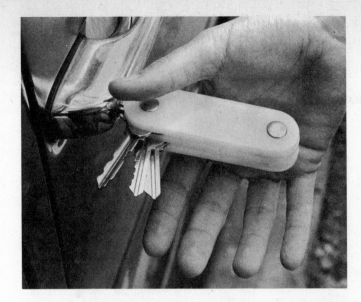

Special key holder
devices allow you to
turn a key by holding
the handle in the palm
of your hand. These
are available through
special-equipment
firms or can be made
by riveting a piece of
wood or metal to the
key.

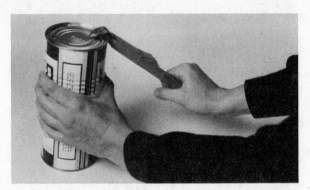

Attach a dowel or a
piece of wood to a can
opener and hold onto
this lengthened handle
when opening cans.
Never use a butterfly
can opener, because
the pressure required
to operate them is
extreme; use an
electric or wall-
mounted type.

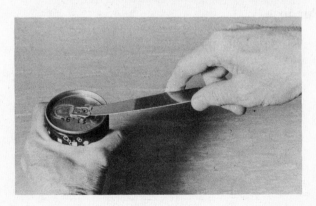

Open flip-top cans
with a knife.

3. USE LIGHTWEIGHT OBJECTS
Purpose

To reduce joint stress and pain and fatigue.

Examples

Items	Lightweight brands	What to avoid
dishes	plastic Corelle Heller	stoneware
pots/pans	Metrolight Prochief Frazier	iron skillet
bowls	plastic aluminum	Pyrex stoneware
baking dishes casseroles	foil pans aluminum microwave cookware Farberware T-fal	Corningware
luggage/briefcases	nylon canvas	leather hardback
fans	plastic	metal
winter coats	fiberfill goose down	leather wool

4. USE ENLARGED HANDLES
Purpose

- To help maintain a secure hold when hands are weak

- To help hold an object if fingers do not fully close

- To lessen tension required to maintain your hold on objects

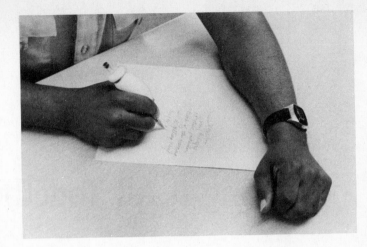

Foam padding added to such articles as a toothbrush, pen, razor, fork, and comb will increase the size of the handle.

5. USE CONVENIENCE ITEMS

Purpose

* To decrease the length of time and number of steps needed to complete task

* To reduce joint stress and pain and fatigue

Examples

Use labor-saving devices, such as food processor, blender, microwave, electric toothbrush, prepared foods, electric hedger, and permanent press clothing.

Putting It All Together

Now you have all the information you need to apply the eight-step problem-solving method to some of the problems interfering with your daily routine. Here are some examples of how the problem-solving method is used. It is important to note that the solution to each problem varies from case to case, depending on the situation surrounding the problem.

Example 1

IDENTIFY: I can't open jars.

PINPOINT: It sometimes causes pain; I'm too weak.

LIST: Ask spouse or neighbor.
Use cans and open with electric can opener.
Buy commercial jar opener.
Use sheet of rubber to produce more friction by placing over lid.
Release suction with a knife.
Tap jar upside down.

SELECT: Tried to release suction.

ASSESS: Worked on some jars but not others.

SUBSTITUTE: Buy commercial jar opener.

ASSESS: It's wonderful!

Example 2

IDENTIFY: My joints are red, hot, and swollen. Activities seem to make them worse. My doctor says rest and do what I can.

LIST: Stay in bed.
Keep up my regular routine.
Meet basic needs by getting sufficient sleep, eat well, reduce tension as possible, and exercise appropriately.
Decrease activities that can wait.
Delegate tasks, modify tasks.

SELECT: Stay in bed.

ASSESS: Stayed in bed and did not move for two days. I feel less fatigue, but my joints are stiff. I think I lost strength.

SUBSTITUTE: Try three ideas at once: meet basic needs, decrease activities that can wait, and delegate tasks or modify tasks.

ASSESS: I feel better. In order to reduce tension, I stopped all activities that can wait, and delegated tasks to family and friends. I move my joints twice a day and feel less stiff. I still shower and dress daily. Note: This period of active arthritis seemed milder than usual.

Example 3

IDENTIFY: I can't go on vacation.

PINPOINT: I can't walk long distances in airports. How will I find accessible bathrooms?

LIST: Bring raised toilet seat.
Call hotel in advance regarding bathrooms.
Call travel agent.
Contact airlines regarding wheelchair.

SELECT: Call travel agent.

ASSESS: Travel agent booked me on an airline with wheelchair service from cab to plane. She contacted the hotel and investigated bathroom status. I still need to bring my raised toilet seat.

Example 4

IDENTIFY: My body aches after working at my desk for an hour.

PINPOINT: Suspect desk is too high.

LIST: Elevate chair by adding cushion.
Work at different location with a lower table.
Purchase new chair.

SELECT: Add cushion.

ASSESS: The cushion improved the work height but now my feet are off the floor. I added a small block under my feet which helped tremendously.

Example 5

IDENTIFY:	I have joint pain during intercourse.
LIST:	Grin and bear it. Make up excuses to avoid. Find resources to learn new positions; i.e., call Arthritis Foundation. Discuss with mate.
SELECT:	Grin and bear it.
ASSESS:	Pain increased and now I am making excuses. My spouse seems frustrated.
SUBSTITUTE:	Call Arthritis Foundation; ask for name of resources.
ASSESS:	Received a copy of "Living and Loving." Tried suggestions in the book and my spouse noticed the difference. I admitted my pain and we are reviewing other resources together.

Example 6

IDENTIFY:	I am afraid to visit friends for brunch. How will I use the toilet?
LIST:	Stay home. Bring raised toilet seat. Call friend and ask about her toilet accessibility. Use toilet before leaving, bring raised toilet seat but leave in car.
SELECT:	Call friend and ask about toilet height.
ASSESS:	Friend suggested I come early and bring toilet seat before other guests arrive to avoid embarrassment. She will store it in the bathroom closet.

Example 7

IDENTIFY:	My knees feel stiff and sore after sitting in a movie theater.
LIST:	Walk to lobby once an hour. Sit in aisle seat and stretch legs every fifteen minutes. Sit in last row and stand when I need to.
SELECT:	Walk to lobby once an hour.
ASSESS:	This wasn't often enough to decrease stiffness. I felt embarrassed to get up more than that.
SUBSTITUTE:	Sit in aisle seat and stretch legs every fifteen minutes.
ASSESS:	This helped, but I decided every ten minutes worked better for me.

Example 8

IDENTIFY: I have trouble unlocking doors.

PINPOINT: My fingers are too weak to turn keys. Repeated attempts hurt my fingers.

LIST: Oil lock.
Lengthen area to grasp—add lever.
Ask in hardware store if larger keys are available.

SELECT: Add lever.

ASSESS: Attached key to piece of plastic with wire. I can open the door on the first or second attempt.

Example 9

IDENTIFY: I'm exhausted when I carry groceries. Sometimes my back hurts.

LIST: Carry smaller loads.
Hold groceries closer to body.
Seek assistance: ask family or friend, pay to have groceries delivered.
Use pelvic tilt when carrying groceries.
Use cart or wagon.
Use backpack.

SELECT: Seek assistance.

ASSESS: Worked well first time, but my friend seemed to resent the third consecutive week and refused.

SUBSTITUTE: Carry smaller loads and hold close to body.

ASSESS: Able to manage one bag half-filled. Contacted friend and asked for help once a month. She said yes. Combining both ideas seems to work well.

12

Self-Helpers

100 + Hints and Aids

The preceding chapter on outsmarting arthritis provided you with basic principles and examples of how to use your joints appropriately. Additional hints are provided in this chapter, not only on how to use your joints, but also on how to perform activities if your general mobility or finger coordination is impaired.

You may find that you are already doing many of the things listed below. It is true that necessity is the mother of invention. If you combine your needs and your common sense, you will probably come up with another 100 hints. Use the suggestions here as a springboard for additional ideas for making your life easier and more comfortable. Then share them with friends and others who might benefit from them.

DRESSING

If buttons are difficult to manipulate, sew Velcro on clothing. Attach buttons permanently to the top side, and use the Velcro as a fastener. Velcro can be found in most sewing stores.

An alternative to buttons on sleeves is elasticized thread sewn on button cuffs. This often provides sufficient give for your hands to slide through.

In the future, buy clothes that are easy to put on and easy to care for. Tops should be large enough or designed so that sleeves are easy to slip

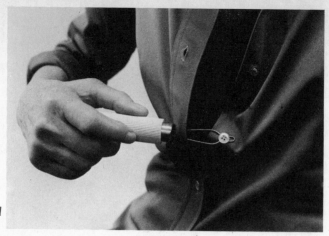

*Buttonhooks work well
to fasten buttons.*

into—you may want to avoid turtlenecks. Elastic waistbands around pants should be loose enough to slip easily over hips. Fastenings should be located in the front and be easy to manipulate.

If reaching the clothes in the closet is difficult, have someone lower the rod.

Special devices to assist with shoes include long-handled shoe horns, elastic shoelaces, and zipper laces.

A bent coat hanger, reacher, or dressing stick can assist with pulling pants up, straightening shirts, or retrieving clothes slightly out of reach.

Place large rings, thread, or leather loops on zipper tabs.

Fasten your bra in front of you. Turn bra around and pull it into place. Try front-closure bras.

When putting on your pantyhose or girdle, first roll them down from the top to the bottom, then step in, pull onto your hips, and unroll. Dusting your thighs with powder makes it easier for the pantyhose or girdle to be pulled into place.

SHOES

When buying shoes, look for the following characteristics:

1. low heel—no higher than one inch (2.5 cm)

2. toe area wide and deep enough to prevent rubbing or crunching of toes

3. cushion sole to pad the ball of your foot—avoid wood

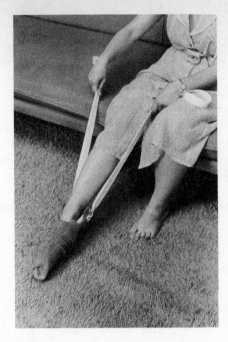
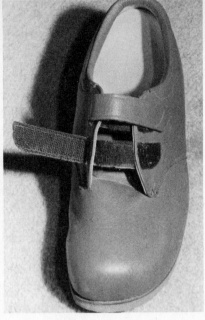

At far left: A stocking device will allow you to put socks on if you can't reach your feet.

At left: Velcro can be useful for fastening shoes as well as clothing.

4. laces, buckles, or Velcro to loosen or tighten when feet swell

5. soft upper material to give or be stretched to relieve pressure on specific areas.

Don't rule out gym shoes. Many of the running and aerobic shoes meet the above criteria. Some now have Velcro closures. If your present shoes have the recommended characteristics but are still uncomfortable, consult your physician or podiatrist.

There are a variety of shoe adaptations available, such as

- soft cushion inserts
- custom-molded inserts
- pads for ball of foot
- external bar under shoe

Most of them take pressure off the ball of the foot. Consult your physician or podiatrist when choosing the proper adaptation for you. Foot problems are very individual.

BATHING AND HYGIENE

A long-handled sponge or brush can be used to soap yourself when bathing.

Tub and shower benches, or a webbed-plastic lawn chair, allow you to sit while showering. This helps prevent fatigue and provides a place to sit when getting down into the tub is difficult.

Safety considerations when bathing include the use of nonskid safety strips or a rubber bathmat on the floor. In addition, grab bars can be permanently installed on the wall or attached to the edge of the bathtub. Grab bars assist with safety when climbing in and out of the tub or shower and also provide a place to pull or push up from when in the tub.

A long shower spray hose makes rinsing easier.

After bathing, put on a terry robe and let it soak up the water as you pat yourself dry.

Use a shower caddy to keep soap and shampoo within easy reach.

Special long-handled combs and brushes are useful when shoulder and elbow limitations prevent you from reaching your head.

In addition, a toilet safety frame or a grab bar installed in the wall next to the toilet will allow you to assist with your arms when sitting and standing.

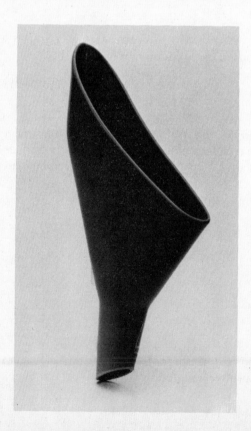

A Sanifem makes it possible for women to urinate while standing.

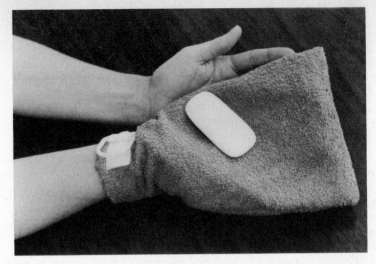

*A bath mitt can be
bought or easily made
by sewing two
facecloths together.
Lather it up and soap
yourself the easy way.*

*A raised toilet seat or
commode over the
toilet provides greater
height and thus makes
standing up easier.*

Electric toothbrushes and Water-Piks make oral hygiene easier. In addition, there is a device that holds dental floss, allowing you to floss your teeth with one hand holding onto the handle—ask your dentist about these or check your local drugstore.

Put foam curlers onto eyeliner and mascara handles for better grip.

Use the heel of your hand to squeeze the toothpaste tube or press down on a toothpaste pump.

For feminine hygiene, wind tampon string around a pencil. Keep pencil horizontal and pull gently with both hands for easier removal. Some brands of tampons have loops rather than straight strings, with which you can more easily use a pencil or your fingers to pull. For those who use pads, a detachable shower hose with an adjustable spray may be useful for more thorough genital area cleaning.

Enlarge the handle of a razor by adding utensil foam or by taping a small sponge around the handle.

Ask family members to fold the end of the toilet paper into a V. This makes the paper easier to grasp.

COOKING

Microwave ovens save time and energy. They are easy to operate, easy to clean, and usually easy to reach since they are often placed on countertops.

To avoid lifting pots heavy with food and the water the food was boiled

Use efficient storage arrangements.

Opener for soda and beer cans

Jar opener

in, consider several alternatives. One is to place a frying basket inside a pot so you can lift the food out with the basket and drain the water later. Spaghetti cookers come with a perforated insert and can serve in the same manner. Or you may want to ladle the contents out.

To open jars, install a jar opener that will grip the lid as you use both hands to turn the jar itself. Also, ask other members of the family not to close lids too tightly.

Use lightweight cooking utensils, bowls, and dishes. Avoid cast-iron skillets and heavy ceramic bowls.

Select appliances with levers or push buttons that are easy to operate.

Store canned goods so that the same items are lined up behind one another. This way you can tell from the front label what is in the back of the shelf.

Plan and prepare meals ahead of time to avoid last-minute preparations. Cook some meals the day before, and then heat them up again the next day. Also, try preparing double or triple portions and freeze the extra.

Use menus that require short preparation and little effort, for example, frozen foods, convenience foods, and ready mixes.

One-pot meals require less cleanup.

Serve foods in the same containers in which they were cooked. Use casseroles, Farberware, and other lightweight, attractive cooking vessels.

Use pie tins and other throw-away utensils. This cuts down on dishwashing.

Line pans with aluminum foil to make cleanup easier.

Use cookie tins and pans with special surfaces that prevent sticking and messy cleanup, or spray them with a nonstick product.

Mixing bowls can be stabilized by placing them on a wet washcloth or on little octopus-like suction cups. You can also place the bowl in a drawer at work height.

Place flour and sugar in containers so you can scoop out the amount needed and avoid lifting heavy bags each time.

Mitt pot holders allow you to lift hot pans with the palms of both hands.

Use a pot with a wet cloth draped over it as a support for a bowl when pouring batter into a baking pan.

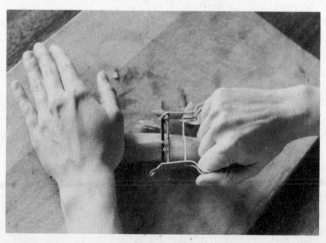

When peeling vegetables, try the kind of peeler with a handle you can slip your fingers through, or build up the handle of a standard peeler.

Use a bent coat hanger or dowel with a hook to pull oven shelves out when checking on the meal.

Attach a spray hose at the kitchen sink so that you can fill pots with water on the countertop; slide pots to the stove to avoid lifting.

Try using a pizza wheel to cut various foods.

Food processors make food preparation a snap, especially when large quantities of food must be chopped, sliced, or grated.

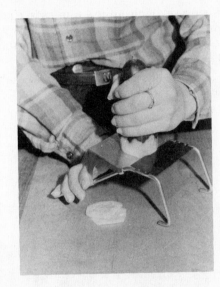

If you can't afford the electric food processors, use an onion chopper, or a Femster.

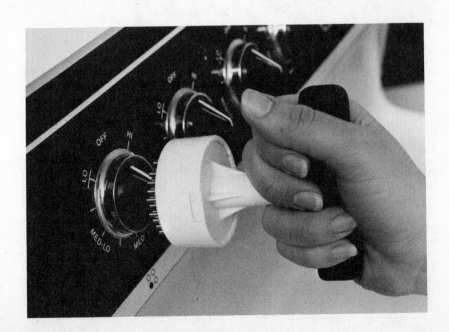

A special device from Sweden makes it easier to turn the knobs on stoves and washing machines.

ENTERTAINING

Arrange a buffet meal. Let your guests select their own silver, plates, and napkins and serve themselves from large dishes of food.

Use nice paper plates and plastic utensils to eliminate dishwashing.

Have a potluck meal, asking each guest to bring a dish of food or some paper goods.

HOUSEKEEPING

Keep a set of cleaning supplies in each area where they are used to eliminate needless walking.

To clean the bathtub, sit on a low stool next to the tub and use a long-handled sponge.

Long-handled sponges can also be used to clean around door sills and other hard-to-reach places.

Use a Back Preserver tool on your floor mop or push broom. Tasks can be performed with better posture and less strain to the back with this special long-handled attachment.

Use a long-handled dustpan and small broom to clean up dry spills from floors.

Use an adjustable-height ironing board so that you can sit to iron. Attach a cord-minder to keep the cord out of your way.

Carpeting or foam-backed rugs help to ease ankle and foot pain when prolonged standing and moving about are necessary.

Use gravity whenever possible. Let your clothes fall from the dryer into the basket. When scooping them out, you may want to use a reacher or stick.

Laundry bags that were originally intended for washing delicate items like nylons can be used for all small pieces of clothing (socks, underwear) and thus eliminate searching in the machine.

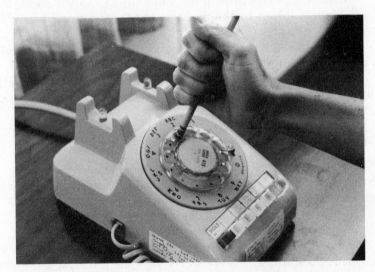

Dialing a phone may be easier with a pencil held in the palm of the hand. Also, interesting and easy-to-operate pushbutton telephones are now widely used. Look into getting one.

Enlarged knobs are available to place on lamps as well as appliances such as washing machines (certain brands only) to increase ease of handling. Check with your washing-machine manufacturer if the controls are difficult to operate.

If lifting detergent boxes is difficult, you can either have someone else pour some into a smaller container or buy the twenty-pound (10 kg) size and scoop it out. Liquid detergents may also be more manageable.

Try using the old-style push-on clothespins rather than pinch clothespins.

Front-loading washers are generally easier to use than top-loading washers. Raising the washer on blocks will also make laundering easier, since bending is eliminated.

Call your local grocery to find out if they deliver at an affordable price. Sometimes a local teenager can shop for you more economically. Also, senior centers often offer shopping services.

Use lockable casters on furniture. It will be easier to move when cleaning.

Use a box or cart to help put things away. As you move from room to room, collect things in the box and put them away when you get to the proper place.

If fitted sheets are difficult to manage, slit the last corner and fasten with a tie. Use an oven shovel to tuck in sheets.

The Touch-tronic, a device that fits into the light socket, allows you to turn lamps on and off by touching them with your fingers. It can be ordered from lighting stores.

DRIVING

When buying a car, look for doors that are easy to open and close, storage that is easy to reach (e.g., hatchback), and a seat positioner that is easy to manipulate.

Attach a loop of fabric to the inside door handle to make it easier to close. (See photo of loop on refrigerator door, page 104.)

Auxiliary or wide-angle mirrors allow for increased visibility when neck movement is limited.

To make driving more comfortable and to prevent low back strain, you may want to look into Sacro Ease seats, which are especially suitable for cars. They are similar to the cooling cushion inserts used when driving during the summer, but can be bent to fit your body curvatures and support your lower back.

Other options include the Wal-Pil-O Luvs Ya Back, which is structurally designed to support muscles and ligaments of the back, and the Bottoms-Up Posture Seat, which improves body posture by helping to eliminate slumping and slouching. Many cars now come equipped with lumbar supports for the driver.

RECREATION OR LEISURE TIME

An embroidery frame that can be attached to a table or chair will allow you to do needlework and sewing without using your hands to stabilize the article. These are available primarily through self-help aids catalogs.

If you like to play cards, try using a card holder. These can be purchased

*If you enjoy gardening,
there is now an
attachment for
shovels. There is a
different attachment to
be used with hoes and
rakes. These Back
Preserver tools can
easily be attached to
your own equipment.*

through mail-order catalogs or easily made by sawing a slit in a piece of
wood.

When gardening, try sitting on a small stool instead of kneeling to weed
and plant.

Gardening can be made even easier by having a planter box or raised
flower beds made. This will eliminate stooping entirely, as you can sit to
work at a comfortable level.

If threading a needle is difficult, self-threading needles or automatic
threading machines are available through catalogs and in some sewing
stores.

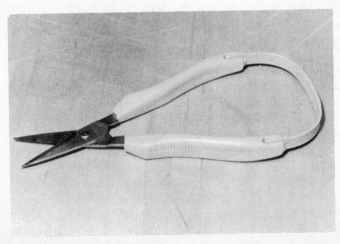

*Use special clipping
scissors when sewing
to avoid pressure and
pain on the thumb
joint.*

Afternoon exercises or sports are a really good way to break up the day. Try to set up a schedule at work where you can take an extended break to swim or exercise during the lunch hour.

KEEPING JOINTS WARM

Use the extra-long heating pads that wrap around an arm or leg and fasten with Velcro to warm an elbow or knee.

Soak stiff, sore, or cold hands in warm water. This is especially useful to loosen them from morning stiffness. At night, warm the hands in this manner; rub hand lotion in and wear cotton gloves while sleeping.

Thermoelastic gloves are especially warming, since they are made from wool and elastic fibers. They are available in some pharmacies.

Thermoelastic products are also available for knees and elbows. A soft, thick knee sock should also be used in the same manner. Cut the sock so you have a tube approximately seven inches (18 cm) long and place the tube over your knee or elbow.

Use electric blankets as a lightweight cover; they are especially useful in warming the bed before you get in it.

An alternative way to stay warm during the night or when resting is to sleep inside a sleeping bag that is placed under a blanket. The bag will turn with you and prevent cold air spaces.

Use a sleeping bag, cozy-wrap, or comforter when reading in a chair.

Use a mug to drink hot tea or coffee and hold it between both hands to warm them.

Slipper socks, worn over a pair of regular socks, will help to keep feet and ankles warm.

A foot bath not only will warm your feet as they soak in the water but also can act as a massager.

Dress warmly. Use long underwear even in the spring and fall.

Place a space heater or heat lamp in your bathroom and turn it on before showering in the morning.

Stand by the radiator to warm up, or build a fire in the fireplace.

COMFORT

When sitting for long periods of time is necessary, such as when riding in a car or flying, you can relax your back muscles by doing the following: place your forearms on your thighs, hands near the knees, and lean forward with your face as near to the knees as possible. Breathe deeply and relax in this position. Repeat several times.

Purchase a padded toilet seat, or sew a cover for it out of thick furry material.

Pad chairs with pillows or foam cushions.

If you don't want to take a pillow with you when going out, take a sweater or jacket along to use as a cushion for hard chairs.

Recliner chairs with head supports are comfortable for many people, especially if you have neck problems.

Electric beds are no longer confined to the hospital. Home models are available that have movable back and foot sections.

Be sure that you have adequate lighting and ventilation for all activities.

If you take Aspirin for pain, you may want to wake up earlier than necessary, take your Aspirin, and go back to sleep until it begins to work. Keep Aspirin and a glass of water at the bedside.

Splints, often made for hands and from special plastics, help to maintain proper joint alignment, prevent stress, and reduce pain. Your physician can refer you to an occupational therapist who can construct one for you.

An Ace bandage can also provide some added stability to joints, as well as serve as a reminder to use them appropriately.

MISCELLANEOUS

To control lamps, equipment, and appliances in inaccessible locations, there is a plug on the market with an on-off switch. This can plug in directly to a wall outlet or can be attached to an extension cord that can be positioned near you.

An easier, though quite expensive, method of controlling appliances and lights is with a Home Control Unit. Available through certain large department stores, this device consists of a command console and up to sixteen module units for each appliance wanted. Pushing the buttons on the console will turn any appliance on or off anywhere in your house.

Use a clipboard to keep writing paper steady.

A felt-tip pen allows you to write with less pressure.

Mechanical reachers extend your reach from two to three feet (60 to 90 cm), allowing you to retrieve items from the floor or high shelves.

When attending lectures, use a cassette recorder to eliminate hurried note taking.

When shaking hands with another person, grasp the fingers or wrist of the person's hands first so that his or her thumb cannot grasp and squeeze your hand too hard.

Use a steak or paring knife at dinner since the sharper the knife, the less pressure needed. Be careful.

Make sure the chairs you use at home are easy to get out of—if not, you may not want to get out of them often enough to move around and loosen up. Avoid soft, low chairs.

13

Getting a Good Night's Sleep

Sleep is vital for maintaining a healthy outlook on life. It allows our bodies to heal and our energy to be replenished.

BEDS

A comfortable bed that allows ease of movement and good body support is the first requirement for a good night's sleep. This usually means a good-quality firm mattress that supports the spine and does not allow the body to sag in the middle of the bed. A bedboard, made of three-quarter or half-inch (1 or 2 cm) plywood, can be placed between the mattress and the box spring to increase firmness. Bedboards can be bought commercially or constructed at home.

Heated waterbeds or airbeds are helpful for some people with arthritis, because they support weight evenly by conforming to the body's shape. Others find these beds uncomfortable. If you are interested, try one out at a friend's home or a hotel for a few nights to decide if it is right for you.

An electric blanket, used at a low heat, is another effective way of providing heat while sleeping, especially for cool or damp nights. Or you might try an electric or wool mattress pad. If you decide to use one or the other, be sure to follow the instructions carefully.

153

154
**Getting a good
night's sleep**

SLEEPING POSITIONS

The best sleeping position depends on which joints are involved. For most people without arthritis of the knees or hips the best position is sleeping on one's side or back. In either case, it is best to use a small soft pillow to support the curvature of the neck and maintain normal neck alignment. Pillows may also be used under the knees to relieve back pain. However, care should be taken not to maintain this position continuously. If you have knee problems, check with your doctor before using a pillow under your knees even for a short period as it can cause knee contractures. In the side-lying position, a small pillow can be placed between the knees.

For people with hip or knee problems, the best sleeping position is one where the knees are straight and the hips are in a neutral position (not rotated to the sides). There are also a few do's and don'ts.

- Do try to rest on your stomach for ten or fifteen minutes a day. This will help prevent flexion contractures of the hips.

- If it does not bother you, try putting a small pillow under your ankles while sleeping on your back. (This will keep your knees straight.)

- Don't sleep with pillows under your knees, even if this is more comfortable.

For people with back problems, often a comfortable way to sleep is the side-lying position, in which you lie on your side with knees bent. In this position it can be helpful to place a pillow between the knees to alleviate stress on the hips and low back. A pillow can also be placed under the upper arm to reduce stress on the shoulder joint. But in most cases, your body will tell you the best position. There is no single right way.

If you have ankylosing spondylitis, there are some specific sleep positions that will help prevent deformity and loss of mobility of the spine. Sleep on your stomach or flat on your back. Avoid using high pillows under your head; sleep without a pillow if possible. Place a small pillow between your shoulder blades when you sleep on your back.

SLEEPING PILLS

Sedatives and sleeping pills should be used with caution. They may be habit forming, suppress important stages of sleep, and cause depression. They only rarely solve sleep problems; the medication taken to control sleep may actually produce a disturbed night's sleep. This is also true of alcohol. If you are using medications and decide to stop, do so gradually.

Strangely, some types of antidepressant medications are sometimes helpful for sleep that is disturbed by pain. Ask your physician about these.

INSOMNIA

There is no known serious complication from lack of sleep. If you go without sleep long enough, you will fall asleep, so don't worry. If you can't sleep, don't lie in bed feeling guilty or bored—get up and do something you enjoy, like reading a book or listening to music, until you are sleepy. Remember that older persons need less sleep, so be sure your insomnia is not due to sleeping too much. There is more worry about sleeping problems than there are problems.

Still, insomnia is a problem that affects all of us at one time or another. It can be a cause of concern if it occurs frequently and involves recurrent daytime fatigue or depression. The causes of insomnia are many, some of which are feelings of anxiety or worry, pain or discomfort due to a medical condition, or an unfamiliar sleeping environment. Other contributing factors may be improper self-treatment or failure to follow the practitioner's recommended dosage or directions for medications. If your sleeping problem continues, you may want to seek a physician's advice.

Some hints for a more comfortable night's sleep include:

- Maintain a regular sleep schedule so that you go to bed and awaken at about the same time each night and morning.

- For relief of pain and inflammation at night, take Aspirin or anti-inflammatory drugs as your doctor prescribes, and be sure to take the proper dose at bedtime. Painkillers should be used with great caution. To maintain a good level of Aspirin throughout the night, try time-released Aspirin.

- Use some of the relaxation techniques described in Chapter 10, or create one of your own that is particularly relaxing to you and will settle the day's thoughts and ease the body's tensions. (Counting backward from 1,000 by twos or threes is especially helpful.)

- Wait until you are sleepy and your body is ready and eager to go to sleep; going to bed early to ensure a good night's sleep is often counterproductive.

- Avoid caffeine (coffee, tea, soft drinks, chocolate) for several hours before bedtime because it can act as a stimulant.

- Moderate your alcohol intake; alcohol may cause an erratic night's sleep and restlessness. Avoid any alcohol for three or four hours before bedtime.

- Provide yourself with a comfortable environment. Your environment includes mattress, lighting, noise level, temperature, and ventilation.

- Try taking a warm bath before going to bed.

- Get as much exercise as you can during the day.

- Don't do things that excite you just before going to sleep.

- Avoid naps if you are having problems sleeping at night.

If you do wake up with stiffness during the night, try some of the easier exercises in Chapter 8 (or small amounts in the pain-free range) right in the bed to reduce discomfort and pain, allowing for a more undisturbed and restful sleep.

References

Coleman, Richard M. *Wide Awake at 3:00* AM: *By Choice or Chance.* New York: W. H. Freeman, 1986.

Oswald, Ian, and Kristine Adam. *Get a Better Night's Sleep.* North Ryde, NSW: Methuen, 1983.

14

Depression and
Other Problems

Depression is like waking up under a big dark cloud every day. Just when
you think you have it licked, back comes the depression, greater than ever.

One of the most frequent problems associated with arthritis is depression. Depression and pain and concerns about growing old are often parts of
a vicious circle. The more depressed you are, the more pain you feel; the
more pain you feel, the more stressed you become. The more stressed you
become, the more depressed you are.

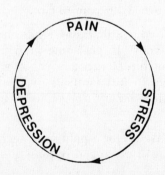

We have already discussed a number of ways to deal with pain, includ-ing heat, relaxation, and exercise. It is when you are the most depressed that you need to pay the most attention to these techniques. Continue to do these things when you are feeling well in order to maintain your good spirits. Take your medicine and do your exercises—even if you don't feel like it. But you also want to lick the depression that is making everything worse.

It is not hard to tell when you have pain. But it is not as easy to recognize when you are depressed. Just as there are many degrees of pain, so there are many different degrees of depression. If your arthritis is a significant prob-lem, you almost certainly have or have had some problems with depression; such problems are normal. Depression is felt by everyone at some time. It is how you handle it that makes the difference. The following fourteen signs have to do with depression, and you probably have had some of them, in either mild or severe form. Learn them. They are not the disease but the reaction to the disease, and you need to be able to cope with them.

1. Loss of interest in friends or activities. Not "being home" to friends, perhaps not even answering the doorbell.

2. Isolation. Not wanting to talk to anyone, only watching television, avoiding friends you happen to meet on the street.

3. Difficulty sleeping, changed sleeping patterns, interrupted sleep, or sleeping more than usual. Often, going to sleep easily, but awakening and being unable to return to sleep. (It is important to remember that older people need less sleep.)

4. Loss of interest in food.

5. Loss of interest in personal care and grooming.

6. Unintentional weight change, either gain or loss, of more than ten pounds (4 kg) in a short period of time.

7. A general feeling of unhappiness lasting longer than six weeks.

8. Loss of interest in being held or in more intimate sex. These problems can sometimes be due to medications and they are very important, so be sure to talk them over with your doctor.

9. Suicidal thoughts. If your unhappiness has caused you to think seri-ously about killing yourself, get some help from your doctor, good friends, a member of the clergy, a psychologist, or a social worker. These are not things to kill yourself over, and these feelings will pass and you will feel better. So get help and don't let a tragedy happen.

10. Frequent accidents. Watch for a pattern of increased carelessness, ac-cidents while walking or driving, dropping things, and so forth.

11. Low self-image. A feeling of worthlessness, a negative image of your body, wondering if it is all worth it. This too will pass.

12. Frequent arguments. A tendency to blow up easily over minor matters, over things that never bothered you before.

13. Loss of energy. Feeling tired all of the time.

14. Inability to make decisions. Feeling confused and unable to concentrate.

If some of these seem familiar, you may well be depressed. There are at least a dozen things you can do to change the situation. But, being depressed, you may not feel like making the effort. Force yourself or get someone to help you into action. Find someone to talk with. Here are the twelve actions:

1. If you feel like hurting yourself or someone else, call your mental health center, doctor, suicide prevention center, a friend, clerical counselor, or senior center. Do not delay. Do it now. These feelings do not mean that you are crazy. Most of us feel this way at one time or another. Often, just talking with an understanding person or health professional will be enough to help you through this mood.

2. Are you taking tranquilizers? These include drugs such as Valium, Librium, reserpine, codeine, sleeping medications, and other "downers." These drugs intensify depression, and the sooner you can stop taking them, the better you will be. Your depression may well be a drug side effect. If you are not sure what you are taking or what the side effects might be, check with the doctor or pharmacist. Before discontinuing a prescription medication, always check, at least by phone, with the prescribing physician, as there may be important reasons for continuing its use or there may be withdrawal reactions.

3. Are you drinking alcohol in order to feel better? Alcohol is also a downer. There is virtually no way to escape depression unless you unload your brain from these negative influences. For most people, one or two drinks in the evening is not a problem, but if your mind is not totally free of alcohol during most of the day, you are having trouble with this drug.

4. Continue your daily activities. Get dressed every day, make your bed, get out of the house, go shopping, walk your dog. Plan and cook meals. Force yourself to do these things even if you don't feel like it.

5. Visit with friends. Call them on the phone, plan to go to the movies or on other outings. Do it.

6. Join a group. Get involved in a church group, a discussion group at a senior citizen club, a community college class, a self-help class, or a senior nutrition program.

7. Make plans and carry them out. Look to the future. Plant some young trees. Look forward to your grandchildren's graduation from college even if they are in kindergarten.

8. Don't move to a new setting without first visiting for a few weeks. Moving can be a sign of withdrawal, and depression often intensifies when you are in a location away from friends and acquaintances. Your troubles may move, too.

9. Take a vacation with relatives or friends. Vacations can be as simple as a few days in a nearby city or a resort just a few miles down the road. Rather than go alone, look into trips sponsored by colleges, senior centers, or church groups.

10. Do twenty to thirty minutes of physical exercise every day.

11. Make a list of self-rewards. Take care of yourself. You can reward yourself by reading at a set time, seeing a special play, or by anything big or small that you can look forward to.

12. Get a pet. Dogs and cats are best, but even goldfish help.

Depression feeds on depression, so break the cycle. The success of everything else in this book depends on it. Depression is not permanent, but you can hasten its disappearance. Focus on your pride, your friends, your future goals, your positive surroundings. How you respond to depression is a self-fulfilling prophecy. When you believe that things will get better, they will.

PAIN

Although we have talked a lot about pain in earlier chapters, here we would like to review some basic principles and discuss the connection between pain and mood.

1. Keep active when you have pain. Get dressed in your favorite clothes; women put on makeup, men shave. Now do something. Go to work, go out shopping, go to a movie you have wanted to see. All of these activities will make you look and feel good, and will help keep your mind off the pain. If instead you stay home in your favorite old robe, stay in bed or mope around the house, you will have too much time to think about your pain and it will seem worse than it is.

2. Do your exercises. Unless you are in a "flare" and have "hot" joints, your exercises will help. Some of the pain of arthritis is due to stiff, unused muscles. Therefore, it is very important to keep your muscles in strong, supple condition. Muscle strength will also help keep your joints stable.

3. Practice relaxation exercises. Relaxed muscles and nerve endings send out fewer pain messages, thus you have less pain.

4. Don't be a martyr. Pain is individual, and it cannot be seen. Therefore, don't be afraid to tell friends and family members that you are in pain. Ask for help in carrying groceries, making beds, or mowing the lawn.

Don't worry if people look at you strangely. Remember that people usually can't see your arthritis or tell that it is hurting you. A direct request for help is not being dependent; it is a direct, honest, and often necessary communication.

5. Pain is closely related to stress and depression. Thus, reducing stress and depression will also reduce pain. Sometimes people are not aware of how closely attitude and pain are related. Thus, we suggest a simple exercise. For a week, keep a Pain/Mood Diary like the one shown here. Each day, put a dot somewhere between "No Pain" and "Terrible Pain" to indicate your pain for that day. Do the same for your mood. After a week, connect all the pain marks and all the mood marks. You may be surprised to see the connections between your mood and your pain.

PAIN/MOOD DIARY

PAIN

	SUN.	MON.	TUES.	WED.	THURS.	FRI.	SAT.
No Pain							
Terrible Pain							

MOOD

	SUN.	MON.	TUES.	WED.	THURS.	FRI.	SAT.
Feeling Great							
Feeling Awful							

FATIGUE

There is no question about it, arthritis can be very draining of energy. This is particularly true of rheumatoid arthritis, but it can be a problem in any type of arthritis. Thus, know that fatigue is a part of the overall problem and that you are not just imagining it. Know also that fatigue can be a sign of depression, so you should consider whether the fatigue might be lessened by treating the depression.

One way of testing the source of your fatigue is to exercise. Next time you are fatigued, take a short walk or do some other exercise. If your fatigue is due to depression, you will probably feel better. In fact, this happens more than 50 percent of the time.

If the fatigue is caused by your disease, then there are several things you can do.

1. Conserve your energy (see Chapter 11).

2. Do the obvious—rest! Take a short nap once or twice a day. If this is impossible, then just relax. Try doing a relaxation exercise.

3. Fatigue, like pain and fear, cannot be seen and is not understood by most people. Therefore, tell your boss, friends, and family that fatigue is one of the problems of your arthritis and that you may have to take short rests from time to time. Gain their support in allowing you to rest. Most employers are more than willing to allow a little extra rest time for good employees. You, your family, your friends, and your employer should understand that there is a difference between fatigue and being lazy.

4. Take a good long look at yourself. Will you allow yourself to rest? Many of us build our self-images around the false ideal of being indestructible—supermom, macho man, or the perfect worker. If this is you, then reassess your position. Fatigue is one of the body's major early warning systems; it is telling you to take heed. Tune into your own body and follow its directions. The ability to rest is a strength and not a weakness.

SEX

Sexuality does not cease with a diagnosis of arthritis; but the pain and burden of the disease may make the expression of our sexuality difficult. It need not be. A full, loving sex life is available to all of us.

Sexuality encompasses much more than physical intercourse; it involves our basic needs for intimacy, for affection, approval, and acceptance. It also reflects our individuality: each of us expresses our sexuality uniquely, depending on the beliefs and values we have adopted as we grow up.

Unfortunately, these beliefs can stifle our sexual pleasure. We tend to hold onto assumptions that limit the enjoyment we will permit ourselves. "Disabled people have no desire for sex." "No one could find my body attractive." "A woman ought not to ask for sex." If we hope to appreciate and enjoy our sexuality, we must understand how these kinds of assumptions about ourselves and our loved ones inhibit us.

Here is an all-too-common example of how our beliefs can get in our way: A woman has arthritis. Her husband is afraid of causing her more pain during intercourse and, being too uncomfortable to talk about it, becomes hesitant to initiate sex. Since she is already insecure about her appearance, she mistakenly thinks that her husband no longer finds her attractive and she feels hurt and becomes a little distant. At this point, the situation serves to reinforce her husband's initial fear that he causes her pain. He may begin to feel deprived or resentful and draw away from his wife emotionally. Or he may begin to have feelings of inadequacy or helplessness about himself, with the same result; he draws away from his wife. Nobody wins; everybody loses.

Clear communication is the tool for resolving this common impasse and, for that matter, most problems concerning sex. Each partner must clearly convey his or her needs and desires to the other, or they are destined to have an unsatisfying relationship.

What do you do if arthritis pain and fatigue is a hindrance to a sexual relationship? Some ideas for coping with pain and fatigue are found earlier in this chapter. We will not address physical positioning or technique, but articles on this topic are available from your doctor or local Arthritis Foundation or Society office. While knowledge of different love-making techniques can be valuable to someone who might otherwise be experiencing pain during intercourse, no technique or position alone will guarantee satisfaction unless there is a willingness to explore and communicate the many aspects of sexuality with one's partner.

Many of us reserve our love and trust for everyone but ourself. We insist on seeing ourselves as unlovable, and when we do, it is not surprising that others around us come to share that view. We have to work at letting go of those "unlovable" assumptions. "Who could love my body?" "I don't deserve love." "I'm being selfish." Few of us compare very well with the magazine ideal of sexual attractiveness. If we persist in trying to live up to this ideal, we are bound to remain dissatisfied. We must instead decide that we need and deserve sexual happiness *now just as we are*.

We have seen a bumper sticker that reads, "Sex Cures Arthritis." While that may not be true, sex can actually help the pain of arthritis. It seems that the excitement of sex stimulates our bodies to produce cortisone, adrenalin, and other chemicals that help to ease pain naturally. Use this information as you see fit!

A note about partners of people with arthritis. Many husbands and wives have told us how hard it is to watch their spouse suffer with arthritis. They feel helpless and sometimes guilty that they can't in some way share in their partner's distress. It is hard to live with arthritis, even if you don't have it. We suggest that you talk these problems over with other partners of people with arthritis. You can find such folks through your doctor, arthritis classes, or your local Arthritis Foundation or Arthritis Society. The important thing is to know that you are not alone and that your feelings are normal. For more discussion of the emotional side of arthritis, see Chapter 15.

15

Feelings and Communication

The problems of living with arthritis are not all physical ones. Many center around emotional and interpersonal issues. Just as pain and loss of function are normal symptoms of arthritis, so are the feelings of denial, fear, frustration, anger, depression, and finally acceptance. Of course, not everyone experiences all of these emotions to the same degree or on the same time schedule, just as everyone's experience with the disease is not the same. However, these feelings are important enough to merit attention.

In this chapter we will look at these feelings and discuss ways to deal with them. We will also explore some of the feelings and concerns of friends, family, and employers. Finally, we'll give you some tools for improving listening skills and communication. Not everyone with arthritis has the same set of problems. Therefore, you may not relate to all the things discussed here. As a good self-manager, take what is useful for you.

IN THE BEGINNING (AND SOMETIMES LATER, TOO)

Disbelief or Denial

When someone is first diagnosed with arthritis, it often comes as a shock. "This can't be happening to me." "The doctor must be wrong." "I'm not old enough to have arthritis." These are all common thoughts. Common reactions are either to ignore the disease or, if this is impossible, to seek a "cure."

165

The "source" of the cure may be going from doctor to doctor, trying special diets, or following the recommendations of other healers.

If you are truly concerned that you may have been misdiagnosed, get a second opinion. If you have osteoarthritis, a second opinion can come from any family doctor or internist. If you have rheumatoid or another type of arthritis, you may want to get the opinion of a rheumatologist. While a second opinion can be valuable, we must caution against going from doctor to doctor. One of the best things to do is to establish a long-term relationship with a physician whom you like and trust. Thus, as the disease changes, he or she can more easily become familiar with you and the tempo of your disease. This is probably one of the best tools any doctor can have in working with patients to manage arthritis.

Fear and Panic

These emotions can surface any time. Some people are afraid they won't be able to do the things they must or want to do. They may be afraid their family and friends won't understand. One of their greatest fears is that they will become dependent on others. Of course, there are other fears. "How can I manage a life of pain?" "My body will change, and I'll be ugly." "If I can't keep up, my partner will leave me." "I'll become a burden to my children." "I won't be able to earn a living." Probably the greatest fears of all are the fears of change and of the unknown.

First, know that your fears are normal. You are not going crazy. Next, begin to deal with your fears by seeking knowledge and communicating. This is the time to begin learning about arthritis. However, before you start you should know your diagnosis so that as you read, you can sort out those things that apply to you. Seek out information. A good place to start is with the Arthritis Foundation or the Arthritis Society; you can find phone numbers in the back of this book. Also, go to your local library and find books on arthritis. If a book is more than five or, at the most, ten years old, the information is probably out of date. Therefore, it should be read with great caution. Other sources of information include your doctor, possibly your pharmacist, other health professionals such as physical and occupational therapists, and, of course, your friends.

This is also a good time to seek out others with arthritis. Join a support group such as those offered by the Arthritis Foundation. See if you can find a friend or a friend of a friend who has a similar problem. You might even ask your doctor to put you in contact with others who have some of the same problems. Meeting people with arthritis who have managed to live full and successful lives is one of the best ways to overcome fear.

Talk about your fears. In this way you may find that many of your fears are not necessary. Recently, we did a study of the fears of children with arthritis and found that many of them were afraid of dying, which rarely occurs. In these cases all it took was a few words from a parent or the doctor to remove what was for these children a major nightmare. We have also met older people who begin to get osteoarthritis of the fingers. They are very concerned about the changes in their hands and fear that they will lose function and become helpless. Again, a few words go a long way toward alleviating fears. Osteoarthritic hands, despite deformities, usually remain completely functional.

Finally, some fears may be realistic. Arthritis may mean a change in lifestyle or relationships. However, these changes are not always negative. Many people have told us that arthritis, while not a welcomed visitor, has helped them to accomplish more in their lives and to gain greater happiness. The road from fear to accomplishment is not an easy one, but it is possible. Finding support and remaining open to new adventures will make the journey easier.

AS TIME GOES ON

Uncertainty and Frustration

In talking with many people with arthritis, we have learned that one of the most difficult tasks in living with this disease is learning to live with uncertainty. Because the disease waxes and wanes in an unpredictable manner, it is very difficult to plan anything. One day it is possible to live an almost normal "pre-arthritis" type of life, and yet the next day finds one barely able to function. "I can't plan anything." "I never know how I will be feeling." "My family is constantly postponing pleasurable activities because of my illness." "My boss gets upset because she can't count on me." "Friends don't understand when I have to cancel at the last minute." There is no way to make living with uncertainty easy. However, there are some ways of easing the uncertainty and the guilt that come from not fulfilling commitments.

Start by keeping a log or diary of your daily activities and your physical symptoms. You will learn what activities make your arthritis worse and can start rearranging your life to do the things you need and want to do.

If there is a very important event coming up in your life, such as a wedding or a reunion, talk with your doctor first. He or she may be able to rearrange your medications for a short period of time so that you can enjoy the event without suffering the fear of uncertainty.

Plan ahead. If there is something you want to do, rest up beforehand.

Talk with your family and friends about the uncertainties. If they know you may not be able to follow through, they will be more understanding.

Don't expect others to cancel plans just because you have to cancel. It is very frustrating, for example, not to be able to go to the zoo with the children or attend a party, but you *can* make sure that the activity goes on without you. This way friends and family won't be unduly denied pleasurable activity because of arthritis. It will also help you avoid guilty feelings.

Anger

Not everyone with arthritis experiences anger; however, it is very common. The anger is usually aimed at an unfair world. "Why me?" "It doesn't matter what I do, nothing works." Sometimes, because of all the frustrations, the anger is expressed—rightly or wrongly—toward family and friends. "Why isn't my spouse more helpful?" "The kids shouldn't be so demanding." "Can't my friends understand that I hurt?" "My doctor doesn't believe me." Unfortunately, anger is often expressed in very unproductive ways. These include giving up, *doing* nothing. "Why bother? Nothing I do works anyway." Another way of expressing anger is *saying* nothing. Rather than expressing it in words, we may act it out in hostile actions, such as refusing to talk to a spouse or dropping a long-time friendship. Of course, the most common way of expressing anger it to shout, blow up, or be verbally hurtful. None of these expressions of anger is helpful. Rather, they often make the situation worse by alienating the very people who can be the most helpful.

First, recognize that being angry is normal. You have a lot to be angry about. This is not a fair world, and arthritis is not a fair disease. At times it may seem that nothing you do works. However, there is another way of looking at this. For example, if you do nothing, you might get worse sooner, or you might develop more serious problems than the ones you already have. Although doing something does not always make you better, it helps to maintain the status quo. At other times it helps in slowing deterioration. For example, one thing we have learned from our studies is that for many people with arthritis, self-management does not improve their daily functioning. However, it does slow the decline. That is, they still have problems of function, but instead of getting worse over time, they remain about the same. Thus, four years later, they still have the same problems, but they haven't gotten worse. A change of perspective sometimes helps.

When the anger is directed at another person, the first thing to do is determine what is making you angry. It may be that a friend is being too helpful, while for someone else the problem may be that a friend is offering no help. The second thing to do is to decide what action the other person could take that would correct the situation.

Once you have done these two things you are ready to express your anger in a way that has a chance of defusing the situation and helping you get what you need and want. One of the best ways to do this is to use "I" messages. These are explained in detail at the end of this chapter. In short, an "I" message is one in which you express your feelings and desires rather than blame the other person. Such messages are aimed at opening up communications rather than closing them down.

Sometimes the anger and frustration of having arthritis needs to be discussed with someone besides your family and friends. This is the role of a professional counselor. Look for someone who has had experience in working with people who have a chronic illness. Psychologists, social workers, family counselors, and religious leaders such as priests, ministers, and rabbis can be very helpful. It is a wise person who seeks help rather than being hurtful to loved ones.

Depression or Sadness

Almost everyone with arthritis suffers some depression or sadness. Again, this is quite normal. After all, you have had many losses and have to make changes in your life. For details on depression, see Chapter 14.

Acceptance

Arthritis often means making changes in life. You may not be able to do everything that you once could. This may be due to physical disability or just a lower energy level. Unfortunately, people sometimes make the wrong choices about what they can and cannot do. One older class participant was very unhappy because he did not have the energy to join his friends for lunch. When we asked him what he did at home in the mornings he gave us a long list of chores, starting with preparing a large breakfast and followed by washing dishes, dusting, working in the garden, and assisting a friend. A woman was very unhappy because she was not able to prepare a huge traditional holiday dinner for her family. When we asked these people if they couldn't do less or ask for help, it was obvious they considered the tasks they were doing as part of their role in life. They thought that doing one's chores came before the pleasure of lunch with friends, and that a good mother fixed holiday meals.

Start by sitting down and deciding what is really important to you. When the gentleman above did this, he discovered that of all his morning activities, having a big breakfast and doing some gardening were most important. The woman decided that it was very important to make the holiday dessert, but the rest of the meal could be done by others.

Next, decide how you are going to get the other things done or what you may leave undone. The man decided that he could do dusting once a week, wash the dishes just once a day, and tell his friend that he was very sorry but that he wasn't able to help. The woman decided she could ask the different members of her family each to contribute a dish for the dinner and the older children to clean up after the meal. In fact, the family had been offering to do this for years, and the woman had refused.

Third, make a list of all the things you really want to do and then prioritize the list. Here the important word is *want*. Next, make a list of all the things you feel you *have to* do and, again, prioritize these.

Finally, look at the two lists. If something appears on both lists, then this is an activity you probably should keep. If there are things on the *have to* list that keep you from doing things on the *want* list, think about how you can get some of the *have to* things done. Or maybe they can be left undone. A house doesn't have to be dusted every day.

This brings us to asking for help. One of the most important but also most difficult things anyone with arthritis can learn to do is ask for help. Because we like being independent, we tend to try to do all the things we feel must be done ourselves, and give up the things we like doing. For example, some people with arthritis will give up outings with family and friends in order to clean the house or maintain the garden, rather than asking for help in order to be able to go out.

There are several sources of help. You can ask family or friends. Many times these people would be more than happy to do some shopping or gardening. They may not have offered because they were afraid of hurting your feelings or they were not aware you needed help. Second, you can employ someone to do the tasks that have to be done but that you cannot do. Maybe a neighbor child will mow the lawn while you garden. Finally, in every community there are organizations set up to give help. Church and temple youth groups, Scouts, and Service Clubs all have members who want to help. Sometimes businesses let you shop by phone. Even if something seems far-fetched, investigate the possibilities. Help usually will not come without your seeking it.

FOR YOUNG ADULTS WITH ARTHRITIS

For young people, arthritis can be an especially devastating burden. It sometimes seems that all of life's promise has been taken away. This need not be so. We know many young people with arthritis, some pictured in this book, who lead full, active, work and family lives. In talking with them we learn to emphasize the 90 percent that can be done, rather than the 10 percent that must be put aside.

Young men and women with arthritis can lead full, happy married lives. It is important that the spouse understand the disease, its changeable ways, and the extra stresses that it can place on a relationship. When arthritis causes marital problems it is often for one of two reasons. The most common reason is that the spouse was not prepared for living with uncertainty. It is hard to understand how one can look the same yet on one day be fully active and on the next barely able to move. Thus, the spouse without arthritis sometimes feels put upon and may wonder if arthritis isn't just an excuse for not doing what one does not want to do.

Along these same lines, some spouses sometimes get annoyed with all the extras. As one put it, "I hate 'would you mind . . . ?' all the time." On the other hand, other spouses have told us that they are more than happy to be of help. What is annoying and grating to one is perfectly acceptable to another.

Another problem is the spouse who is too helpful. In one case, a new mother with rheumatoid arthritis was not allowed by her husband to do anything for their baby except feed him. It is therefore no wonder that the child turned to his father for love and support while seeing his mother as a feeding machine. Being too helpful can be just as devastating as not being helpful enough.

Most young women with almost any type of arthritis can conceive and bear a child. If you are thinking of becoming pregnant, it is important to discuss this with your doctor. You may need to change medications and be more carefully monitored than someone without arthritis. However, just because you have arthritis is no reason why you must give up your dream of having children.

Unfortunately, some young people with arthritis find themselves divorced and caring for one or more children just when they most need help. This is a sad and complex set of problems. Our suggestion is to both seek *and* accept help. Help comes in many forms: family, friends, and neighbors, as well as professionals from your personal physician to social workers and psychologists.

In short, having arthritis when you are young is a challenge. However, there is no reason that—with a little thought and care—you can't lead a full and active life.

POSITIVE OUTCOMES

So far we have talked mostly about the negative aspects of arthritis. However, there are also some positive aspects. Arthritis, like other adversity, often brings families and friends closer together. Where they once took each other for granted, they now cherish their relationships and use them to the fullest. We have even heard some people say that while no one wants arthritis, it was one of the most positive things to have happened in their lives.

For others, arthritis has become a challenge, another mountain to conquer. Using some of the techniques we outlined in Chapter 6, they set goals and worked little by little to accomplish them. Sometimes the challenges are small, such as being able to climb the steps of a daughter's home in order to share in holiday festivities. Other times the challenges are greater: arranging a trip to a foreign country to see the things one has always wanted to see. The challenges can also be personal. One elderly gentleman we know had very severe rheumatoid arthritis. His pain was such that even getting out of the house was an effort. All his life he had wanted to be a swimming instructor. With this goal in mind he had both hips replaced, underwent lengthy rehabilitation, and is now taking classes in lifesaving. We expect that he will soon be teaching swimming.

ADVICE FOR FAMILY, FRIENDS, AND EMPLOYERS

When you have arthritis, you're not the only person who has to deal with the problem. Your family, friends, colleagues, and employers, as well as many other people in your life, must also learn about and adapt to the disease. Often, however, people have misconceptions about arthritis, and may feel uncomfortable about asking you for the truth. Some of the most common problems and concerns are discussed below. Share this section with others so they'll know what to do to help make everybody's life easier.

Learning about Arthritis

Most people have an image of arthritis. Usually these images are either of someone badly deformed and handicapped, often bedridden, or of an older person hobbling about with a walking stick. Today, neither image is correct. Most people with arthritis are neither badly handicapped nor bedridden. They are usually able to maintain full and active lives. While it is true that many older people have arthritis, arthritis is not an old person's disease. Anyone can be affected, including infants, children, and young adults.

Learn about arthritis and rid yourself of those stereotypes. Good sources of accurate information are your physician, the Arthritis Foundation and Arthritis Society, and the references listed throughout this book.

Not Knowing What to Do

When we are faced with someone who has a problem, we often don't know what to do. Will he be insulted if we help? Should we keep asking her how she feels? Should we ignore the problem?

The solution is to ask. This seems very simple, but it may not be. Before giving help, ask the person, "How can I help you?" If the answer is, "I don't need any help," then accept this. If the person is a friend or family member you might say, "I won't keep offering help. However, know that I am willing to help anytime. Just ask." Such a statement makes life less awkward for everyone.

Employing Someone with Arthritis

This is a big concern. The bottom line is that most people with arthritis require little or no help and can be fully employed. However, if you are considering hiring someone with arthritis, or learn that one of your employees has arthritis, ask what can be done to help if help is needed.

It has been our experience that there are two kinds of help that employees with arthritis usually need. Sometimes the workplace needs some slight modification. In our office this has meant buying special scissors, as well as a wheeled cart to move things around from place to place. Workplace modifications need not be expensive. Small things can often make a big difference.

The second type of assistance has to do with working hours and conditions. People with arthritis often need to move frequently. They should be free to stand up and stretch. If the job requires standing, they may need to sit a few minutes every hour or so. Also, early morning is an especially difficult time for many people who have morning stiffness. If possible, these people like to come to work late and leave late. Others prefer to work only part-time. Once the needs of the person are known, and working conditions negotiated, people with arthritis *can* work, and are often more reliable than those without the disease.

Dealing with Anger and Depression

It is not only the person with arthritis who suffers from anger and depression. These emotions often affect family and friends, too. "I'm so frustrated, there is nothing I can do." "I hate to see her suffer." "It's not fair, we can't do the things we used to do." "I can never count on him for anything." "Why can't I share some of the pain?" All of these things are often said, or at least thought.

First, know that your feelings are not bad or selfish. They are perfectly normal. The best way to deal with these feelings is to communicate them. This next section will give you some concrete ways in which to start. In addition, you may want to discuss your feelings with others who have arthritis in the family. You will quickly find you are not alone. In some cases, talking with a social worker, psychologist, or marriage and family counselor may be helpful. In short, don't keep these feelings to yourself. Deal with them honestly. This will result in many benefits for you and your loved one with arthritis.

COMMUNICATION SKILLS

Probably the single most important way to deal with the emotions of arthritis is through communication. This is true not only for the person with arthritis but for family, friends, and employers as well. Here are some suggestions for improving your listening and verbalizing skills.

Listening

This is probably the most important communication skill. Most of us are much better at talking than we are at listening. There are several levels involved in being a good listener.

1. **Acknowledge having heard the other person.** Let the person know you heard them. This may be a simple "uh huh." Many times the only thing the other person wants is acknowledgment, or just someone to listen because sometimes merely talking to a sympathetic listener is helpful.

2. **Acknowledge the content of the problem.** Let the other person know you heard the content and emotional level of the problem. You can do this by restating what you heard. For example, the content: "You are planning a trip." Or you can respond by acknowledging the emotions: "That must be difficult," or "How sad you must feel." When you respond on an emotional level, the results are often very startling. These responses tend to open the gates for more expression of feelings.

3. **Respond by seeking more information.** This is especially important if you are not completely clear about what is being said or what is wanted. "Can you tell me more about . . . ?" "I don't understand . . . please explain." "I would like to know more about . . ." "How can I help?"

Verbalizing Feelings

When we are angry or upset, most of us tend to blame someone else. This is natural. However, the result is that the other person also becomes angry, defensive, and sometimes hurt. As this cycle escalates, nothing is accomplished except an excess of bad feelings.

One way to avoid this unpleasantness and still voice our displeasure is to use "I" messages. The concept is simple. Whenever you want to express feelings, express them in terms of how *you* feel, not how the other person *makes you feel*. Take responsibility for your feelings instead of blaming the other person. The following are some examples.

INSTEAD OF: "Why can't you kids be more helpful? You are just selfish and inconsiderate."

TRY: "I am really upset that you kids haven't made your beds and picked up your room."

INSTEAD OF: "Why are you always late? We can never get anywhere on time."

TRY: "I get really angry when you are late."

INSTEAD OF: "Why aren't you ever any help? Do you just want me to have more pain?

TRY: "I could really use some help."

The secret is to avoid the use of the word *you* and instead report your personal feelings using the word *I*. Of course, like any new skill, "I" messages take practice. Start by really listening, both to yourself and to others. How often do you hear blaming? Then try to use "I" messages at least once a day. You will be surprised at how fast they become a habit.

There are some cautions to note when using "I" messages. First, they are not panaceas. Sometimes the listener has to have time to hear them. This is especially true if blaming has been the more usual way of communicating. Even if at first "I" messages seem ineffective, continue using them. Time is on your side. Second, "I" messages can become a game or a means of manipulation. If used in this way, then they escalate problems. To be used effectively, "I" messages must report honest feelings.

One last note: "I" messages should also be used to express positive feelings. "I really like that color on you." "I can see that you are walking much better." "I like it when you give me a hug."

Arthritis can bring out many kinds of feelings and emotions. Communicating becomes even more important than it usually is in everyday life. This chapter only begins to scratch the surface. The suggestions made here are merely places to start. For assistance, you may want to see a professional, such as a psychologist, or read some of the references that follow.

References

LeMaistre, JoAnne. *Beyond Rage: The Emotional Impact of Chronic Physical Illness.* Oak Park, IL: Alpine Guild, 1985.

Lewis, Kathleen. *Successful Living with Chronic Illness.* Wayne, NJ: Avery, 1985.

Ziebell, Beth. *Wellness: An Arthritis Reality.* Dubuque, IA: Kendall-Hunt, 1981.

16

Nutrition *Is* Important

Foods, diet, and nutrition are special concerns of people with arthritis. Questions come up—"Will this food help my arthritis?" "Are there any foods I should avoid?" "How can I lose weight?"—but reliable answers can be hard to find.

Your diet is simply what you eat and drink each day. Learning about foods and nutrition and putting that knowledge to work *can* help you deal with your arthritis. It can help you

- improve the nutritional quality of your diet

- keep your weight under control

- cope with medications

- avoid constipation

- decide whether to take extra vitamins and minerals or other supplements

- avoid unproven and potentially unhealthy "arthritis diets" and "miracle cures"

- feel and be as healthy, fit, and energetic as you can

175

However, foods and nutrition *can't* cure your arthritis. Unless you have gout, no special foods, diets, or supplements will directly affect your arthritis.

IMPROVING THE NUTRITIONAL QUALITY OF YOUR DIET

Nutrients are the substances in food that the body needs to work correctly. Your body needs over forty essential nutrients (see the accompanying chart). It needs water, carbohydrates, protein, and fat. It also needs a number of vitamins and minerals. But while your body needs a certain amount of each nutrient, consuming large amounts of specific nutrients can be dangerous. Good nutrition means giving your body the right amounts of all the nutrients it needs—not too little, not too much.

The single most important step you can take to make sure that your body gets enough of each nutrient is to eat a wide variety of different foods. Yes, variety still works. People who eat many different vegetables, fruits, grain products, fish, poultry, and other meats improve their chance of getting the right amounts of the nutrients they need.

Variety helps because nutrients are distributed throughout the foods we eat. No food contains every nutrient. Many supply only a few. If you eat the same foods all the time, you may get plenty (even too much) of several nutrients but too little of the others. If you open up your diet to more foods, you are more likely to get what you need—adequate but moderate amounts of each nutrient.

ESSENTIAL NUTRIENTS

Type of Nutrient	Basic Functions
1. Water	Water is the "main ingredient" of the body. It provides the proper environment for the various bodily processes.
2. Carbohydrates	Carbohydrates include starches, sugars, and fiber. Starches and sugars are a primary source of the energy (calories) that fuels the activities of the body. Fiber influences both bowel function and blood cholesterol levels.
3. Protein	Protein is essential for growth and for the maintenance and repair of bone, muscle, and the various organs. Protein also can supply calories and energy.
4. Fat	Fat is a concentrated source of calories and a carrier of certain vitamins that dissolve only in fat. Certain fats also supply essential fatty acids.
5. Minerals	Minerals help regulate a number of bodily activities. They are essential to proper muscle and nerve function. They also play a significant role in the growth, maintenance, and repair of bone.
6. Vitamins	Vitamins help regulate various processes that go on inside the body. Each vitamin has specific roles that do not change. Vitamins do not supply energy.

Keep in mind that variety only works if you eat many different foods from all the food groups. Eating different dishes prepared from the same small group of foods won't do the job.

Increasing variety isn't the only step you can take to improve your diet. You can also shift the focus of your diet. Instead of eating foods that are rich in fat (especially animal fat, milk fat, and hydrogenated oils) and foods made with lots of salt and sugar, you can switch to eating more breads, cereals, pasta (especially whole-grain), and more vegetables and fruits.

Making this change in emphasis can help you control your weight and help ensure that you get enough vitamins and minerals. Because it will add fiber to your diet, it also can help you maintain proper bowel function. It may even reduce the risk of heart disease, stroke, and cancer.

Our Nutrition Guidelines are designed to help you put these basic principles—more variety; less fat, salt, and sugar; more vegetables, fruits, and grains—into practice. Begin with the "basics," then move to the "improvements." Make a few changes, take time to get used to them, then try a few more.

1. For variety, experiment with unfamiliar foods and foods you don't eat very often. Don't rely on just one or two foods from each group. This is especially important for vegetables, fruit, and grain products.

2. Adapt the basic pattern to suit your needs. If you are sedentary or want to lose weight, emphasize the lower calorie (lower fat) foods within each group, especially the meat and milk groups. If you are large and active, you may need to add some extra food. Breads, other low-fat grain products, vegetables, and fruits are good choices.

3. Don't ignore milk. People with arthritis need calcium; milk products supply calcium. (For more about calcium, see Chapter 4.) Fortified fluid milk also supplies vitamin D. To avoid excess fat, it is generally best to use low-fat or nonfat milk. If you find it difficult to consume two servings of milk a day, try to drink small amounts of milk throughout the day and think about taking a calcium supplement. If you don't drink much milk, try to get out in the sunshine three times a week for about fifteen minutes each time. The body can produce its own vitamin D provided the skin is regularly exposed to sunlight.

4. Pay attention to protein sources, but don't go overboard with meat. You don't need much meat to get enough protein. If you consume far more protein than you need, you may make it more difficult for your body to meet its needs for other nutrients. Three ounces (85g) of meat looks about as big as a deck of standard playing cards. Two three-ounce (85g) servings a day of poultry, fish, or other meats is usually plenty. (A small third serving may be a good idea if you can't or don't eat any milk, yogurt, or cheese.)

NUTRITION GUIDELINES: THE FOOD GROUPS

Food Group	Includes		Typical Serving Sizes
Grain Products	Grain and cereal products prepared with little or no fat or sugar:		
	Breads, muffins, rolls		1 slice bread 1 muffin or roll
	Breakfast cereals Noodles and pasta Rice and barley Tortillas		1 oz (28 g) cold cereal ½ cup (120 mL) noodles, pasta, rice, or hot cereal 1 tortilla
Vegetables & Fruits	All vegetables and fruits		½ cup (120 mL) vegetables or small fruits 1 medium-size piece of fruit ½ cup (120 mL) pure juice
Vitamin C Sources	Citrus fruits Berries Currants Guava Kiwi Melon	Broccoli Cabbage Cauliflower Greens Potato Tomato	
Vitamin A Sources	Deep yellow and orange fruits and vegetables Dark green vegetables		
	Apricot Cantaloupe Mango Pumpkin Tomato	Broccoli Carrot Chard Spinach Sweet potato	
Milk Products	Milk Cheese Cottage cheese Ice milk and ice cream Yogurt		1 cup (235 mL) milk 1 oz (28 g) cheese 1 cup (235 mL) cottage cheese 1 cup (235 mL) ice milk 1 cup (235 mL) yogurt
Meats	Fish, poultry, seafood Beef, lamb, pork, veal Dried beans and peas Eggs Nuts		3 oz (85 g) of cooked meat (excluding bones) 1 cup (235 mL) cooked beans 2 eggs
Other Foods			
Alcohol	Beer, wine, liquor		
Fats & Oils	Butter, margarine, cooking oils, cream, cream cheese, sour cream Salad dressing		
Sugar & Sweets	Cakes, cookies, pastries, pies Soft drinks Syrup, honey, candy		

5. In general, spend more effort reducing the amount of fat you eat and less effort worrying about the exact number of eggs you eat. Eggs are a good source of high-quality protein. Even if your doctor has advised you to limit egg yolks because of your blood cholesterol level, you can probably eat three or four large eggs a week. Ask to be sure.

6. Remember that you can get protein by eating grains and legumes (dried beans or peas) in the same meal. You don't have to eat meat or eggs. A meal that combines beans with rice, corn, wheat, or sesame will provide high-quality protein. So will one that combines peanuts and wheat with milk, or greens with rice.

NUTRITION GUIDELINES: RECOMMENDATIONS FOR ADULTS

Food Group	Basic Pattern	Suggested Improvements
Grain Products	4 to 6 (or more) servings a day	Emphasize whole-grain breads and cereals
Vegetables & Fruits	5 (or more) servings a day	Eat foods rich in vitamin A and vitamin C daily Include daily servings of lightly cooked or raw vegetables Eat pickles only occasionally
Milk Products	2 servings a day	Switch to nonfat and low-fat milk products Drink at least some fluid milk every day Eat ice cream only occasionally
Meats	2 servings a day	Emphasize fish, poultry (eaten without the skin), beans, and lean meats Trim visible fat off meats before cooking or eating Limit consumption of bacon, ham, and sausage
Other Foods		
Alcohol		If you drink, do so in moderation (no more than one or two drinks a day)
Fats & Oils		Avoid fried foods (including snack foods) Limit rich sauces, gravies, and desserts Use spreads and salad dressings sparingly For cooking, use small amounts of vegetable oil rather than butter, margarine, or lard
Sugar & Sweets		Avoid "filling up" on sugars and sweets; use only small amounts unless you are very active

CONTROLLING YOUR WEIGHT

If you are overweight, you are putting extra loads and extra stress on your weight-bearing joints. This makes little sense if you have arthritis because it often makes the pain or inflammation worse. Losing weight makes more sense: it will ease the strain, lessen the pain, and improve your agility. Also, joint replacement surgery is often not possible for someone who is seriously overweight.

Losing weight and keeping it off is a challenge. It takes time. If you want to reduce, keep in mind that there is nothing sinful about weighing a lot and nothing magic about any particular weight. Losing weight is only a tool to help you feel better now and in the years to come. To manage your arthritis, you should control your weight. But there is no need to let your weight control you.

"Super" Diets Are Bad Ideas

Most people associate losing weight with going on a special diet. But the truth is that most weight-loss diets are bad ideas. Why? Think about a diet you've tried or heard about:

- Did it tell you to cut out whole groups of foods or nutrients (no fat, no carbohydrates)?

- Did it tell you to eat just a few foods (only cottage cheese and celery, only fruit, only meat)?

- Did it rely on "dietetic" foods or special formulas?

- Did it promise quick weight loss (five pounds in three days, five kilos in two weeks)?

Diets like these are a problem. They may help you lose weight, but only temporarily. They won't help you keep the weight off.

To lose weight and keep it off, you must change your eating habits permanently. If you don't, you will start regaining weight once you go off the diet and back to your usual pattern. Does avoiding sugar and starches for months, eating only cottage cheese for weeks, or relying on special drinks teach you realistic new eating habits that you can keep for the rest of your life? No.

Fad or "miracle" diets also can threaten your health. To stay healthy while you reduce, which is crucial for people with arthritis, it is important to continue to eat modest but reasonable quantities of a wide variety of nutritious foods. If you eat very little, you may lose valuable lean muscle tissue rather than fat—muscle that will not necessarily return even if you gain weight. And if you eat only a small range of foods, you run the risk of getting too little of a number of nutrients. Your bone health may suffer as a result.

If special diets are not the answer, what is? Changing your eating habits, food choices, and cooking practices, and adopting a realistic attitude toward your weight. There is no one right way to do this, but the following suggestions may help.

Adopt a Realistic Attitude

1. Check with your doctor. Make sure your physician recommends that you lose weight. If you weigh just a few pounds more than you would like, you may not need to lose weight at all. Try to accept your weight and devote your energy to some other concern.

2. Set a reasonable goal that you know you can reach within a few months. If you want to lose more than ten or fifteen pounds (5 to 7 kg), think about losing five or ten pounds (2 to 4 kg) initially. (Five pounds (2 kg) is more realistic if you are inactive.) Once you reach your goal, stop and take the time to get used to the changes that got you there. For a month or so, focus on keeping your weight stable rather than getting it lower. If all goes well, decide to lose another five or ten pounds (2 to 4 kg). When you achieve your second goal, remember to practice your new habits. Become comfortable with your new weight before you continue.

3. Lose weight gradually. Two to five pounds (1 to 2 kg) a month is a reasonable rate.

4. Don't weigh yourself every day—once every week or two is enough. Remember, losing weight isn't your only aim. Learning the new habits that will help you keep the weight off is just as important.

5. Don't get discouraged by a bit of inconsistency. Your life changes from week to week. It is only natural that changing your eating habits is easier some weeks than others. Expect gradual improvements but don't demand perfection.

6. Don't worry or give up if your weight reaches a plateau after a few weeks. When you first lose weight, much of what you lose is water. After two or three weeks, this water weight comes back. When it does, it can keep your weight from going down for a week or so even though you continue to eat less and lose fat.

Change Your Eating Habits

Lifelong changes in eating habits are the key to permanent weight loss. A Food Diary can help you identify the changes that will help you. Write down everything you eat and drink for three days (better yet, a week) on a chart like the example we've shown here. Examine the diary for clues to why you weigh what you do. For example:

- Is cooking one of your hobbies? Do you eat when you cook or clean up? It may help to share the cooking with someone else, or to prepare less and serve smaller portions.

DAY AND TIME	WHAT I ATE	HOW MUCH I ATE	WHERE I ATE	WHAT MOOD I WAS IN	WHAT I WAS DOING BESIDES EATING

- Do you (over)eat when you get depressed, bored, or nervous? Make a habit of eating only when you feel hungry. It may help to plan in advance something cheering or calming to do—call a friend, take a warm bath, read, take a walk, listen to music—when the difficult mood strikes.

- Do you eat more than you notice when you watch television, read, or talk on the telephone? Focus on what you eat. Don't do anything else while you eat. Eat slowly.

- Do you eat too fast? Your body needs time to signal that you have eaten enough. If you eat rapidly, you may not feel full until after you have already eaten far too much. Slow down. Take smaller bites, and put down your fork after each mouthful. Pause several times during each meal.

- Do you eat less than three times a day? Some people find that they eat less when they eat three, four, or even five small meals a day instead of just one or two relatively large meals. Try it.

Change Your Food Choices

Follow the Nutrition Guidelines, emphasizing the foods that are low in fat and relatively low in sugar. Some suggestions:

- Eat more poultry and fish; less red meat. When you do eat red meat, choose the leaner cuts. Keep in mind that for any particular cut, USDA

182

Select grade meat has less fat than USDA Choice, and both have less fat than USDA Prime.

- Drink low-fat or nonfat milk. Avoid eating large amounts of cheese because most cheeses are high in fat.

- Eat fruits raw or canned in their own juice instead of fruits canned in heavy syrup.

- Substitute fruits and raw vegetables for some or all of your usual snacks.

- Eat fewer "luxury foods"—foods that contain quite a lot of fat or sugar but little else. Most such foods are either greasy, "rich," or very sweet. Some examples:

    gravies, sauces, dressings

    bacon

    butter, margarine, cream, cream cheese

    cakes, pies, pastries, soft or crumbly cookies

    soft drinks

    beer, wine, liquor

Change Your Cooking Practices

Before cooking, trim visible fat off meats and remove skin from poultry. Find and use recipes that require only small amounts of fats (including butter, margarine, cream, and sour cream) and oils. Avoid frying, especially deep-fat frying. When you do fry, use nonstick pans and a minimum of oil. If you see fat or oil on or in a cooked food, try to cut, spoon, or drain out most of it.

Become More Active

If your first response to this suggestion is, "I'm too tired to do anything else after I get home from work," or "I get enough exercise just running the house," think about this: exercise helps people develop stamina and tire less easily. Regular exercise doesn't wear you down. It peps you up. And even a relatively mild exercise program can help you lose weight (so your joints carry lighter loads) and firm and tone your muscles (so they provide stronger support for your joints).

To minimize the pain and stress of exercise, choose a program that uses the painful joint the least but still provides a good general workout. (See Chapter 7.)

Maintain Your Weight

If you follow these suggestions, you won't suddenly need to learn a whole new set of eating habits designed to keep weight off, because you will be learning the new habits you need while you lose weight. But keeping the weight off will still be a challenge. This section presents some ideas to help you meet that challenge.

1. Join a support group and stay with it for at least four to six months. If you aren't already part of a weight-loss group, joining one now can give you important assistance. Look for one that

    *   emphasizes the importance of good nutrition and the use of a wide variety of foods,

    *   gives you support in the form of ongoing meetings and long-term follow-up, and

    *   emphasizes changes in eating habits and patterns.

2. Gradually increase the amount of food you eat but continue to follow the eating habits and practices you learned while you were losing weight. It is especially important to continue to keep the amount of fat in your diet relatively low. The same is true of alcohol.

3. Keep active. If you exercise three to five times a week you will improve your odds of success noticeably. Gradually increase your activity level if possible.

4. Weigh yourself once or twice a week, preferably soon after you get up in the morning. Think about keeping a record of your weights.

5. Set a "maximum acceptable weight." Weights naturally fluctuate, but it can help to set a limit on the amount of fluctuation you will allow. Five pounds (2½ kg) over your current weight may be a reasonable limit, but make your own decision based on your own knowledge of your body.

6. When and if you reach your maximum acceptable weight, review and follow the suggestions in the preceding sections and start keeping a *daily* Food Diary. Don't stop until you are at least two or three (1 to 1½ kg) pounds below your maximum acceptable weight.

COPING WITH MEDICATIONS

Food and medicines affect one another. Some drugs used for arthritis are best absorbed when taken on an empty stomach. Others can irritate or upset your stomach unless you take them with food. Some even alter your nutritional needs. Learn how the medicines you use interact with food, and you may be able to prevent a few problems.

Whenever you get a new medication, find out whether you should take it with meals or on an empty stomach. Aspirin, for example, should be taken with meals and ample fluids. Doing this helps prevent stomach irritation and upset. Prednisone, Indocin, and Clinoril also become less irritating when taken with meals or milk. Ask your doctor or pharmacist, or check Chapter 17 of this book.

Also, remember that if your physician asks you to take a drug "with every meal," he or she probably assumes that you eat three meals a day. If you don't, be sure to say so. You may need different directions.

Aspirin, corticosteroids (such as prednisone), laxatives, and antacids are examples of drugs that can affect your nutrient needs.

Aspirin often causes a small amount of bleeding in the gastrointestinal tract. If you regularly take large amounts of Aspirin, you may well need extra iron to compensate for the blood loss. You may also need somewhat more folic acid (a vitamin) and vitamin C. Green leafy vegetables, asparagus, liver, kidney, and whole-grain cereals are good sources of folic acid. Citrus fruits, tomatoes, cabbage, potatoes, berries, melon, and dark green vegetables supply vitamin C. Meats are a main source of iron; legumes and whole-grain breads and cereals provide additional iron. But if you need more iron, taking an iron supplement may be preferable to eating large quantities of meat; more about this later.

Prednisone and other steroid drugs can cause people with arthritis to hold too much water in their bodies. If this happens to you, your doctor may ask you to limit the amount of salt or sodium in your diet (ordinary table salt is *sodium* chloride). Each of us needs some sodium for our muscles and nerves to work properly. But keeping the amount you consume relatively low can help minimize problems with water retention.

To control your intake of sodium:

- Don't add salt to your food at the table.

- Use less salt in cooking. Many recipes work fine with only one-quarter or one-half of the suggested amount of salt.

- Avoid foods that taste very salty or contain a lot of salt:

  pickles, sauerkraut, other foods made with brine

  ham, bacon, sausage

  cold cuts, processed or canned meats

  canned soups, bouillon

  salted snack foods (salted popcorn, pretzels, nuts, crackers, chips)

  soy sauce, steak sauce, other salty condiments

Softened water, antacids that rely on sodium compounds (AlkaSeltzer, BromoSeltzer, Brioschi, Rolaids), and baking soda used as an antacid can significantly add to your intake of sodium. If your physician prescribes a diet that contains a specific amount of sodium, ask for further instructions.

Prednisone may also increase your need for protein, calcium, potassium, and certain vitamins. If you need to take prednisone or another corticosteroid for an extended period of time, make a special effort to follow the Nutrition Guidelines. Be sure to eat at least the recommended amount of meat and milk products. You may want to take supplements that supply moderate amounts of calcium and other vitamins and minerals. If you are on steroids, your doctor may prescribe vitamin D in large doses (e.g., 50,000 I.U. twice a week) to help protect your bones.

Antacids and laxatives may seem like harmless medicines, but they're not. *Antacids* that contain calcium (Tums, Alka–2, Di–Gel) can be constipating. Those that contain aluminum hydroxide (Mylanta, Maalox, Gelusil, Amphogel, Gaviscon) can interfere with your body's use of phosphorus, a mineral crucial for bone health. Frequent use of laxatives can lead to dependency. *Laxatives* may also reduce your ability to absorb a number of the nutrients in your food. This is especially true of mineral oil, milk of magnesia, and products that rely on phenolphthalein or bisacodyl.

If you frequently use antacids and laxatives, try to cut down. And take special care with your diet.

AVOIDING CONSTIPATION

Constipation is common among people with arthritis. One reason for this is that many people with arthritis are not as physically active as they once were. Another is that a number of arthritis medications tend to be constipating.

To prevent or deal with constipation, keep these suggestions in mind:

1. **Pay attention to your body's signals.** If you feel you need to go to the bathroom, don't wait. Go. It is easier for your body to develop its own natural schedule for bowel movements when you pay attention to the warning signals.

2. **Take your time in the bathroom.**

   - Take deep breaths to relax the muscles.

   - Tuck in your belly and navel, then raise one leg toward your chest. Rest your foot on the seat if you can do so comfortably.

   - Don't strain.

   - To make sure you take your time, have something to read or a radio in your bathroom.

3. **Don't force your body onto a rigid schedule. Don't overuse laxatives.** There is no need to have a bowel movement every day. If you don't feel pain or discomfort when you go to the bathroom, don't take laxatives to force yourself onto a different schedule.

   Laxatives can make minor problems with constipation more persistent. If you use one frequently your intestines can become dependent on it, with the result that you become constipated when you stop the laxative. If this happens, don't try to solve the problem by going back to the laxative. Instead, give your system time to adjust to functioning on its own. Help it along by following the other suggestions in this section.

If you must use a laxative, use one based on psyllium (Metamucil, Hydrocil Instant, Fiberall, Serutan). Psyllium is a natural product that holds water and adds bulk. When using one of these products be sure to drink plenty of water or other fluid (6–8 glasses a day).

In general, try to avoid antacids; many can be constipating. If you must take an antacid while constipated, choose one that tends not to be constipating. Try to avoid milk of magnesia. (Maalox, Mylanta, and Gelusil are possibilities.)

4. **Manage your stress level.** Organize your work schedule to minimize your efforts and maximize your strength. For example, do all the upstairs work at one time, all downstairs work another time. Take rest periods. Also, try out the relaxation techniques discussed in Chapter 10.

5. **Eat slowly.** Mealtime should be a period of rest. When you eat, sit down, concentrate on eating, and try to enjoy your food. Don't think about problems or things you have to do. *Chew slowly and thoroughly.*

6. **Drink plenty of fluids.** Water adds bulk to the stool. This keeps the stool soft and makes it easier for your muscles to move it through your intestinal tract. Try to drink at least two quarts or liters of fluids each day—about eight large glasses. Plain water is good (warm or cool) but mineral water, club soda, coffee, tea, juice, milk, and soup also count.

7. **Exercise.** Physical activity will help your body eliminate waste more smoothly and easily.

8. **Eat prunes or drink prune juice.** Prunes and prune juice naturally contain a chemical substance that eases constipation. (If you are trying to lose weight, keep in mind that prune juice has more calories than most juices.)

9. **Gradually add fiber to your diet.** Our bodies cannot digest certain parts of most fruits, vegetables, and whole-grain products. The parts we cannot digest are referred to as "fiber." Fiber, especially "insoluble fiber," is a natural laxative. It holds water in and adds bulk to the stool, which makes it softer and easier to expel. Fiber also helps waste pass through the lower intestine more quickly.

You can increase the amount of fiber (including insoluble fiber) in your diet by eating more fruits and vegetables and more whole-grain breads, cereals, and crackers. Both cooked and raw vegetables and fruits provide significant amounts of fiber. Whole-wheat bread is a good source of insoluble fiber, as are whole-grain cereals made from wheat. Wheat bran and bran cereal are excellent sources of insoluble fiber, but should always be eaten in small quantities with plenty of fluids. If dry cereals or wheat bran seem to irritate your system, try hot cereals instead.

When you add fiber to your diet, be sure to do it *gradually* over weeks or months. If you don't, you may overwhelm your digestive system, experience problems with gas, and become very uncomfortable.

SUPPLEMENTS

People with arthritis often take dietary supplements of one kind or another—extra vitamins, bone meal, fish oil capsules, the list goes on. Do supplements make sense? Sometimes yes, often no. It certainly doesn't make sense to take supplements haphazardly. Many supplements are a waste of money. They won't cure your arthritis. They may even endanger your health. But some people with arthritis can benefit from supplements that contain *moderate* amounts of specific nutrients.

Problems with Supplements

- Supplements are not a cure. There is no proof that any nutrient or food substance cures arthritis.

- Supplements cannot guarantee good nutrition. Our bodies need at least forty different nutrients. No supplement contains all of the nutrients we need in the amounts we need them. When you take a supplement, you get only the particular nutrients and amounts the manufacturer chooses to include. To be fairly certain of receiving appropriate amounts of all the known nutrients (and have a respectable chance of obtaining any unidentified nutrients), you still need a healthy varied diet.

- Supplements can create health problems. Some nutrients, such as vitamin A and vitamin D, accumulate in the body. If you regularly take a supplement that provides much more of a nutrient than your body needs, the accumulation may reach toxic levels. Also, giving your body large amounts of some nutrients but not others can lead to harmful imbalances. Just recently, health authorities initiated an investigation after they noticed that many of the people who developed a particular blood disease had been taking L-Tryptophan, an amino acid available as a dietary supplement.

Unless your doctor or a trained nutritionist advises you personally to do so, don't take double doses of any supplement and avoid supplements that supply more than 100 percent of the Recommended Daily Allowance [the "RDA"] for a nutrient. Virtually any healthy person who consumes 100 percent of the RDA for a nutrient receives more than enough of that nutrient.

Reasonable Use

While it is best to avoid most dietary supplements, there are situations where taking a moderate amount of one or more nutrients can make sense.

Do you eat very little? If you eat little, whether because you are inactive or because you are losing weight, you may not get enough of certain nutrients even though you make good food choices. Taking a moderate multi-vitamin *and mineral* supplement once every day or two can fill the gap for some (but not all) nutrients.

Supplements that provide between 50 and 100 percent of the RDA for a relatively wide range of vitamins and minerals include Centrum, Life-Line Maximum Daily, Life-Line Centra Life, One-a-Day Maximum Formula, Unicap M, and Unicap Sr. Many drugstore chains sell store-brand supplements that are very similar to these brand name supplements but are significantly less expensive.

If you take a multivitamin-mineral supplement, avoid breakfast cereals that are "fortified" with vitamins. ("Enriched" foods are fine.) Eating vitamin-fortified cereals will only give you expensive, unnecessary, and possibly excessive amounts of a few of the nutrients you already consume. Instead of emphasizing fortified foods, spend your money on other healthy foods that you don't eat very often.

Are you elderly? If you are elderly and sense that you don't digest many foods as well as you used to, you too may want to take a moderate strength multivitamin-mineral supplement. It is relatively common for people to develop some trouble absorbing nutrients from their food as they grow older. Taking a moderate supplement once a day won't let you ignore what you eat, but it may give you a needed boost.

Do you avoid milk and cheese? Milk and milk products are rich in calcium and protein. While other types of food also supply protein, few other foods are rich in calcium. Unless you consume a substantial amount of milk or milk products every day (two glasses of milk, two ounces (60 g) of hard cheese, or several cups (500 mL) of cottage cheese), there is a real chance that your body does not get all the calcium it should.

If you enjoy milk and tolerate it well, a good (perhaps the best) way to prevent difficulties with calcium is to drink two glasses of low-fat or skim milk daily and eat a healthy varied diet. (Chapter 4 lists nondairy foods that can provide significant amounts of calcium.) But if you can't or won't drink milk, a calcium supplement may be in order. If you have had problems with kidney stones, consult your doctor before taking calcium.

Different types of calcium supplements are available. In general, look for a supplement that will provide between 50 and 100 percent of the RDA for calcium. (This translates to 500 to 1,000 mg of "elemental calcium" a day.) Avoid bone meal and dolomite. Try to stay away from tablets that are heavily compressed to reduce their size—they can be harder to absorb. If you already take a multivitamin-mineral supplement, avoid calcium supplements that contain added vitamin D.

If constipation is a problem, try a supplement that supplies no more than 250 mg of elemental calcium per tablet. (Os-Cal 250 and Citracal 950 fall into this category.) If you tolerate one tablet a day, try taking two or three over the course of a day.

Always take calcium tablets with plenty of fluids. Try not to take them at the same time as supplements that contain iron.

Do you regularly take large doses of Aspirin? If you take many Aspirin each day, you probably need more than the average amount of iron. (If you take Indocin, Butazolidin, or corticosteroids, you may also need extra iron.) Many foods contain some iron, but meat tends to be our primary source. So if you don't eat much meat, supplemental iron can be a wise idea.

Iron is available alone and in multivitamin-mineral supplements. Be cautious with any supplement that contains well over 100 percent of the RDA for iron. It may cause constipation. It may also reduce your ability to absorb other minerals.

Fish oils have been in the news for some time now. Researchers are examining connections between fish oil consumption, cholesterol levels, and heart disease. And they are investigating whether fish oils—more precisely the "omega-3 fatty acids" present in fish oils—may be useful in treating certain forms of arthritis.

Fish oils are also in the drugstore. Omega-3 fatty acid supplements are widely available under names such as Cardi-Omega 3, EPA Plus, MaxEPA, ProMega, and Proto-Chol. Most contain 300 mg of omega-3 fatty acids per capsule. Their labels often suggest taking six capsules a day.

Are fish oil supplements likely to help people with arthritis? At this point, the answer is no. There is no reason to take omega-3 fatty acids for osteoarthritis. The ongoing research focuses on rheumatoid arthritis and other forms of inflammatory arthritis, *not* osteoarthritis. As for rheumatoid arthritis, the most we can say now is that large doses of omega-3 fatty acids (doses equivalent to fifteen or so capsules a day) may give modest temporary relief to some people with rheumatoid arthritis. Smaller doses are unlikely to be of any benefit. And we do *not* know whether long-term use of fish oil supplements is safe. Among other things, frequent use of fish oil supplements (including bottled fish liver oils) may contribute to anemia and may lead to potentially toxic overloads of vitamins A and D.

One thing that is fairly certain is that fish oil supplements will affect your budget. Six capsules daily can cost over $25 a month.

Of course, there are still many good reasons to eat fish regularly. If you rarely have fish, try eating fish instead of meat in three or four meals each week. Cold-water marine fish such as salmon, mackerel, trout, sardines, tuna, herring, bluefish, and halibut are natural sources of omega-3 fatty acids. Soybean, walnut, wheat-germ, and canola oils also contain omega-3 fatty acids.

ARTHRITIS DIETS AND "CURES"—HOW TO AVOID TRAPS

We have already mentioned that there are no proven nutritional cures or treatments for arthritis, except in the case of gout. Yet diet "cures" for arthritis appear regularly in magazines and books and many people are interested. At the Stanford Arthritis Center we have studied the effects of diets; those who follow the fad diets do not feel any better than those who do not.

If you want to learn how to judge for yourself those articles and books on "miracle" cures—so that you won't get trapped into unhealthy practices—this final section is for you.

Step 1: Get a copy of the book or article in which the originator of the diet explains the diet and the "proof" of its effectiveness.

Step 2: Read the entire article. Figure out what kind of evidence the author has. Does he or she try to persuade you with anecdotes—short stories of what happened to individual patients? Or does he or she present the results of scientific studies ("clinical trials")?

Step 3: If the evidence consists of anecdotes or case reports, analyze them as follows:

1. Get the facts.

   - Who was involved?

   - What was the treatment?

   - What was the result?

   - Were there any side effects from the treatment?

   - What claims does the author make, based on the result?

2. Think about the facts, asking yourself:
   a. Could anything else have caused the claimed results?

   - Was anything beside the diet changed (medications, exercise)?

   - Could the change have been caused by a psychological effect—"positive thinking" on the part of the patient?

   - Could it have been a coincidence? Arthritis pain tends to come and go.

   People often try new cures when they have the most pain, improve naturally, and then conclude that the cure works. Usually, the improvement comes about because the arthritis is at the "peak" of the pain cycle when the person tries the cure. The arthritis would have improved with or without the "cure," because the arthritis was going into remission anyway.

   b. Were the patients different from other people with arthritis or from you in any important ways?

   c. If the author presents several anecdotes as evidence, are there any patterns other than that the patients followed the diet and improved? In one popular book that deals with nutrition and arthritis, the author describes a number of cases in which patients followed a specific diet and improved. But if one looks closely, there is another pattern—many of the patients also lost considerable amounts of weight. This sort of thing should make you suspect that it isn't the specific diet but rather the weight loss that causes the improvement.

Step 4: If the author presents clinical trials or studies, you have to analyze the evidence differently. When you read anecdotes, you probably will find that it is difficult to answer the questions suggested above. Observations of single cases simply do not give enough information to tell whether treatments really work. That is the reason clinical trials are done—they help us sort out the effects of the treatment from psychological effects, coincidence, and other such factors.

A clinical trial is an experiment in which one group of people gets a treatment ("Treatment X"), a similar group receives no treatment or a "traditional" treatment, and the results for the two groups are compared. If the group with the new treatment does better than the other group (the "control" group), the conclusion is that the new treatment helps. But if roughly the same proportion of people improve in both groups, the conclusion is that the new treatment has no effect or at least no greater effect than the traditional treatment.

The following diagram may clarify matters. In this trial, the conclusion is that Treatment X does not help, because the same number of people got better in both groups. Notice that if the researcher had observed only the people getting Treatment X, it would have looked as though Treatment X works, even though it does not.

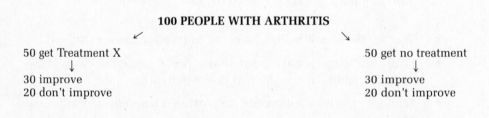

100 PEOPLE WITH ARTHRITIS

50 get Treatment X
↓
30 improve
20 don't improve

50 get no treatment
↓
30 improve
20 don't improve

Here are some questions to ask yourself about results from clinical studies:

1. **Were the two groups of people really similar?** If they were not, the differences between them may have confused the study and made the results deceptive. For example, if the group that receives no treatment has more severe arthritis, its members may not improve as much as members of the group whose problems are less severe. If this happens, it may seem that Treatment X works better than no treatment, but it was not a fair comparison. Some things that may need to be similar in compared groups are age, sex, weight, exercise and activity patterns, and the severity and type of arthritis

2. **Were the researchers looking for a specific outcome?** If they wanted to prove that one group does better than the other, it may have biased their observation and affected the way they saw things. "You see what you want to see" can apply to scientific research, too, if you're not careful.

193
Arthritis diets and
"cures"—how to
avoid traps

3. **Is the study published in a recent scientific journal?** Editors of such magazines usually screen articles quite thoroughly. If a study is not published, it may mean that there were serious flaws in the procedures.

Step 5: If you are still not sure whether you should try the diet (after you evaluate the evidence), try to contact your doctor or nutritionist for advice.

Step 6: If you are unable to contact anyone, or if you still think that the diet may be good, ask yourself these questions:

1. Does the diet eliminate any of the basic foods or nutrients? If so, you may harm your health if you follow it.

2. Does the diet stress a few special foods, so that you will have little variety in your meals? Again, if it does, it may harm your health.

3. Do the foods or supplements cost more than you can afford? If so, following the diet may force you to cut back on other essentials.

4. Are you willing to put up with the trouble and expense involved, knowing that the chances are good that it will not be a cure?

If you answer no to the first three questions and yes to the last, it probably won't harm you to try the diet and see if it works for you. Remember, though, that even if it does seem to work for you, it may not work for someone else.

References

Brody, Jane. *Jane Brody's Nutrition Book.* New York: Bantam, 1982.

Vegetarian Eating

Lappé, Frances. *Diet for a Small Planet.* New York: Ballantine, 1985.

Robertson, Laurel, Carol Flinders, and Bronwen Godfrey. *Laurel's Kitchen: A Handbook for Vegetarian Cookery and Nutrition.* New York: Bantam, 1978.

Weight Control

Ferguson, James M. *Learning to Eat: Behavior Modification for Weight Control.* Palo Alto, CA: Bull Publishing, 1975.

Nash, Joyce D., and Linda Ormiston. *Taking Charge of Your Weight and Well-Being.* 2nd ed. Palo Alto, CA: Bull Publishing, 1989.

Waltz, Julie. *Food Habit Management: A Comprehensive Guide to Dietary Change.* ed. Fay Ainsworth and Susan Sommerman. Edmonds, WA: Northwest Learning Associates, 1982.

17

The Drug Scene
Medications That Help Arthritis

Knowing all about your drugs is not easy. All drugs are complex, and full explanations from family doctors invariably take lots of time. Unfortunately, that time is not always available to physicians. The interview with your doctor is an intensive experience, and all too frequently discussion of prescribed treatment merely serves to end it quickly. Too little time is spent on this important subject. Here, the discussions you have been having with your physician are repeated. Read the ones you need. Reread those you forgot.

INFLAMMATION

Many important arthritis medicines reduce inflammation, and you have to know a little bit about this concept. Inflammation is part of the normal healing process. The body increases blood flow and sends inflammatory cells to repair wounded tissues and to kill bacterial invaders. The inflammation causes the area to be warm, red, tender, and often swollen. To understand the potential problems of drugs that reduce inflammation, it is important to recognize first that inflammation is a normal process.

In rheumatoid arthritis the inflammation causes damage, and thus suppression of the inflammation can be helpful in treatment. In osteoarthritis there is little inflammation or the inflammation may be necessary for the

195

healing process. So you don't always want an anti-inflammatory drug just because you have arthritis—in rheumatoid arthritis, yes; in osteoarthritis, probably no.

ASPIRIN AND OTHER NONSTEROIDAL ANTI-INFLAMMATORY DRUGS (NSAIDs)

Aspirin is one of the most important drugs for arthritis. Not only is it useful itself, but it also serves as a model for understanding the benefits and problems of medical treatments for arthritis.

Aspirin is the most frequently used drug in the world and the most misunderstood. It is among the safest drugs currently used, yet we constantly hear of its dangers. It has become so familiar that people fail to take it seriously: "Take two Aspirin and call me in the morning." Yet it is said to be so powerful that today the United States Food & Drug Administration would not license it if it were a new drug. The scare press reports the hazards of bleeding from the stomach or of liver damage. The same press reports the next day that Aspirin may prevent heart attacks by thinning the blood. These contradictions dominate our daily encounters with Aspirin.

If used properly, Aspirin is a marvelous drug for many kinds of arthritis. If not used correctly, it can lead to real frustration. Read the next several paragraphs carefully; they illustrate things you need to know about Aspirin specifically, but also illustrate general principles you need to know about all arthritis medications.

What You Need to Know About Anti-inflammatory Medications

1. **You must know the difference between the terms** *analgesic* **and** *anti-inflammatory.* *Analgesic* means "pain-killing." *Anti-inflammatory* means that the redness and swelling are reduced. Aspirin provides minor pain relief and is helpful for headaches, sunburn, or other familiar problems. But it can be a major anti-inflammatory agent and can actually decrease the swelling and tissue damage in rheumatoid arthritis.

With Aspirin the dosage is the difference. The pain-killing effects of Aspirin are best after you take two tablets (10 grains). If you take more Aspirin, you do not really get any more pain relief. You can repeat this analgesic (pain-killing) dose every four hours because it tends to wear off in about that time. In contrast, the anti-inflammatory effect requires high and continuous levels of Aspirin in the blood. A person must take twelve to twenty-four tablets (5 grains each) each day and the process must be continued for three to four weeks to obtain the full effect.

2. **You need to know the difference between allergy and side effects.** People often maintain that they cannot tolerate a drug because of problems they have had with it in the past. When the doctor asks what drugs you are allergic to, you may mention such drugs because of the problems you have had. Most of the time, you have had a side effect from the drug, not an allergy.

Allergy is relatively rare; side effects are common. Only a few people get an allergy, but everyone experiences side effects if they get enough of a drug. There are different symptoms. A skin rash, wheezing in the lungs, or a runny nose generally mean allergy. Nausea, abdominal pain, ringing in the ears, and headache usually mean side effects. If you have an allergy, that is a good reason to avoid that drug in the future. If you have side effects to a drug, usually it means that you need one or another trick to get your body to tolerate the drug better, or perhaps just a little lower dose.

These considerations are particularly important with Aspirin. The treatment range is just below the level that gives side effects. So most patients receiving Aspirin for anti-inflammatory purposes will have some ringing in the ears or some nausea. This is just a signal to slow down a little bit and to establish what dose is exactly the correct one for you. If you do not know this principle, you are going to give up too soon on a superb drug, and you will not get better.

3. **You also need to know about drug absorption and drug interactions.** Food delays the absorption of a medicine into your body. With some drugs the presence of food in your stomach will totally prevent the absorption of the medication. But food also protects the stomach lining and can make taking a drug more comfortable. Thus, although food may decrease the effectiveness of a medication, it also may decrease certain side effects by protecting the stomach. By and large, antacids (Maalox, Mylantin, Gelusil) act just about the same as food; they decrease absorption but protect the stomach.

Some medications are coated to protect the stomach; the coating is designed to dissolve after the tablet has passed through the stomach into the small bowel. These coatings work for some people. On occasion, the coating never dissolves and the person derives no benefit whatsoever from the drug; it passes unaltered into the toilet. On other occasions the coating doesn't last long enough and nausea is encountered anyway.

Drugs are chemicals. Interactions between two drugs (two chemicals) are extremely common. Aspirin blocks absorption from the stomach of some of the newer anti-inflammatory agents discussed in the next section. By and large, the fewer medicines you take at one time, the more predictable your response to treatment will be. Most reactions having to do with absorption or interactions with other drugs are not perfectly predictable. You may have them or you may not. The treatment for your arthritis will ultimately be unique to you. You may need to discover by trial and error some of the reactions of your own body. To figure things out, it helps if you know the final general point.

4. **You should know about dosage equivalents, generic names, and product differences.** Aspirin is huckstered more than any other drug. It is found in the drugstore in several hundred different formulations. It is "the drug doctors recommend most." Manufacturers compete to find tiny areas of difference among products which can be exploited by advertising campaigns. There are "arthritis extra-strength" Aspirin, buffered Aspirin, and

coated Aspirin. There is Aspirin with extra ingredients, such as caffeine or phenacetin. There is Aspirin in cold formulations with antihistamines or other compounds. There is Aspirin that is advertised for its purity.

A standard Aspirin tablet is 325 mg, and the amount of drug is accurate to government standards. You always pay more for a brand-name formulation. For arthritis, do not buy Aspirin that is compounded with any drugs other than possibly an antacid (Bufferin, Ascriptin). Even then, you may find it less expensive to take Aspirin with an antacid such as Maalox rather than to buy buffered Aspirin. You do not want the caffeine, the phenacetin, or the antihistamine ingredients. Do not use a coated Aspirin (Ecotrin, Enseals) unless you have stomach problems with regular Aspirin. They are more expensive and you may not get as good absorption from your stomach. All of the Aspirin rated by USP or other legal standards are pure enough for your use. If your body can tell a difference, stay with a product that seems to work for you. Otherwise, buy the cheapest USP Aspirin that you can find. If it smells like vinegar when you open the bottle, it is too old and you should throw it out. If you have problems with the new child-proof caps, ask your pharmacist for a regular top.

5. **You must treat Aspirin and other NSAIDs with respect.**   Aspirin and other NSAIDs, despite their familiarity, are not safe medications. They have side effects that include nausea, headache, upset stomach, skin rash, and liver and kidney problems. These effects have been known for a long time and are generally minor.

The major side effect is the development of serious ulcers in the stomach and severe bleeding from the gastrointestinal tract. This process usually occurs silently, without any preceding symptoms. It can result in hospitalization or even death. Because these medications are so widely used, it has been estimated that in the Unites States serious side effects are more common with these drugs than with all other drugs put together.

This is not to say that these drugs should be feared or avoided, since in many patients, probably a majority, the good they do far outweighs the risk of side effects. Yet you should always ask yourself if you need to continue long-term treatment with these or any other drug, and whether there are safer medications for you. Since these drugs are taken for symptomatic relief, if you are not obtaining such relief from one of these medications, it is reasonable to ask your doctor about discontinuing it.

Gastric ulcers from NSAID therapy are usually located around the outlet from the stomach. These ulcers form and heal periodically in most of the patients who are taking full doses of these drugs and have been for a long time. Occasionally, an ulcer is located near one of the larger arteries to the stomach lining and severe bleeding can result. The risk of bleeding requiring hospitalization is about 1 percent for each year that you take these medications in full doses. The risk of death is approximately one in ten hospitalizations, or about one in 1,000 patients per year of full therapy.

All patients are not at the same risk for these problems, which are more than three times as common in people over sixty. They are twice as common in people who smoke cigarettes. They are higher in people who are taking corticosteroids (prednisone; see below), and more likely in people who have already had an episode of bleeding from their stomachs. They are more common in people who have had stomach problems already and had to stop using several of these drugs. They occur more commonly in women, but only because women use these drugs more. Many studies are now underway to determine more precisely those subjects who are at greatest risk.

Can these problems be prevented? At this time the answer is "probably so." Antacids such as Maalox seem to help prevent the upset stomach but perhaps not the bleeding episodes. Similarly, drugs like cimetidine and ranitidine, which decrease stomach acid, seem to prevent the minor symptoms more than the development of ulcers. Sucralfates may help a little, but again do not appear definitive.

Recently, the U.S. Food and Drug Administration has licensed a new drug called misoprostol, used specifically to prevent NSAID ulcers. This is a promising development and may help to deal with this serious side effect. For patients with several risk factors, the current recommendation is to consider prophylactic treatment with misoprostol. The disadvantages: misoprostol, while preventing the development of ulcers, doesn't always help with the symptoms you may be having from the NSAID drugs. It may actually cause symptoms, particularly diarrhea during the first few days. It has not yet been shown definitely to prevent hospitalizations and deaths, although this effect seems likely from the studies that have been reported to date. Taking any preventative medication costs money, in the case of Cytotec about $500 per year. Our recommendation at this writing is to consider misoprostol for patients over sixty-five, for those who have had a previous bleeding episode, and for those who are already getting preventive treatment with another agent and hence would spend no more money by switching to misoprostol.

What follows is general advice. If your doctor's advice differs, then listen to your doctor. He or she is most familiar with your specific needs. The doses and precautions listed are those known at the time of this writing and are subject to changes your doctor may know about. But if you receive advice that doesn't make sense according to the principles outlined in this section, don't hesitate to ask questions or get another opinion.

Acetylsalicylic acid (Aspirin)

Purpose: To relieve pain; to reduce inflammation.

Indications: Pain relief for osteoarthritis and local conditions such as bursitis. Anti-inflammatory agent for rheumatoid arthritis.

Dosage: For pain, two 5-grain tablets (10 grains) every four hours as needed. For anti-inflammatory action, three to four tablets, four to six times daily (with medical supervision if these doses are continued for longer than one week). The time to maximum effect is thirty minutes to one hour for pain and one to six weeks for the anti-inflammatory action.

Side effects: Common effects include nausea, vomiting, ringing in the ears, and decreased hearing. Each of these is reversible within a few hours if the drug dosage is decreased. Allergic reactions are rare but include development of nasal polyps and wheezing. Prolonged nausea or vomiting that persists after the drug is stopped for a few days suggest the possibility of a stomach ulcer caused by the irritation of the Aspirin. With an overdose of Aspirin, there is very rapid and heavy breathing, and there can even be unconsciousness and coma. Be sure to keep Aspirin (and all medications) out of reach of all children.

Aspirin has some predictable effects that occur in just about everyone. Blood loss through the bowel occurs in almost all persons who take Aspirin, because the blood clotting function is altered, the stomach is irritated, and Aspirin acts as a minor blood-thinning agent. Up to 10 percent of those taking high doses of Aspirin will have some abnormalities in the function of the liver; although these are seldom noticed by the person taking Aspirin, they can be identified by blood tests. Since serious liver damage does not occur, routine blood tests to check for this complication are not required. Hospitalization for gastrointestinal hemorrhage occurs in about 1 percent of people taking full doses for one year.

Aspirin is not recommended when you have influenza, chicken pox, or high fevers because of the possibility of a rare complication called Reye's syndrome.

Special hints: If you note ringing in the ears or a decrease in your hearing, then decrease the dose of Aspirin. Your dose is just a little bit too high for the best result. If you notice nausea, an upset stomach, or vomiting, there are a variety of things you can do. First, try spreading out the dose with more frequent use of smaller numbers of pills. Perhaps instead of taking four tablets four times a day, you might take three tablets five or six times a day. Second, try taking the Aspirin after meals or after an antacid, which will coat the stomach and provide some protection. Third, you can change brands and see if the nausea is related to the particular brand of Aspirin you were using. Fourth, you can try coated Aspirin. These are absorbed variably, but are often effective in protecting the stomach and decreasing nausea. Ecotrin is the best absorbed, and Enseals is next best. Probably other brands of coated preparations should be avoided, since some of them are absorbed by very few people. Although it is a nuisance, you can get good relief from the nausea by taking a suspension of Aspirin rather than the tablet. Put the Aspirin in a half glass of water and swirl it until the Aspirin particles are suspended in the water. Fill another glass half full of water, drink the suspended Aspirin, and wash it down with the other glass of water. This is an effective and inexpensive way to avoid nausea once you get used to the taste.

Keep track of your Aspirin and always tell your doctor exactly how much you are taking. Aspirin is so familiar that sometimes we forget that we are taking a drug. Be as careful with Aspirin as you would be with any drug. In particular, you may want to ask your doctor about interactions with the newer anti-inflammatory agents, with probenecid, or with blood-thinning agents, if you are taking those drugs. Pay special attention to your stomach. So many drugs cause irritation to the stomach lining that you run the risk of adding insult to injury. Two drugs that irritate the stomach lining may be more than twice as dangerous; again, the fewer medications at one time the better. Every time you talk to a doctor about drugs, be sure to describe all the drugs you are taking, not just your arthritis drugs. It is a good idea to keep a list of all the drugs you take and have it ready to show any doctor you visit, including your dentist.

Ecotrin

325 mg, 500 mg tablets and caplets
See Acetylsalicylic acid (Aspirin).

Disalcid (salicylate)

500 mg round, aqua, scored, film-coated tablet
500 mg aqua and white capsule
750 mg capsule-shaped, aqua, scored, film-coated tablet

Purpose: To relieve pain; to reduce inflammation.

Indications: For mild pain relief of osteoarthritis and in local conditions. As an anti-inflammatory agent for synovitis or attachment arthritis, as in rheumatoid arthritis and ankylosing spondylitis.

Dosage: For pain, one or two 750 mg capsule-shaped aqua tablets every twelve hours. Each 750 mg Disalcid tablet is equivalent in salicylate content to about two and a half normal-sized Aspirin tablets. Occasionally, higher doses may be needed. For pain, the maximum effect is reached in two hours; one to six weeks are required for anti-inflammatory action to take full effect.

Side effects: Common side effects include nausea, vomiting, ringing in the ears, and decreased hearing. Each of these is reversible within a few hours if the drug dosage is decreased. Allergic reactions are rare but potentially include development of nasal polyps and wheezing. With an overdose of any salicylate there can be very heavy and rapid breathing, and even unconsciousness and coma.

Disalcid is being used more frequently in arthritis because it appears to be less toxic to the stomach than Aspirin and the other NSAIDs, although definitive data are not yet available. Additionally, Disalcid has less effect upon the platelets, so there is less chance of minor bleeding problems. The blood salicylate level rises more slowly and lasts longer than with Aspirin, therefore the drug does not have to be taken as often as Aspirin.

Disalcid should be avoided during chicken pox or influenza because of the possibility of Reye's syndrome, as mentioned before.

Some physicians do not believe that the anti-inflammatory activity of Disalcid is as good as that of Aspirin. Other physicians believe that the effects are identical. So it seems likely that Disalcid is less toxic than ordinary Aspirin, but it is not clear that it is as effective a drug. It finds particular use in patients who have had problems with stomach upset from ordinary Aspirin or who are in high-risk groups for gastrointestinal bleeding episodes.

Special hints: If you note ringing in the ears or a decrease in your hearing, decrease the dose of Disalcid; it is just a little bit too high for best results. Keep track of your Disalcid intake and always tell the doctor exactly how much you are taking.

Trilisate (choline magnesium trisalicylate)

500 mg scored, pale pink, capsule-shaped tablet
750 mg scored, white, film-coated, capsule-shaped tablet
1,000 mg scored, red, film-coated, capsule-shaped tablet

Purpose: To relieve pain; to reduce inflammation.

Indications: For mild pain relief of cartilage degeneration and local conditions. Also an anti-inflammatory agent for synovitis and attachment arthritis.

Dosage: For pain, one or two 500 mg tablets every twelve hours. For anti-inflammatory activity, two to three tablets every twelve hours. Each Trilisate tablet is equivalent in salicylate content to 10 grains of Aspirin (two usual-sized Aspirin tablets). Occasionally higher doses may be needed. The maximum effect is reached in two hours for pain effects; one to six weeks are required for anti-inflammatory action to take full effect.

Side effects: Common effects include nausea, vomiting, ringing in the ears, and decreased hearing. Each of these is reversible within a few hours if the drug dosage is decreased. Allergic reactions are rare but potentially include development of nasal polyps and wheezing. With an overdose of salicylate, there can be very rapid and heavy breathing, and even unconsciousness and coma.

Trilisate has been urged as a drug of choice in arthritis because it is much less toxic to the stomach than Aspirin. Additionally, there is less effect upon the platelets, so there is less chance of a bleeding problem. The blood salicylate level rises more slowly and lasts longer; hence, the drug does not have to be taken as often as Aspirin.

But a controversy has arisen because some physicians do not believe that the anti-inflammatory activity of Trilisate is nearly as good as that of Aspirin. Other physicians believe that the effects are identical. So, it seems clear that Trilisate is less toxic than ordinary Aspirin, but it is not clear that it is as effective a drug. It finds particular use in patients who have had problems with stomach upset from ordinary Aspirin. Trilisate does require a prescription; it is not clear why a prescription should be required for this drug any more than for regular Aspirin.

Special hints: If you note ringing in the ears or a decrease in your hearing, decrease the dose of Trilisate; it is just a little bit too high for the best results. Keep track of your Trilisate intake, and always tell the doctor exactly how much you are taking. It is possible that there may be drug interference between Trilisate and the nonsteroidal anti-inflammatory agents discussed in the following pages, so you will usually not want to take them at the same time.

OTHER NSAIDs

Aspirin is a *nonsteroidal anti-inflammatory agent*. That is, it is not a corticosteroid (like prednisone), but it is an anti-inflammatory agent because it fights inflammation. Some of the disadvantages of Aspirin have been noted above. In anti-inflammatory doses, side effects such as nausea, vomiting, and ringing in the ears are common. Some persons can't tolerate these side effects. Others, either ill-advised or not persistent, don't really try. Aspirin requires many tablets and regular attention to the medication schedule. So, a class of "Aspirin substitutes," given the cumbersome name of nonsteroidal anti-inflammatory drugs (NSAIDs) has been developed. In common medical usage, Aspirin is not included in this group. To further simplify, we use the term *anti-inflammatory drugs* in this book. In the over-the-counter market, "Aspirin substitute" usually refers to acetaminophen (Tylenol), which is discussed below as a pain reliever; acetaminophen is not an anti-inflammatory drug.

There is a huge market for NSAIDs. Nearly every drug company has tried to invent one and has promoted heavily whatever has been developed. Some of these drugs have been promoted in the financial pages of the newspaper or announced in press releases before the scientific evidence was complete. Clearly, you have to be careful about what you read under such circumstances. But there is some substance to the claims. Many of these drugs are good ones. They may be better for those truly unable to tolerate Aspirin. Unfortunately, they are more expensive, newer, and their long-term side effects are less well known. While present evidence suggests that they are slightly safer than Aspirin because of fewer stomach symptoms, they probably should not yet be accepted as less hazardous. Aspirin has been used for centuries, and experience with these new drugs is sufficiently short that some side effects may not yet have been discovered.

In perspective, the development of these drugs represents a substantial advance. In part, this is because of the difficult problems posed by the corticosteroids (discussed in the next section). The use of the term *nonsteroidal* to distinguish these compounds underscores the importance of this feature.

In average potency, full doses of these drugs are roughly equivalent to full-dose Aspirin. Gastrointestinal side effects, such as heartburn and nausea, are usually less frequent than with Aspirin—hence an advantage for those with intolerant stomachs. Available evidence indicates that different drugs can be best for different individuals. These drugs come from several different chemical families and are not interchangeable. You may have to try several to find the best. The major medications in this category are discussed below in alphabetical order, according to brand name. The generic name is given in parentheses.

Advil (ibuprofen)

200 mg brown tablets and caplets
See Motrin.

Ansaid (flurbiprofen)

50 mg white tablet
100 mg blue tablet

Purpose: To reduce inflammation; to slightly reduce pain.

Indications: For relief of mild pain in rheumatoid arthritis or osteoarthritis.

Dosage: Usually prescribed as one tablet (50 mg or 100 mg, depending) two or three times per day. The maximum recommended dosage is 300 mg per day.

Side effects: The most frequent side effects are gastrointestinal, as with other drugs of this group. Diarrhea is a frequent problem and can be quite severe. Irritation of the stomach lining can cause nausea, heartburn, and indigestion. Occasionally, individuals note fluid retention. Allergic reactions such as rash or asthma are very rare. Hospitalization for gastrointestinal bleeding probably occurs in about 1 percent of those taking full doses for one year.

Special hints: For irritation of the stomach, decrease the dose or spread the tablets out throughout the day. Absorption will be slightly decreased if you take the drug after meals or after antacids, but greater comfort may result. For the diarrhea, you have to eliminate the drug and then, if it is desired, start again at a lower dose. Flurbiprofen has been found useful in rheumatoid arthritis, degenerative arthritis, and for treatment of local conditions. Perhaps because it is one of the more recent drugs to be approved, and perhaps because of the problem with diarrhea, Ansaid has not been as widely used as many of the other agents. However, like any other drug of this group, it may be preferred by certain individuals.

Butazolidin (phenylbutazone), Tandearil (oxyphenbutazone)

100 mg round, red, film-coated tablet
100 mg orange and white capsule

Purpose: To reduce inflammation.

Indications: For reduction of inflammation when inflammation is causing harm, as in rheumatoid arthritis.

Dosage: Three or four 100 mg capsules spread throughout the day. Short courses of treatment given for gout or local conditions may be six capsules the first day, then five, four, three, two, and one on successive days for a six-day course.

Side effects: Unfortunately, phenylbutazone and oxyphenbutazone can be hazardous. These were the first anti-inflammatory agents to be developed and we have had some twenty years of experience with them. We now know that on rare occasions they can cause serious problems with the blood, essentially killing all of the white cells or red cells. These conditions, termed *aplastic anemia* or *agranulocytosis*, can be fatal. They are very rare, occurring in perhaps one person in every 10,000. When encountered, the conditions are sometimes reversible after the drug is stopped, and they don't seem to occur if the drug is used only for a short period. Because of this toxicity, most doctors use the other drugs described below in preference to Butazolidin. This may be unfortunate, since Butazolidin is a very effective medication in many instances.

Irritation of the stomach lining may also occur, with nausea, heartburn, indigestion, and occasionally vomiting. Some persons retain fluid with Butazolidin and a low-salt diet is recommended. Allergic reactions, including rash, are rare. Hospitalization for gastrointestinal bleeding occurs in 1 to 2 percent of those taking full doses for one year.

Special hints: For nausea, spread the dose out a little throughout the day and take the capsules on a full stomach, perhaps half an hour after meals. If you don't have a meal at that time, take an antacid half an hour before the medication. Occasionally, some people will have better luck with Tandearil if stomach upset with Butazolidin is a major problem. Watch your weight; if it goes up you are probably retaining fluid. If so, reduce the salt in your diet (see Chapter 16), and be alert for any signs of shortness of breath. If shortness of breath occurs, call the doctor without delay.

While you are taking this drug, blood counts are recommended by most doctors, even though these tests do not protect you against the bad reaction. Possibly, however, they may allow an adverse reaction to be discovered more quickly. Blood counts every two weeks for the first three months and once a month thereafter are recommended by many doctors. For a short six-day course, no blood tests are required by most doctors. You should be able to tell if this is going to be a good drug for you within one week. If you haven't noticed major benefit, you may want to discuss a change in medication with your doctor.

Clinoril (sulindac)

150 mg, 200 mg bright yellow, hexagon-shaped tablets

Purpose: To reduce inflammation; to reduce pain slightly.

Indications: For anti-inflammatory action and mild pain relief.

Dosage: One 150 mg tablet twice a day. This drug also comes in a 200 mg tablet, and dosage may be increased to 200 mg twice a day if needed. Maximum recommended dose is 400 mg a day.

Side effects: Gastrointestinal side effects, with irritation of the stomach lining, are the most common, and include nausea, indigestion, and heartburn. Stomach pain has been reported in 10 percent of subjects, and nausea, diarrhea, constipation, headache, and rash in from 3 to 9 percent. Ringing in the ears, fluid retention, itching, and nervousness have been reported. Allergic reactions are rare. The use of Aspirin in combination with this drug is not recommended by the manufacturer, since Aspirin apparently decreases absorption from the intestine. Hospitalization for gastrointestinal bleeding occurs in about 1 percent of those taking full doses for one year.

Special hints: Sulindac has no particular advantages or disadvantages over the other anti-inflammatory agents described in this section, except that it may cause the minor kidney side effects less frequently and therefore is sometimes used for people with heart or kidney problems.

For stomach upset, take the pills after meals; skip a dose or two if necessary. Antacids may be used for gastrointestinal problems and may sometimes help. Check with your doctor if the distress continues. Maximum therapeutic effect is achieved after about six weeks of treatment, but you should be able to see a major effect in the first week if Clinoril is going to be a really good drug for you.

Dolobid (diflunisal)

250 mg light orange, film-coated, capsule-shaped tablet
500 mg orange, film-coated, capsule-shaped tablet

Purpose: To reduce inflammation and slightly reduce pain.

Indications: For anti-inflammatory action and mild pain relief.

Dosage: For osteoarthritis, 500 to 700 mg daily is equal to six to ten 300 mg regular Aspirin. For rheumatoid arthritis 1,000 mg daily has been shown to be as effective as twelve to fourteen 300 mg (regular) Aspirin.

Side effects: This drug is generally well tolerated. Three to 9 percent of people taking this drug may have some stomach pain or diarrhea. The frequency of gastrointestinal bleeding is probably similar to other drugs of this class.

Special hints: Dolobid is one of the newest of the nonsteroidal drugs. More studies are needed to determine its usefulness when compared to other non-steroidal anti-inflammatory drugs. At this time, it does not seem to have any particular advantages or disadvantages.

Feldene (piroxicam)

10 mg dark red and blue capsule
20 mg dark red capsule

Purpose: To reduce inflammation; to reduce pain slightly.

Indications: For anti-inflammatory activity and mild pain in rheumatoid arthritis, local conditions, and sometimes cartilage degeneration (osteoarthritis).

Dosage: One 20 mg tablet once daily. Do not exceed this dosage. This is a long-acting drug, and it need be taken only once daily.

Side effects: The drug has been generally well tolerated, although gastrointestinal symptoms including irritation of the stomach lining do still occur, as well as nausea, indigestion, and heartburn. Allergic reactions, including skin rashes and asthma, are very rare. Peptic ulceration can occur, and hospitalization for gastrointestinal bleeding is seen in 1 to 2 percent of those who take full doses for one year. Since Feldene is so long-lasting, concern has been expressed that it might be unusually toxic for elderly people or for people with liver or kidney problems.

Special hints: Some seven to twelve days are required before the benefits of Feldene are apparent, and full benefits may not be clear until six weeks or more. Aspirin should be avoided in general. Dosage recommendations and indications for use in children have not been established. Some patients with rheumatoid arthritis or osteoarthritis prefer Feldene, particularly because of the convenience of once-a-day dosage.

Indocin (indomethacin)

25 mg, 50 mg blue and white capsules
75 mg sustained-release, blue/white capsules
50 mg blue suppositories

Purpose: To reduce inflammation; to slightly reduce pain.

Indications: For reduction of inflammation and for mild pain relief.

Dosage: One 25 mg capsule three to four times daily. For men or large women, doses totaling as high as 150 to 200 mg (six to eight capsules) may be required and tolerated each day. It is also available in 50 mg capsules and in a 75 mg sustained-release form which needs to be taken only twice daily.

Side effects: Irritation of the stomach lining, including nausea, indigestion, and heartburn, occurs with a number of people. Allergic reactions (including skin rash and asthma) are very rare. A substantial problem, not present with other drugs of this class, is headache and a bit of a goofy feeling. Hospitalization for gastrointestinal bleeding is seen in 1 to 2 percent of those on full doses for one year.

Special hints: Many doctors find Indocin to be rather weak for treatment of rheumatoid arthritis in early stages, although it is sometimes effective in later stages. In a long-term illness, maximum effect may take six weeks or so, but you should be able to tell within one week if it is going to be a major help. This is the cheapest of the new nonsteroidal drugs, so if it works you may save money. On the other hand, it may be one of the most toxic drugs. Some studies suggest that Indocin actually *increases* the rate of cartilage destruction in osteoarthritis of the hip.

There are also some problems with absorption of Indocin from the intestine. If you take it after meals, you have less stomach irritation, but some people do not absorb the drug very well. So, for maximum effect you need to take it on an empty stomach and for maximum comfort on a full stomach. Trial and error may be necessary to establish the best regimen for you. Aspirin poses another problem. When some individuals take Aspirin with Indocin, the Indocin is not absorbed from the intestine. Usually you will not want to take these two drugs together, since you will get more irritation of the stomach lining but no more therapeutic effect than if you just took the Aspirin. If this drug makes you feel mentally or emotionally fuzzy for more than the first few weeks, we think that is a good reason to discuss a change in medication with your doctor.

Meclomen (meclofenamate)

50 mg dark yellow/light yellow capsule
100 mg dark yellow/off-white capsule

Purpose: To reduce inflammation; to reduce pain slightly.

Indications: For anti-inflammatory action in attachment arthritis, synovitis, local conditions, and occasionally degenerative cartilage changes.

Dosage: The total daily dosage is 200 to 400 mg, usually administered in three or four equal doses. The drug is supplied in 50 mg and 100 mg capsules.

Side effects: Gastrointestinal side effects are most commonly reported and include diarrhea in approximately one-quarter of patients, nausea in 11 percent, and other gastrointestinal problems in 10 percent. Over the long term, at least one-third of patients will have at least one episode of diarrhea. With this drug the diarrhea is more severe than with any of the other drugs of this class, and sufficiently so to require discontinuation of treatment in approximately 4 percent of patients. A variety of other generally minor side effects have been reported but do not appear to be at all common. Hospitalization for gastrointestinal bleeding is seen in 1 to 2 percent of those on full doses for one year.

Special hints: This drug was introduced in 1980, and has been used relatively little. It is probably comparable in effectiveness to the other nonsteroidal agents. It is not yet recommended for children, and its effects have not been studied in patients with very severe rheumatoid arthritis. It may be taken with meals or milk to control gastrointestinal complaints. Maximum effect is achieved after about six weeks of treatment, but you should be able to see a major effect in the first week if it is going to be a really good drug for you. Avoidance of Aspirin and other medications while taking this drug is advisable but not essential.

Motrin (ibuprofen)
Also called **Rufen, Advil,** and **Nuprin**

300 mg round, white tablet
400 mg round, red-orange tablet
600 mg oval, peach tablet
800 mg apricot, capsule-shaped tablet

Motrin and Rufen are the same drug, ibuprofen, produced by two different companies. Advil and Nuprin are smaller doses of ibuprofen available without a prescription.

Purpose: To reduce inflammation; to slightly reduce pain.

Indications: For anti-inflammatory action and mild pain relief.

Dosage: One or two 400 mg tablets three times daily. Maximum daily recommended dosage is 2,400 mg, or six tablets.

Side effects: Gastrointestinal side effects, with irritation of the stomach lining, are the most common, and include nausea, indigestion, and heartburn. Allergic reactions are rare and the drug is generally well tolerated. A very few individuals have been observed who have had *aseptic meningitis* apparently related to this drug. Here, the person experiences headache, fever, and stiff neck, and examination of the spinal fluid shows an increase in the protein and cells. The syndrome resolves when the drug is stopped, but can come back if the drug is given again. Occasionally, individuals may retain fluid with this medication. Hospitalization for gastrointestinal bleeding is seen in about 1 percent of those who take full doses of 2,400 mg per day or more for one year.

Special hints: Motrin is not consistently useful for the treatment of rheumatoid arthritis. Overall, many doctors are beginning to feel that it is one of the weaker therapeutic agents in this group. If you are not getting enough relief from it, you may wish to discuss a change in medication with your doctor. Avoidance of Aspirin and other medications while taking Motrin is advisable but not essential. It is absorbed reasonably well even on a full stomach, so if you have problems with irritation of the stomach take the drug after an antacid or after a meal. Maximum effect is achieved after about six weeks of treatment, but you should be able to see a major effect in the first week if it is going to be a really good drug for you.

Over-the-Counter Ibuprofen

Recently, the U.S. Food and Drug Administration has allowed the sale of ibuprofen without a prescription in a smaller, 200 mg, tablet size. This historic ruling has added a third minor analgesic to Aspirin and acetaminophen. The decision was made after careful review of many studies indicating that ibuprofen was at least as effective as these two previously available drugs, and possibly less toxic, at relieving minor pain. Advil and Nuprin are the trade names for over-the-counter ibuprofen, and they are already heavily advertised and heavily used. Ibuprofen is now also present in many different over-the-counter medications, including Midol.

What does this mean for the patient with arthritis? Relatively little. Most arthritis patients need at least 2,400 mg of ibuprofen per day, and twelve Advil tablets a day rather than four to six Rufen is a bit of a nuisance. And it is hard to save money, since the cost per milligram is set so that it is about the same by prescription or over-the-counter. If you need anti-inflammatory doses of ibuprofen, you should be seeing your doctor every so often anyway, so do not use the availability of the product over the counter as an excuse to stay away from the doctor. Also, many health insurance plans will not pay for medication unless it is purchased by prescription. So, our recommendation remains that ibuprofen for arthritis be used on a prescription basis unless just an occasional tablet is required for pain.

Nalfon (fenoprofen)

200 mg orange/white capsule
300 mg orange/yellow capsule
600 mg orange/yellow capsule-shaped tablet

Purpose: To reduce inflammation, to slightly reduce pain.

Indications: For anti-inflammatory activity and mild pain relief in rheumatoid arthritis, local conditions, and sometimes cartilage degeneration (osteoarthritis).

Dosage: One or two 300 mg capsules three to four times a day. Maximum recommended dosage is ten tablets daily. It is now available in 600 mg capsules, with a maximum dosage of five tablets daily.

Side effects: Irritation of the stomach lining is the most frequent side effect and includes nausea, indigestion, and heartburn. Allergic reactions including skin rash or asthma are very rare. Fluid retention is only very occasionally a problem. Hospitalization for gastrointestinal bleeding is required in approximately 1 percent of patients taking full doses for one year.

Special hints: For stomach irritation, reduce the dose, spread it out more throughout the day, or take the drug after meals or after antacid. Maximum effect may take six weeks or more, but you should see major benefit in the first week if the drug is going to be a great help to you. Aspirin should be avoided in general, although the evidence for its effect on the absorption of Nalfon is controversial. Nalfon is quite useful in rheumatoid arthritis and is preferred by many individuals to Aspirin on the basis of better effect on the disease as well as less bothersome side effects. It has found uses in osteoarthritis, particularly of the hip.

Naprosyn (naproxen)

250 mg round, light yellow tablet
375 mg capsule-shaped, peach tablet
500 mg capsule-shaped, light yellow tablet

Purpose: To reduce inflammation; to slightly reduce pain.

Indications: For anti-inflammatory action and mild pain relief.

Dosage: One tablet two or three times a day. Maximum recommended dosage is 1,000 mg a day.

Side effects: Gastrointestinal side effects, with irritation of the stomach lining, are the most common and include nausea, indigestion, and heartburn. Skin rash and other allergic problems are very rare. Fluid retention has been reported in a few individuals. Hospitalization for gastrointestinal bleeding is required in approximately 1 percent of patients taking full doses for one year.

Special hints: Naprosyn has an advantage over some drugs in this class by having a longer "half-life." Thus, you do not have to take as many tablets as with the other medicines in this group. Each tablet lasts from eight to twelve hours. It is one of the most popular of the drugs of this class.

In general, Aspirin should be avoided, since it interferes with Naprosyn in some individuals. If you notice fluid retention, reduce your salt and sodium intake (see Chapter 16), and discuss a change in medication with your doctor. If you have stomach irritation, try taking the tablets on a full stomach or after antacids. Although absorption may be slightly decreased, you may be more comfortable overall.

Nuprin (ibuprofen)

200 mg yellow tablets and caplets
See Motrin.

Orudis (ketoprofen)

25 mg dark green/red capsule
50 mg dark green/light green capsule
75 mg dark green/white capsule

Purpose: To reduce inflammation; to slightly reduce pain.

Indications: For anti-inflammatory action and mild pain relief.

Dosage: Orudis comes in 25 mg, 50 mg, and 75 mg capsules. Recommended daily dose is 150 to 300 mg, divided into three or four doses daily.

Side effects: Like other drugs of this group, the most frequent side effects are gastrointestinal. Irritation of the stomach lining can cause nausea, heartburn, and indigestion. Occasionally, individuals note fluid retention. Allergic reactions such as rash or asthma are very rare. Hospitalization for gastrointestinal bleeding occurs in over 1 percent of those taking full doses for one year.

Special hints: This is a relatively new drug of this class, but there is wide experience with it in other countries and chemically it is closely related to ibuprofen, naproxen, and fenoprofen. For irritation of the stomach, decrease the dose or spread the tablets out throughout the day. Absorption will be slightly decreased if you take the drug after meals or after antacids, but greater comfort may result. Ketoprofen is useful in rheumatoid arthritis. It has found use in degenerative arthritis of the hip and for treatment of local conditions. As is true for other drugs of this group, ketoprofen will be the preferred drug for certain individuals.

Rufen (ibuprofen)

400 mg round, bright pink tablet
600 mg white, capsule-shaped tablet
800 mg white, capsule-shaped tablet
See Motrin.

Tolectin (tolmetin sodium)

200 mg round, white tablet
400 mg orange capsule

Purpose: To reduce inflammation; to reduce pain slightly.

Indications: For anti-inflammatory action and mild pain relief.

Dosage: Two 200 mg tablets three or four times daily. Maximum recommended dosage is 2,000 mg, or ten tablets daily. Larger tablet sizes may soon be available.

Side effects: Like other drugs of this group, the most frequent side effects are gastrointestinal. Irritation of the stomach lining can cause nausea, heartburn, and indigestion. Occasionally, individuals note fluid retention. Allergic reactions such as rash or asthma are very rare. Hospitalization for gastrointestinal bleeding occurs in about 1 percent of those taking full doses for one year.

Special hints: For irritation of the stomach, decrease the dose or spread the tablets out throughout the day. Absorption will be slightly decreased if you take the drug after meals or after antacids, but greater comfort may result. Aspirin and other drugs of this class may potentially interfere with absorption and the best rule is to take just one drug at a time. Tolectin is useful in rheumatoid arthritis. It has found use in degenerative arthritis of the hip and for treatment of local conditions. Certain individuals will prefer Tolectin to all other drugs of the group.

Voltaren (diclofenac)

25 mg yellow, round, film-coated tablet
50 mg light brown, round, film-coated tablet
75 mg white, round, film-coated tablet

Purpose: To reduce inflammation; to slightly reduce pain.

Indications: For anti-inflammatory action and mild pain relief.

Dosage: Usually given as one tablet (25 mg, 50 mg, or 75 mg, depending) two or three times a day. The maximum recommended dosage is 200 mg per day.

Side effects: The most frequent side effects are gastrointestinal, as with other drugs of this group; irritation of the stomach lining can cause nausea, heartburn, and indigestion. Occasionally, individuals may note fluid retention. Allergic reactions such as rash or asthma are very rare. Hospitalization for gastrointestinal bleeding probably occurs in about 1 percent of those taking full doses for one year.

Special hints: Voltaren, one of the most recently released nonsteroidal medications in the United States, has had extensive international experience. In fact, it is the most frequently used nonsteroidal medication worldwide. The USFDA was slow in review, in part because of fear of more frequent liver problems. This does not appear to be the case, but periodic blood tests for liver toxicity are recommended by some.

Voltaren comes with an "enteric coating" designed to improve stomach tolerance; this is probably not effective. For irritation of the stomach, decrease the dose or spread the tablets out throughout the day. Absorption will be slightly decreased if you take the drug after meals or after antacids, but greater comfort may result.

Voltaren is useful in rheumatoid arthritis, degenerative arthritis, and treatment of local conditions. Certain individuals will prefer Voltaren over other drugs of this group.

SOON-TO-BE-RELEASED NONSTEROIDAL MEDICATIONS

A number of new, nonsteroidal anti-inflammatory drugs (NSAIDs), relatively similar to those just discussed, are in the process of review by the Food and Drug Administration of the United States. Many of these drugs are currently being used in other countries and appear to have a role in the treatment of osteoarthritis and rheumatoid arthritis. The review process by the USFDA now takes approximately four to five years, and it is not possible to predict whether or not a new agent will be released or after what period. Given current knowledge, none of these new drugs will be dramatically different from drugs already available, so not too much is being lost by these delays. Also, a new drug is less well understood in terms of toxicity and benefits than a drug for which there has already been wide use. On the other hand, individual patients often do better with one or another nonsteroidal drug; therefore a wide choice of drugs is helpful for finding the drug that causes you the least toxicity and gives you the most benefit.

Some of these drugs have been formulated to have less gastrointestinal toxicity than their predecessors, and they may actually be safer agents. Often, on the other hand, the agents that cause the fewest side effects turn out to be the least powerful drugs for the management of arthritis.

In general, when considering one of the new agents, rely on your doctor's advice. If you have been having a lot of trouble with stomach upset from drugs, then it might be a good idea to try one of the agents that causes less gastrointestinal difficulty such as Disalcid, Trilisate, or ibuprofen. If you have not been getting the desired effect from the drugs of one chemical class, sometimes it is useful to try the drugs of a different class. It is possible that some new drugs will be better for rheumatoid arthritis and others better for osteoarthritis or other forms of arthritis. But treat each of these drugs with respect and consider that it is always possible for a drug, particularly a new drug, to be responsible for a new symptom problem that develops while you are taking the medication.

CORTICOSTEROIDS

About 1950, a widely heralded miracle occurred—the introduction of cortisone for the treatment of arthritis. The Nobel Prize for Medicine was awarded to the doctors who developed this drug. People with rheumatoid arthritis and other forms of synovitis suddenly noted that the swelling and pain in their joints decreased and that the overall toxicity of the disease disappeared. They felt fine.

The initial enthusiasm for cortisone in arthritis was tremendous. But over the following years, a number of major cautions began to be voiced. Slowly, the cumulative side effects of the cortisonelike drugs began to be recognized. For many individuals, the side effects were clearly greater than any benefits obtained. Cortisone became the model of a drug that provides early benefits but late penalties. Now, with a quarter of a century of experience with corticosteroids, our perspective is more complete. They represent a major treatment for arthritis, but their use is appropriate in only a relatively small number of cases and then only with full attention to potential complications.

Steroids are natural hormones manufactured by the adrenal glands. When used medically, they are given in doses somewhat higher than the amounts the body generally makes. In these doses they suppress the function of your own adrenal glands and lead to a kind of drug dependency as the gland slowly shrinks. After many months of steroid use, the drug must be withdrawn slowly to allow your own adrenal gland to return to full function; otherwise an "adrenal crisis" can occur in which you just don't have enough hormone. Steroids must be taken exactly as directed, and a physician's close advice is always required.

Steroids used in arthritis are very different from the sex steroids, or androgens, taken by athletes, which have no role in treating arthritis and, indeed, shouldn't be used by athletes either.

Let's discuss the side effects. They can be divided into categories depending upon the length of time you have been taking the steroid and the dose prescribed. Side effects result from a combination of how high the dose is and how long you have been taking it. If you have been taking steroids for less than one week, side effects are quite rare, even if the dose has been high.

If you have been taking high doses for one week to one month, you are at risk for development of ulcers, mental changes including psychosis or depression, infection with bacterial germs, or acne over the skin. The side effects of steroid treatment become most apparent after one month to one year of medium to high dosage. The individual becomes fat in the central parts of the body, with a buffalo hump on the lower neck and wasting of the muscles in the arms and legs. Hair growth increases over the face, skin bruises appear, and stretch marks develop over the abdomen. After years of steroid treatment (even with low doses) there is loss of calcium, resulting in fragile bones. Fractures can occur with only slight injury, particularly in the spine. Cataracts slowly develop and the skin becomes thin and translucent. Some physicians believe that hardening of the arteries occurs more rapidly and that there may be complications of inflammation of the arteries.

Many of these side effects will occur in everyone who takes sufficient doses of cortisone or its relatives for a sufficient period of time. The art of managing arthritis with corticosteroids involves knowing how to minimize these side effects. The physician will work with you to keep the dose as low as possible at all times. If possible, you may be instructed to take the drug only once daily rather than several times daily, since there are fewer side effects when it is taken this way. If you are able to tolerate the drug only every other day, this is even better, for the side effects are then quite minimal. Unfortunately, many people find that the dosage schedules that cause the fewest side effects also give them the least relief.

Steroids are always to be used with great respect and caution. The tendency is slightly increasing for experienced doctors to use low-dose corticosteroid treatment in rheumatoid arthritis, demonstrating that the proper indications for use of these drugs are still somewhat controversial. High-dose cortisone treatment for uncomplicated rheumatoid arthritis has long been considered bad practice in the United States; it remains the essence of some quack treatments of arthritis, such as those available in Mexican border towns. Corticosteroids are harmful in infectious arthritis and should not be given by mouth in local conditions or in osteoarthritis.

There are three ways to give corticosteroids. They can be taken by mouth, they can be given by injection into the painful area, or an injection of adrenal cortical stimulating hormone (ACTH) can be given to cause an individual's own adrenal gland to increase production of hormones. Prednisone (or prednisolone) is the steroid usually given by mouth and is the reference steroid discussed here. There are perhaps twenty different steroid drugs now available. Cortisone itself retains too much fluid and the second drug developed, hydrocortisone, has the same deficit. The fluorinated steroids, such as triamcinolone, cause greater problems with muscle wasting than does prednisone. The steroids sold by brand name are about twenty times as expensive as prednisone and do not have any major advantages. Hence, there is little reason to use any of these other compounds for administration of steroids by mouth. Use prednisone.

Prednisone

Many doses (1 mg to 50 mg) white round tablets

Purpose: To reduce inflammation; to suppress immunological responses.

Indications: For suppression of serious systemic manifestations of connective tissue disease, such as kidney involvement. In selected cases, for use in low dose suppressing the inflammation of rheumatoid arthritis.

Dosage: The normal body makes the equivalent of about 5 to 7.5 mg of prednisone each day. "Low-dose" prednisone treatment is from 5 to 10 mg. A "moderate dose" ranges from 15 to 30 mg per day and a "high dose" from 40 to 60 mg per day, or even higher. The drug is often most effective when given in several doses throughout the day, but side effects are least when the same total daily dose is given as infrequently as possible.

Side effects: Prednisone causes all of the side effects of the corticosteroids listed above. Allergy is extremely rare. Side effects are related to dose and to duration of treatment. The side effects are major and include fatal complications. Psychological dependency often occurs and complicates efforts to get off the drug once you have begun.

Special hints: Discuss the need for prednisone very carefully with your doctor before beginning. The decision to start steroid treatment for a chronic disease is a major one and you want to be sure that the drug is essential. You may want a second opinion if the explanation does not completely satisfy you. When you take prednisone, follow your doctor's instructions very closely. With some drugs it does not make much difference if you start and stop them on your own, but prednisone must be taken extremely regularly and exactly as prescribed. You will want to help your doctor decrease your dose of prednisone whenever possible, even if this does cause some increase in your symptoms.

A strange thing can happen when you reduce the dose of prednisone; a syndrome called *steroid fibrositis* causes increased stiffness and pain for a week to ten days after each dose reduction. Sometimes this is interpreted as a return of the arthritis and reduction of dosage is stopped. If you are going to take prednisone for a long time, ask your doctor about taking some vitamin D along with it. There is some evidence that the loss of bone, the most critical long-term side effect, can be reduced if you take vitamin D (usually prescribed as 50,000 units twice a week) together with adequate calcium.

If you are having some side effects, ask your doctor about once-a-day or every-other-day use of the prednisone. Watch your salt and sodium intake and keep it low, since there is already a tendency to retain fluid with prednisone. Watch your diet as well, since you will be fighting an increase in appetite and a tendency to put on fat. If you stay active and limit the calories you take in, you can minimize many of the ugly side effects of the steroid medication and can improve the strength of the bones and the muscles. If you are taking a corticosteroid other than prednisone by mouth, ask your physician if it is all right to switch to the equivalent dose of prednisone. (See Chapter 16 for further hints on nutrition.)

STEROID INJECTIONS
Depo-medrol, other brands

Purpose: To reduce inflammation in a local area.

Indications: Noninfectious inflammation and pain in a particular region of the body. Or a widespread arthritis with one or two areas causing most of the problem.

Dosage: Dosage varies depending on the preparation and purpose. The frequency of injection is more important. Usually injections should be no more than every six weeks. Many physicians set a limit of three injections in a single area.

Side Effects: Steroid injections resemble a very short course of prednisone by mouth and therefore have few side effects. They result in a high concentration of the steroid in the area that is inflamed and can have quite a pronounced effect in reducing this inflammation. If a single area is injected many times, the injection appears to cause damage in that area. This has resulted in serious problems in frequently injected areas, such as the elbows of baseball pitchers. Some studies suggest that as few as ten injections can cause increased bone destruction; hence, most doctors stop injecting well before this time.

Special hints: If one area of your body is giving you a lot of trouble, an injection frequently makes sense. The response to the first injection will tell you quite accurately how much sense it makes. If you get excellent relief that lasts for many months, reinjection is indicated if the problem returns. The steroid injections contain a "long-acting" steroid, but it is in the body for only a few days. The effects may last much longer than this, however, since a cycle of inflammation and injury may be broken by the injection. If you get relief for only a few days, then injection is not going to be a very useful treatment for you. If you get no relief at all or an increase in pain, this is an obvious sign that other kinds of treatment should be sought. If you can find a "trigger point" on your body where pressure reproduces your major pain, then injection of this trigger point is frequently beneficial. Occasionally, persons with osteoarthritis get benefit from injections, but injections are usually not helpful unless there is inflammation in the area.

DISEASE-MODIFYING ANTI-RHEUMATIC DRUGS (DMARDs)

The anti-inflammatory drugs discussed above are symptomatic medications only. They don't do anything basic to control arthritis. In rheumatoid arthritis and other forms of synovitis, however, there is a much more important class of drugs. Collectively, these drugs are usually called disease-modifying anti-rheumatic drugs or DMARDs. They have also been called slow-acting anti-rheumatic drugs (SAARDs) or, inappropriately, remission-inducing drugs (RIDs). While they rarely induce true remission, they are much more effective anti-inflammatory agents than the NSAIDs and in a number of cases have been shown to slow the process of joint destruction in rheumatoid arthritis.

A revolution in thinking about rheumatoid arthritis treatment is occurring. It used to be thought the DMARDs were reserved for later in the care of patients with exceptionally severe disease that could not be controlled with lesser agents. Now it is increasingly recognized that these drugs should be started early in the course, and should be regarded as the backbone of treatment for rheumatoid arthritis. In general, patients with significant rheumatoid arthritis should be on one or another of these agents *throughout* the course of their disease. If you suspect rheumatoid arthritis, you should see a rheumatologist familiar with DMARDs *as early as possible*.

This shift from considering DMARDs as powerful drugs to be kept in reserve to considering them as front-line treatment came about because of a recognition of the serious complications of rheumatoid arthritis, the substantial side effects related to gastrointestinal bleeding of the NSAIDs, a reassuring safety profile for these stronger drugs, and the availability of a larger number of drugs of this class. Usually the good effects from these agents will only last a year or so, and so a strategy of sequentially using them one after another (or even in combination) is required.

There are now eight of these agents available, and more are under development. These are intramuscular gold, oral gold, D-penicillamine, hydroxychloroquine, sulfasalazine, methotrexate, azathioprine, and cyclophosphamide. Methotrexate has become the most frequently used of these agents, while cyclophosphamide, which is much more toxic than the other drugs, has fallen into disuse except in very extreme situations.

GOLD SALTS AND PENICILLAMINE

These are major-league drugs, although no one knows exactly why they are so effective in so many individuals. They provide dramatic benefits to over two-thirds of persons with severe rheumatoid arthritis. Each has major side effects that require stopping treatment for at least one-quarter of the users and that may in rare cases be fatal. Gold salts and penicillamine are two very different kinds of drugs, but there are striking similarities in the type and magnitude of good effects and in the type of side effects. Neither appears to be of use in any category other than rheumatoid arthritis, but the scientific proof of their effectiveness in rheumatoid arthritis is impressive.

These agents can result in remission of the arthritis. In perhaps one-quarter of users the disease will actually be so well controlled that neither doctor nor patient can find any evidence of it. Usually these drugs have to be continued in order to maintain the remission, but, to reduce inflammation, the effects can be more dramatic than with any other agent, except possibly methotrexate or azathioprine. Individuals who use these drugs must accept certain significant hazards, but there is a good chance of very major benefit. In rheumatoid arthritis, these drugs have also been shown to retard the process of joint destruction.

If you are not able to tolerate one of these drugs, you may be able to tolerate the other. If you don't get a good response from one, you may from the other. After failure with one drug, the chances decrease a little, but success with the second drug is still common.

Which should be used first? No one knows. In England, penicillamine is usually used first. In the United States, it is gold. Gold requires a visit to the doctor every week for a while. With costs of blood tests, the total dollar cost of the initial course of injectable gold may be $1,200 or more. Penicillamine can be taken by mouth, and while the drug itself is expensive, the total cost may be less. In terms of effectiveness and in risk, you can consider these two drugs about the same.

Myochrisine, solganol (Gold Salts)

Purpose: To reduce inflammation and retard disease progression.

Indications: Rheumatoid arthritis and some other forms of synovitis.

Dosage: 50 mg per week by intramuscular injection for twenty weeks, then one to two injections per month thereafter. Many doctors use smaller doses for the first two injections to test for allergic reactions to the injections. Sometimes doctors will give more or less than this standard dosage depending upon your body size and response to treatment. "Maintenance" gold treatment refers to injections after the first twenty weeks (which result in about 1,000 mg of total gold). The dosage and duration of maintenance therapy varies quite a bit; with good responses, the gold maintenance may be continued for many years, with injection given every two to four weeks.

Side effects: The gold salts accumulate very slowly in the tissues of the joints and in other parts of the body. Hence, side effects usually occur only after a considerable amount of gold has been received, although allergic reactions can occur even with the initial injection. The major side effects have to do with the skin, the kidneys, and the blood cells. The skin may develop a rash, usually occurring after ten or more injections, with big red spots or blotches, often itchy. If the rash remains a minor problem, the drug may be cautiously continued, but occasionally a very serious rash occurs following gold injections.

The kidney can be damaged so that protein leaks out of the body through the urine. This is called *nephrosis* or the *nephrotic syndrome* if it is severe. When it is recognized and the drug is stopped, the nephrosis usually goes away, but cases have been reported in which it did not reverse. The blood cell problems are the most dangerous. They can affect either the white blood cells or the platelets, those blood cells that control the clotting of the blood. In each case, the gold causes the bone marrow to stop making the particular blood cell. If the white cells are not made, the body becomes susceptible to serious infections that can be fatal. If the platelets are not made, the body is subject to serious bleeding episodes that can be fatal. These problems almost always reverse when the drug is stopped, but reversal may take a number of weeks, during which time the person is at risk for a major medical problem.

There are other side effects, such as ulcers in the mouth, a mild toxic effect on the liver, or nausea, but they usually are not as troublesome. Overall, about one-quarter of users have to stop their course of treatment because of the side effects. One or 2 percent of users experience a significant side effect; the other users don't really notice very much of a problem, even though a serious side effect may be about to occur. Less than one in a thousand times there may be a fatal side effect. With careful monitoring, the drug is reasonably safe and its benefits justify its use, since over 70 percent of those treated with gold show moderate or marked improvement. However, you must maintain your respect for this treatment and keep up regular blood tests to detect early side effects. One final note: Most side effects occur during the initial period of twenty injections. Serious side effects during the maintenance period are less common.

Special hints: You must learn to be patient with gold treatment. The gold accumulates slowly in the body and good responses are almost never seen in the first ten weeks of treatment. Improvement begins slowly after that and major improvement is usually evident by the end of 1,000 mg, or twenty weeks. Similarly, if the drug is stopped, it requires many months before the effect is totally lost. In one famous study, the gold group was still doing better than the control group two years after the drug had been stopped, although most of the effect of the drug had been lost by that time. After a side effect, many doctors will suggest that the drug be tried again. Often, this can be worthwhile if the approach is very cautious, since the drug is frequently tolerated the second time around. At our Arthritis Center we do not try gold salts again if there has been a problem with the blood, but we will use it again cautiously after mild skin reactions or mild amounts of protein loss through the urine.

To minimize the chance of serious side effects, most doctors recommend that a check be made of the urine for protein leakage, of the white cells and the platelets, and that the patient be questioned about skin rash before every injection. This is good practice. Unfortunately, the combination of twenty doctor visits, twenty injections, twenty urinalyses, twenty blood counts, and so forth, makes the cost of initiating gold treatment approximately $1,200 when pursued in this manner. There are some ways to decrease this cost while preserving the safety. You can ask your doctor to prescribe some test kits so that you can test your urine for protein at home. This is a very easy technique. You can ask if it is possible to have just a platelet smear and a white count rather than a complete blood count each time. You can inquire whether it is possible to have the nurse give an injection after checking the blood count without actually having a doctor visit every week. And, some people have successfully been given their own shots at home with the help of their family, although this is not acceptable to many. By using such techniques, you can save half to three-quarters of the cost of a course of gold treatment.

Ridaura (auranofin)

3 mg brown/white capsule with tapered ends

Purpose: To reduce inflammation in rheumatoid arthritis and retard disease progression. (This drug is "oral gold.")

Indications: For anti-inflammatory activity in rheumatoid arthritis.

Dosage: Average dosage is 6 mg daily. The drug is slowly absorbed and distributed through the body, and weeks to months may be required before full therapeutic effect is achieved.

Side effects: The most common side effect is dose-related diarrhea, which occurs at some time in approximately one-third of treated patients and requires discontinuation in 10 to 20 percent of patients. Skin rash has occurred in 4 percent, mild kidney problems in 1 percent, and problems with the platelets in half of 1 percent of patients.

Special hints: Ridaura, useful in rheumatoid arthritis, is an important drug for some patients. It is not believed to be effective in osteoarthritis, gout, or minor rheumatic conditions. It may or may not have an eventual role in psoriatic arthritis, ankylosing spondylitis, and the arthritis of children. If diarrhea is encountered, the dose should be reduced. As with intramuscular gold injections, patients should be monitored periodically for blood complications, skin rash, and protein loss in the urine. Follow your doctor's advice for the particular tests required and the frequencies with which they are needed. This is a powerful drug and needs to be used with respect.

Penicillamine (cuprimine)

125 mg gray/yellow capsule
250 mg yellow capsule

Purpose: To reduce inflammation and retard disease progression.

Indications: Rheumatoid arthritis and some other forms of synovitis.

Dosage: Usually 250 mg (one tablet or two 125 mg tablets) per day for one month, then two tablets (500 mg) a day for one month, then three tablets (750 mg) per day for one month, and finally four tablets (1,000 mg) per day. Dosage is usually not increased rapidly, and may be increased even more slowly than this. After remission, the drug can be continued indefinitely, usually at a reduced dosage. And if a good result is obtained earlier, you can stop with the lower dose.

Side effects: These closely parallel those noted above for gold injections. The major side effects are skin rash, protein leakage through the urine, or a decrease in production of the blood cells. Additionally, individuals may have nausea, and some notice a metallic taste in their mouth or a decreased sense of taste.

Penicillamine weakens the connective tissue so that the healing of a cut is delayed, and a scar may not have the same strength it would have without the penicillamine. So, stitches following a cut should be left in for a longer period of time, and wound healing should be expected to be delayed. Surgery under these circumstances may be more difficult.

Special hints: Penicillamine takes a number of months to reach its full therapeutic effect and the effect persists for a long time after you stop taking the drug. Responses usually take from three to six months but can be as late as nine months after the drug is begun. Because of the risk of side effects, doctors have now adopted the "go low, go slow" approach given in the dosage schedule above. When full doses were begun earlier, the frequency of side effects was higher. Even now, only about three-quarters of individuals will complete the treatment and the remainder will have some side effects, approximately the same as those listed for gold salts. The drug may be tried again after a side effect if the side effect has been mild. We do not try the drug again if there has been a problem with the blood counts, but may cautiously try it if there has been a minor problem with protein in the urine, a minor skin rash, or minor nausea.

Monitoring for side effects has to be carefully performed. Usually a blood count or smear, a urinalysis for protein leakage, and questioning of the person about side effects are required every two weeks or even more frequently. It should be noted that with both penicillamine and gold, careful monitoring improves your chances of not having a serious side effect, but does not eliminate them. These drugs contain an intrinsic hazard that no physician can eliminate. Again, you can negotiate to have some of the drug monitoring done by a local laboratory and review the results yourself, check your own urine for protein, and so forth, if you desire. Most doctors who use these drugs a good deal have evolved some method of minimizing the cost of the monitoring. Again, after the first six months, side effects are relatively rare but still do occur. Some individuals will have an excellent response to the penicillamine even though they never get up to the full dosage of 1,000 mg per day.

Plaquenil (hydroxychloroquine)

200 mg white, scored, round tablet

Purpose: To reduce inflammation and possibly to retard disease progression in rheumatoid arthritis; to reduce disease activity in systemic lupus erythematosus.

Indications: Rheumatoid arthritis that is active.

Dosage: One to two tablets (200 to 400 mg) per day.

Side effects: This is the best tolerated of all drugs used for rheumatoid arthritis, and side effects are unusual. With a very few people, gastric upset or muscular weakness may result. Consideration needs to be given to the possibility of eye toxicity, which is an occasional complication of antimalarial drugs. This is a rare complication and appears to be always reversible if the possibility is regularly monitored by periodic eye examinations after the first year of treatment.

Special hints: Plaquenil takes six weeks to begin to show an effect, and full effect can take up to twelve weeks, so plan on at least a twelve-month trial. The eye complications appear to be much less common with Plaquenil than with chloroquine, the antimalarial drug that used to be used most often. They seldom if ever are seen with less than one year of treatment at recommended dosage. Bright sunlight seems to increase the frequency of eye damage, so we recommend using sunglasses and wide-brimmed hats for sun protection. We recommend eye examinations after one year of continuous treatment and at three-month intervals thereafter. This should give ample warning of any problems. Do not exceed two tablets daily. Since the drug is so well tolerated, both tablets may be taken together in the morning. The good effects of this drug are long-lasting, and continue for weeks or months after the drug is stopped. Overall, this is the safest drug available for treatment of rheumatoid arthritis; it should be used with respect but not fear.

Azulfidine (sulphasalazine)

Azulfidine EN-tabs
500 mg orange, film-coated tablets

Purpose: To reduce inflammation and possibly to retard disease progression in rheumatoid arthritis.

Indications: Rheumatoid arthritis and some other forms of synovitis.

Dosage: Three or four 500 mg tablets daily, taken spread out as two or three doses over the day. Dosage may be increased to as many as six 500 mg tablets, usually taken as two tablets three times daily.

Side effects: This is a sulfa drug, and should not be taken by people with an allergy to sulfa. Allergy is unusual, and may take the form of a rash, wheezing, itching, fever, or jaundice. Azulfidine may cause gastric distress or other side effects in some patients. Blood tests should be done every so often to detect any (rare) effects on the blood cells or platelets. Most people, probably four out of five, experience no trouble whatsoever.

Special hints: Azulfidine is used in patients with inflammatory problems with the bowels, where it reduces the inflammation, at least in part because of an antibiotic effect on the bacteria that live in the bowel. Recently, British scientists have found that it has a major effect on rheumatoid arthritis, and this has been confirmed by investigators in the United States. No one knows how it works, but it is very effective in some patients. It takes a month or more before the effects begin to be noticed, and full effects may take three or more months. Usually if you are not going to tolerate the drug, you will know in a week or so.

IMMUNOSUPPRESSANT DRUGS

Immunosuppressant drugs are very important agents for management of rheumatoid arthritis. They are prescribed in certain cases of rheumatoid arthritis because they can reduce the number of inflammatory cells present around the joint.

The immune response helps the body recognize and fight foreign particles and viruses. When it goes wrong, it can cause allergy or autoimmune disease. In this case, antibodies from the immune system attack the body's own tissues, causing disease. Immunosuppressant drugs can tone down this reaction.

Some of these drugs work by *cytotoxic* action. They kill rapidly dividing cells much like an X-ray beam. Since in some diseases the most rapidly dividing cells are the bad ones, the overall effect of the drugs is good. Others of these drugs antagonize the chemical system inside the cell, such as the purine system or the folate system. From the patient's standpoint, it doesn't really make too much difference how they work.

The major short-term worry with these drugs is that they can destroy bone-marrow cells. The bone-marrow cells make red cells that carry oxgyen, white cells that fight infection, and platelets that stop bleeding. Any of these blood-cell types can be suppressed by taking enough of these drugs, and even if there seem to be enough white cells, dangerous infections can occur.

These infections are often called "opportunistic"; caused by different kinds of germs than those that cause infections in healthy people. For example, patients are often afflicted with herpes zoster (shingles) and can be prone to infections from types of fungus that are around all the time but seldom cause disease. Or, a rare bacterial infection can occur. These infections can be difficult to treat and sometimes hard to diagnose.

For patients who have taken immunosuppressant drugs for several years, there is some concern about cancer. Although this seems to be extremely rare or absent in humans, these drugs do cause cancer in some laboratory animals. It seems that if humans are afflicted, it is only after years of treatment. Present evidence suggests that leukemia can occasionally be caused by cytotoxic drugs such as cyclophosphamide, but not by methotrexate or azathioprine.

After considering all these dangers, we really don't know how to compare them to other drugs. Although there is some potential danger of cancer, the alternative might be prednisone with all of its potential problems. It is possible that these drugs are actually less dangerous than some of the drugs with which we have been more comfortable.

The diseases for which these drugs may be most useful are as follows: in Wegener's granulomatosis, previously fatal, these drugs are usually curative. They are very helpful in severe polyarteritis. They are probably useful in resistant severe dermatomyositis or polymyositis. They are probably helpful in severe kidney disease of systemic lupus. They are very helpful and increasingly used in psoriatic arthritis and rheumatoid arthritis.

Methotrexate

2.5 mg yellow, round tablet

Purpose: For reduction of inflammation.

Indications: Steroid-resistant dermatomyositis or polymyositis, psoriatic arthritis, rheumatoid arthritis, other forms of synovitis.

Dosage: Often this drug is given intravenously or intramuscularly in intervals of one week to ten days followed by a week during which no drug is taken. The dose ranges from 20 to 50 mg each injection. If taken orally, as is usual in rheumatoid arthritis, the dose is usually 5 to 15 mg *per week* given in two or three doses, twelve hours apart; sometimes as a single weekly dose.

Side effects: These include opportunistic infections, mouth ulcers, and stomach problems. Damage to the liver, a special side effect of this drug, is particularly a problem if the drug is taken orally every day. When taken orally, this drug is absorbed by the intestine and passes through the liver on the way to general circulation. As a result, most doctors have discontinued this daily method of administration. Instead the drug is given intermittently, once a week, so that the liver has an opportunity to heal. Problems can still occur with the newer dose schedules, but are much less frequent. A severe problem with the lungs is occasionally seen with methotrexate. Cancer has *not* been reported.

Special hints: This drug is remarkably effective in many cases of rheumatoid arthritis and has become the preferred drug for many patients. Because of its remarkable effectiveness, it is now the most frequently used of the DMARDs. Regular blood tests are required, as with all of these drugs. Some doctors recommend liver biopsy to be sure that the liver is normal before starting the drug. However, this procedure is hazardous and seems unnecessary as long as blood liver tests are normal before the drug is started. We don't think that you should have a "baseline" liver biopsy like this. The blood liver tests should be checked every so often—perhaps at three- or six-week intervals during treatment—and the drug should be stopped if there is any suspicion of difficulty. Since alcohol also can damage the liver, alcohol intake should be extremely moderate during this period of methotrexate treatment. Some doctors recommend liver biopsy after a few years of treatment to make sure that no scarring has occurred. We believe that a follow-up biopsy is very seldom required, but this is a controversial question. At this time, there seem to be worse complications from liver biopsies (the death rate is between 1 in 1,000 and 1 in 10,000) than from methotrexate liver disease (no serious events reported yet). Patients who are taking Plaquenil together with methotrexate seem to have fewer liver test abnormalities.

Cytoxan (cyclophosphamide)

25 mg, 50 mg white with blue flecks, round tablets

Purpose: For immunosuppression.

Indications: Wegener's granulomatosis, severe systemic lupus erythematosus, polyarteritis, possibly severe rheumatoid arthritis.

Dosage: Usual dose is 100 to 150 mg (two to three tablets) daily.

Side effects: The dosage can be adjusted so that the white count is maintained in the low normal range. Severe bone-marrow cell depression can occur and cancer has followed use in laboratory animals. Opportunistic infections can result. Special side effects of Cytoxan include hair loss, which can be quite extensive, but usually reverses after the drug is discontinued, and bladder irritation. The drug is eliminated from the body through the kidneys and the eliminated products can cause blisters on the inside of the bladder. Scarring of the bladder and possibly even cancer of the bladder can occur after long-term use. Additionally, there is a decrease in the sperm count and, in women of childbearing age, there is damage to the eggs which can cause sterility. These effects are reversible at first, but irreversible later. Stomach or intestinal upset is noted by some patients. Leukemia has also been reported.

Special hints: Cytoxan may be the strongest of the immunosuppressant agents and it is probably the most toxic. Nitrogen mustard, which must be given intravenously, is a similar drug with many of the same side effects. It is not used frequently. Another drug that works similarly, chlorambucil, now is very seldom used because of its toxicity.

The bladder side effects can be minimized by drinking large amounts of water, and all patients taking this drug should try to drink an extra two quarts of liquid each day beyond their usual intake. This dilutes the toxic products in the bladder and minimizes the damage. Don't take this drug at bedtime because the urine concentrates overnight and stays in your bladder too long. Use of this drug should be reconsidered by patients planning to have children. Regular blood counts, every one or two weeks to start and no less frequently than once a month later, are required.

Imuran (azathioprine), 6-MP (6-mercaptopurine)

50 mg yellow to off-white, scored, overlapping circle-shaped tablet

Purpose: For immunosuppression.

Indications: Severe systemic lupus erythematosus, rheumatoid arthritis, psoriatic arthritis, steroid-resistant polymyositis or dermatomyositis.

Dosage: 100 to 150 mg (two or three tablets) daily is the usual dose.

Side effects: Azathioprine and 6-mercaptopurine are closely related drugs with almost identical actions. Azathioprine is the more frequently used. Side effects include opportunistic infections and possibility of late development of cancer, so far rare to absent in humans. Gastrointestinal (stomach) distress is occasionally noted. Hair loss is unusual, and there appears to be little effect on the sperm or the eggs. There are no bladder problems. Although liver damage has been reported, the drug is usually well tolerated.

Special hints: Regular blood tests are required. Patients taking these drugs should never take allopurinol (Zyloprim) at the same time since the combination of drugs can be fatal. Once the patient responds to this drug, it is often possible to reduce the dose. Theoretically, this decreases the risk of late side effects. Azathioprine has been shown to slow down the progression of rheumatoid arthritis and is very effective in some patients. Most people seem not to have any side effects but there is still concern about what might happen over the long run.

DRUGS TO REDUCE PAIN

This section is included mainly to emphasize that pain-reducing drugs except plain acetaminophen (Tylenol) have little place in the treatment of arthritis. Consider their four major disadvantages. First, they don't do anything for the arthritis; they just cover it up. Second, they help defeat the pain mechanism that tells you when you are doing something that is injuring your body. If you suppress it, you may injure your body without being aware of it. Third, the body adjusts to pain medicines, so that they aren't very effective over the long term. This phenomenon is called *tolerance* and develops to some extent with all of the drugs we commonly used. Fourth, pain medicines can have major side effects. The side effects range from stomach distress to constipation to mental changes. Most of these drugs are "downers," which you don't need if you have arthritis. You need to be able to cope with a somewhat more difficult living situation than the average person. These drugs decrease your ability to solve problems.

Many individuals develop a tragic dependence on these agents. In arthritis, the addiction is somewhat different from what we usually imagine. Most persons with arthritis are not truly addicted to codeine or Percodan or Demerol. They are psychologically dependent on these drugs as a crutch and become inordinately concerned with an attempt to eliminate every last symptom. These agents conflict with the attempt to achieve independent living.

By and large, use these drugs only for the short term and only when resting the sore part, so that you don't reinjure it while the pain is suppressed. Drugs mentioned first in this list are less harmful than those listed later. Drugs to reduce inflammation, discussed above, may reduce pain through direct pain action as well as through reduction of inflammation. This is preferable in inflammatory arthritis. In osteoarthritis plain acetaminophen (Tylenol, other brands) is often very useful as a non-toxic pain reliever.

These same principles hold for a number of less common pain relievers not described in the following section.

Acetaminophen (Tylenol, Other Brands)

325 mg white tablet or caplet
500 mg white tablet or caplet
500 mg yellow/red gel capsule

Purpose: For temporary relief of minor pain.

Indications: Mild temporary pain, particularly with cartilage degeneration (osteoarthritis).

Dosage: Two tablets (10 grains) every four hours as needed.

Side effects: Minimal. Unlike Aspirin, acetaminophen usually does not upset the stomach, does not cause ringing in the ears, does not affect the clotting of the blood, does not interact with other medications, and is about as safe as can be. Of course, as with any drug, there are occasional problems, but this drug is frequently recommended in place of Aspirin for children because of its greater safety. Acetaminophen is the only drug in this category that is not addictive.

Special hints: Acetaminophen is not anti-inflammatory; thus it is not an Aspirin substitute in the treatment of arthritis. If the condition is a noninflammatory one such as osteoarthrosis, then it may be approximately as useful as Aspirin with fewer side effects. It is only a mild pain reliever and therefore has fewer disadvantages than the following agents. It is relatively inexpensive. Advertised names, such as Tylenol, may be more expensive than other acetaminophens.

Darvon (Darvon Compound, Darvotran, Darvocet, Darvocet-N, propoxyphene)

Darvon
32 mg, 65 mg pink capsule
Darvon Compound
32 mg gray/pink capsule
65 mg gray/red capsule
Darvocet-N
50 mg, 100 mg dark orange, coated, capsule-shaped tablets

Purpose: Mild pain relief.

Indications: For short-term use in decreasing mild pain.

Dosage: One-half grain (32 mg) or one grain (65 mg) every four hours as needed for pain.

Side effects: These drugs are widely promoted and widely used with a reasonably good safety record. In some cases, side effects may be due to the Aspirin or other medication in combination with the Darvon. Most worrisome to us has been the mentally dull feeling that many individuals report, sometimes described as a gray semi-unhappy fog. Others do not seem to notice this effect. Side reactions include dizziness, headache, sedation, paradoxical excitement, skin rash, and gastrointestinal disturbances.

Special hints: Darvon is not anti-inflammatory and is thus not an Aspirin substitute. The pain relief given is approximately equal to Aspirin in most cases. The drug is more expensive than Aspirin or acetaminophen. It can induce dependence, particularly after long-term use.

Codeine (Empirin #1, 2, 3, 4; Aspirin with codeine #1, 2, 3, 4; Vicodin)

Codeine (Empirin)
15 mg, 30 mg, 60 mg white, round tablets
Vicodin
5 mg, 500 mg Aspirin white, capsule-shaped tablet

Purpose: Moderate pain relief.

Indications: For moderate pain relief over the short term.

Dosage: For some curious reason, the strength of codeine is often coded by number. For example, Empirin with codeine #1 or just Empirin #1 contains one-eighth grain or 8 mg of codeine per tablet, #2 contains one-fourth grain or 16 mg, #3 contains one-half grain or 32 mg, and #4 contains one grain or 65 mg of codeine phosphate. A common dosage is a #3 tablet (32 mg codeine) every four hours as needed for pain.

Side effects: The side effects are proportional to the dosage. The more you take, the more side effects you are likely to have. Allergic reactions are quite rare.

Codeine is a narcotic. Thus, it can lead to addiction, with tolerance and drug dependence. Frequently in persons with arthritis it leads to constipation and sometimes a set of complications including fecal impaction and diverticuli. More worrisome is the way that persons using codeine seem to lose their will to cope. The person taking codeine for many years sometimes seems sluggish and generally depressed. We don't really know if the codeine is responsible, but we do think that codeine often makes it more difficult for the person with arthritis to cope with the very real problems that abound. The older patient can develop substantial complications from constipation caused by the codeine.

Percodan (Percobarb, Percodan-Demi, Percogesic)

Percodan
yellow tablets
Percodan-Demi
pink tablets

Purpose: For pain relief.

Indications: For short-term relief of moderate to severe pain.

Dosage: One tablet every six hours as needed.

Side effects: Percodan is a curious combination drug. The basic narcotic is oxycodone, to which is added Aspirin and other minor pain relievers. Combination drugs have a number of theoretical disadvantages, but Percodan is a strong and effective reliever of pain. It does require a special prescription because it is a strong narcotic and the hazards of serious addiction are present. The manufacturers state that the habit-forming potentialities are somewhat less than morphine and somewhat greater than codeine. The drug is usually well tolerated.

Special hints: Percodan is a good drug for people with cancer, but it is very dangerous in the treatment of arthritis. It is not an anti-inflammatory agent and does not work directly on any of the disease processes. It is habit forming and it does break the pain reflex. It is a mental depressant, and serious addiction can result.

Demerol (meperidine)

Demerol-Hydrochloride
50 mg, 100 mg white, scored, round tablet
Demerol APAP
50 mg pink/dark pink splotches tablet

Purpose: For relief of severe pain such as in cancer, heart attacks, kidney stones.

Indications: For relief of severe pain, as with a bad fracture that has been immobilized.

Dosage: Various preparations come with 25 mg, 50 mg, or 100 mg of Demerol. One tablet every four hours for pain is a typical dose. Dose is increased for more severe pain and decreased for milder pain.

Side effects: Demerol is a major narcotic approximately equivalent to morphine in pain relief and in addiction potential. Tolerance develops and increasing doses may be required. Drug dependence and severe withdrawal symptoms may be seen if the drug is stopped. Psychological dependence also occurs. The underlying disease may be covered up and serious symptoms may be masked. Nausea, vomiting, constipation, and a variety of other side effects may occur.

Special hints: This is not a drug for the treatment of arthritis. Stay away from it.

TRANQUILIZERS

Valium, Librium, and other tranquilizers are among the most prescribed drugs in North America. They do not help arthritis. These drugs depress the patient and should be avoided by persons with arthritis whenever possible.

MUSCLE RELAXANTS

Soma, Flexeril, and a number of other agents are prescribed frequently as "muscle relaxants." In general, these act like tranquilizers. They treat only symptoms, and are usually not helpful in arthritis. One exception: Flexeril is sometimes useful against fibromyalgia.

NAMES AND AVAILABILITIES

Some drugs are known by different names in the United States, Canada, New Zealand, and Australia. In addition, because of the different governments' approvals, some drugs available in one country are not available in another. All prescription drugs must be taken under the direction of a medical doctor, however, so follow his or her guidelines on what to use.

U.S.	Canada	Great Britain	Australia	New Zealand
(Acetylsalicylic Acid) Aspirin, Ecotrin, Disalcid	Aspirin, Arthrinol, Arthrin, Ecotrin, Entrophen, Artria, Arthrisan	Palaprin, Benoral	Ecotrin, Arthritis-strength aspirin	Aspro, Ecotrin, Disprin, SRA, Aspec, Hedex
Trilisate (Choline Magnesium Trisalicylate)	Same	Same	Unavailable	Unavailable
Nuprin, Advil (Ibuprofen)	Amersol, Advil (APO-Ibuprofen)	Brufen	Brufen	Nurofen, Pamored
Ansaid (Flurbiprofen)	Ansaid, Froben	Froben	Unavailable	Unavailable
Butazolidin (Phenylbutazone)	Same	Same	Same (for hospital treatment of Ankylosing Spondylitis only)	Same (for resistant Ankylosing Spondylitis only)
Tandearil (Oxyphenbutazone)	(Oxybutazone)	Tanderil	Unavailable	Unavailable
Clinoril (Sulindac)	Same (APO-Sulin)	Same	Same	Clinoril, Daclin, Saldac
Dolobid (Diflunisal)	Same	Same	Same	Same

U.S.	Canada	Great Britain	Australia	New Zealand
Feldene (Piroxicam)	Same (APO-Piroxicam)	Same	Same	Same
Indocin (Indomethacin)	Indocid, Indocid SR (APO-Indomethacin)	Indocid	Indocid	Indocid, Arthrexin, Rheumacin
Meclomen (Meclofenamate)	Unavailable	Unavailable	Unavailable	Unavailable
Motrin, Rufen (Ibuprofen)	Motrin, Medipren, Actiprofen (Ibuprofen)	Same	Rafen, Inflam, Rheumacin	Brufen, Inflam
Nalfon (Fenoprofen)	Same	Fenopron	Unavailable	Fenopron
Naprosyn (Naproxen)	Same (APO-Naproxen)	Same	Same	Naprosyn, Naxen, Noflam
Tolectin (Tolmetin Sodium)	Same	Same	Unavailable	Unavailable
Voltaren (Diclofenac)	Voltaren SR	Voltarol	Same	Same
Prednisone (oral steroid)	Prednisone, Delfasone, Paracort	Prednisolene, Betamethasone, Dexamethasone	Same	Prednisone, Delta Cortelan
Depo-Medrol (injectable steroid)	Same	Depo-Medrone	Same	Depot-Medrol
Myochrisine, Solganol (injectable gold salts)	Same	Same	Myocrisin	Myocrisin
Ridaura (Auranofin)	Same	Same	Same	Same
Penicillamine (Cuprimine)	Cuprimine, Depen	Penicillamine, Depamine (Distamine, pendramine)	D. Penamine, Perdolat	D. Penamine
Plaquenil (Hydroxychloroquine)	Plaquenil, Aralen	Same	Same	Same
Azulfidine (Sulfasalazine)	Salazopyrine	Salazopyrin	Salazopyrin	Salazopyrin, Colizine
Methotrexate	Same	Same	Ledertrexate	Same
Cytoxan (Cyclophosphamide)	Cytoxan, Procytox	(Cyclophosphamide)	Cycloblastin (Cyclophosphamide)	Cycloblastin (Cyclophosphamide)
Imuran (Azathioprine)	Same	Same	Same	Imuran, Azamun, Thioprine

U.S.	Canada	Great Britain	Australia	New Zealand
(Acetaminophin) Tylenol	Tylenol, Atasol	(Paracetamol), Panadol	(Paracetamol), Panadol	(Paracetamol), Panadol, Pamol, Disprol, P-500
Darvon (Propoxyphene)	Darvon-N, Frosst 642	Doloxene, Distalgesic (Dextropropoxyphene)	Digesic (Dextropropoxyphene and paracetamol)	Doloxene (Dextropropoxyphene and paracetamol, Digesic, Capadex)
Codeine	Frosst Codeine Phosphate	Same	Same	Same
Percodan (Percobarb, Percogesic)	Percodan-Demi (Percocet)	Unavailable	Unavailable	Unavailable
Demerol (Meperidine)	Same	Pamergan (Pethidine)	Unavailable	Unavailable

Generic names are listed in parenthesis.

18

Working with Your Doctor

A Joint Venture

CHOOSING A DOCTOR

There are many different kinds of doctors and sometimes it is difficult to know what kind to work with for what. Fortunately, most people with arthritis do not need a specialist on a regular basis. Therefore, it often is best to find a doctor who can help you with all of your health problems. For most of you, this will be an internist or a family practitioner.

An *internist* is a doctor who has had special training in the care of adults. Internists take care of all common adult health problems, including arthritis. A *family practitioner* has special training in taking care of all the common health problems that occur in a family. Thus, a family practitioner may assist at the birth of a baby and also take care of grandmother's arthritis. As a general rule, the fewer doctors you have, the better coordinated your health care will be.

For people with difficult arthritis, a *rheumatologist* can be a big help. Rheumatologists are internists with additional training in arthritis and rheumatic diseases. If your arthritis is resistant to treatment, or if you have any kind of inflammatory arthritis such as psoriatic arthritis, systemic lupus, or juvenile arthritis, seek out a rheumatologist.

Most important, if you have rheumatoid arthritis, we strongly advise that you see a rheumatologist as early in the disease as possible and periodically thereafter. As we noted in Chapter 17, rheumatoid arthritis is sometimes best managed by early and continued use of the disease-modifying drugs (DMARDs). Rheumatologists are the doctors most familiar with these drugs and are most comfortable with their early use; other doctors tend to use them "too little, too late."

To find a rheumatologist, look in your telephone directory or ask your doctor if he or she thinks that a referral might be of help. (Unfortunately, not all communities have physicians listed by specialty.) You can also get a list of rheumatologists in your area from the nearest office of the Arthritis Foundation or Arthritis Society. An orthopedic surgeon can be of great help in particular instances, and do not hesitate to ask your doctor to arrange a consultation.

A word of warning: Some people spend a great deal of time and money doctor shopping. They go from doctor to doctor looking for a cure. Unfortunately, doctor shoppers lose out by not having one physician get to know them and be able to build an optimal treatment plan over time. The best advice is to find a doctor you like and stick with him or her. Often, with severe arthritis, nearly all of your care should be provided by a rheumatologist.

COMMUNICATING WITH YOUR DOCTOR

This is a huge subject and probably causes more concern than anyone wishes to admit. Let us first examine expectations.

When someone goes to the doctor, he or she usually wants relief of symptoms and/or reassurance that all is well. He or she may also want information about health or illness. On the other hand, the doctor wants the person to get well and usually feels that the best way to accomplish this is by following medical advice. The patient often recognizes the need for communication more than the doctor does.

A shortened version of a typical encounter with a doctor might go something like this:

PATIENT: Doctor, I have a pain in my knee.

DOCTOR: How long have you had the pain? (Meanwhile, the knee is being examined.)

PATIENT: Six months.

DOCTOR: I think you have arthritis. I want you to exercise, take Aspirin, and lose some weight. Let me know how you are feeling in a month or so.

Meanwhile, the patient is thinking: "How much Aspirin? Does he want me to jog at my age? What does weight have to do with all this? Is this just what he tells everyone? Why doesn't he give me some good medicine? He just wants to get rid of me."

And the doctor is thinking: "I know he or she won't do those things; my patients never do. I wish I knew how to get people to realize that Aspirin, proper exercise, and weight control are the best treatment for osteoarthritis. Patients always want a miracle cure, and we just don't have one."

The fact is that arthritis can be a very frustrating disease for both doctor and patient because there often is not any quick, easy answer.

Before continuing, let's look at some research answers about doctors and patients. Doctors think that patients ought to know a great deal about arthritis. They also believe that patients know very little. The reality is that patients know more than doctors think they know, but patients often don't ask questions or seek information. And some of the information patients have is wrong.

Thus, there are several important things you can do to communicate with your doctor:

1.   Ask questions. To be sure you don't forget, go to your appointment with a written list of two or three important questions. Think about exactly what you want from this visit. Don't wait for the doctor to ask for questions. Ask them when you first enter the office. Research has shown that it is important to ask questions early in the appointment. Later, if you don't understand something, ask. "How many Aspirin?" "What kind of exercise?" "Why should I lose weight?" "What do you mean by *synovitis?*"

2.   If for some reason you know you won't or can't follow the doctor's advice, let the doctor know. For example, "I won't take Aspirin. It gives me stomach problems." "Clinoril may be good but I can't afford it." "I hate exercise." "I would like to lose weight, but I can't seem to give up chocolate and need help."

       Often, if your doctor knows why you can't or won't follow advice, alternative suggestions can be made to help you over the hump. If you don't share your problems, there is no hope of finding solutions.

3.   If you have problems with your treatment, let your doctor know. Don't just stop or change doctors. Since much arthritis treatment is trial and error, you must work with your doctor.

4.   Finally, don't be afraid to ask financial questions. You have a right to know how much an appointment will cost. You can ask the receptionist when you call the doctor's office. If you feel a treatment is too expensive, ask if there are any alternatives. For example, an exercise class at the Y or senior citizen center may be as effective as working with a physical therapist. You may be able to test your own urine at home. There are almost always solutions to such problems if they are discussed.

In short to get the most from your doctor, be a **CAD:**

Come prepared, **A**sk questions, **D**iscuss problems

PROBLEMS

Over the years, we have heard many complaints about doctors and would like to discuss a few of these.

1. **My doctor never has time.**   It is true that physicians are busy. Unlike people in business, they do not have a product to sell. All they have is time. If you know you want to talk with your doctor, ask for more time when you make your appointment. Most offices are run so that a certain amount of time is allotted for each type of visit. For example, five to ten minutes for a brief follow-up, fifteen to twenty minutes for a short visit, and thirty to forty-five minutes for a complete physical. You can ask for as much time as you need. However, you must indicate the amount of time you want when you make your appointment, not when you arrive at the office. Also, you should expect to pay for this extra time.

Another way you can make time is to go to the office prepared. Bring a written list of your questions. Give this list to the doctor when you first start the visit and be sure they are answered before you leave. Don't count on remembering. All of us are a little nervous when we visit the doctor, and it's very easy to forget.

2. **All my doctor does is try one pill after another.**   Unfortunately, there is no way your physician can know for sure what medication will work for you. You may need to try a number of medications before you find the right combination. This trial-and-error method can be expensive. Therefore, when you start a new medication, ask how long it will be until you know if the drug will be good for you. If you will know in a short time, request a prescription for only a week or two, with refills of the prescription permitted. In this way, you can try the medication, and if it doesn't work, you will not have a lot of expensive pills to throw away. Sometimes the doctor will have free sample packages available. Don't be discouraged if you have to try several different medications. Also, don't hesitate to let your doctor know if you have problems with a medication or if it is not working. If you have a problem with a drug and do not have an appointment in the near future, contact your doctor by phone.

3. **My doctor never tells me anything about my medications.**   Again, time is often a factor, or maybe you didn't ask. If you want more information about your medications, first ask your physician. If this is not satisfactory, you can ask the pharmacist. Pharmacists are an underutilized resource for drug information. This book can answer some of the most common questions.

4. **There is no cure; there is nothing my doctor can do anyway.**   Yes and no. While it is true there is no cure for many types of arthritis, there is a great deal that can be done. Diabetes is another disease with no cure. However, insulin and appropriate medical care enable diabetics to live nearly normal lives. No diabetic would think of saying that because there was no cure, physicians can't do anything.

For people with arthritis, medical attention can do a number of things. First, just knowing what one has relieves a lot of worry; this in itself is valuable. Second, physicians may be able to prescribe treatment to make life easier. Third, with many types of arthritis, medical treatment can control the disease or keep it from progressing. Thus, while it is true that doctors often can't cure arthritis, they often can help you help yourself in living more comfortably.

5. **My doctor uses language I can't understand.** Unfortunately, doctors are so used to talking "doctor-talk" that they sometimes exclude the rest of us. They don't do this on purpose or even realize they are doing it. The situation is simple. If you don't understand something, ask. Never be afraid to speak up.

6. **My doctor ignores my ideas about self-care.** Now, this is a hard one. Often, doctors are not trained in use of alternative therapies and, like all of us, tend to downplay things they don't know about. On the other hand, physicians have a responsibility to let you know when a proposed treatment has little scientific merit or is just plain harmful. At our Arthritis Center, we get hundreds of calls a year about all kinds of treatments. We tell people what we know or don't know and try to warn them of possible harms. We, and your doctor, also feel a responsibility to prevent folks from spending large amounts of money on treatments with potential harm or no effect.

If your doctor disregards your ideas, then you have an extra responsibility to find out about the treatment. Generally, if the treatment is free or inexpensive and does not have harmful side effects, go ahead and try it if you wish. On the other hand, be very conscious of expensive treatments (someone is making money off of you). Treatments that promise a cure, or anything with the word *miracle* attached to it, are *never* miracle cures!

7. **My doctor never listens to me.** A good relationship takes two people, people who have similar ideas and are able to communicate. If you feel your doctor is not listening to you, we suggest you discuss it. You can start by saying something like, "Dr. Jones, sometimes I feel you don't hear what I'm saying." This takes some nerve, but we can promise that it will open up the communication process.

Another way to get your doctor to listen is to be brief and to the point. You might even practice before going in. Think out exactly what you want to say; this will make it easier.

8. **I don't feel comfortable talking with my doctor.** This is a problem common to many of us. We have already discussed many ways you can make communication easier. Here is one more. Whenever you want to have a serious conversation with your doctor, plan to do it while you are dressed. It is hard to feel comfortable in your underwear or an examination gown.

Sometimes the personalities of the physician and the patient just don't fit. If you have tried to open up communications and it hasn't worked, then maybe it is time to find a new doctor. Not every patient can like every doctor and vice versa. Doctors sometimes wish they had the option of changing patients. You do have this option, and when necessary, don't be afraid to use it. Good patient-physician relationships are important.

A doctor's addendum: I have never seen a person with arthritis that I couldn't help. There are some individuals, however, that I have not helped. In every such case, the communication broke down. Sometimes I am short of time or short of temper. Sometimes the person doesn't listen or doesn't hear or doesn't understand. Often, a preconceived opinion is the problem. "Aspirin won't work." "My neighbor couldn't tolerate that drug." "I hardly eat a thing." "She seems too old to exercise." "I don't think he would understand." Or a person who reports being worse never filled a prescription, stopped an exercise program after two days, decreased medication ("It was too expensive"), and never mentioned the problem. A solid half of the blame lies with the doctor. Sometimes we do not listen or have our own preconceived ideas. No matter how hard we try we don't always get it right. But the other half of the blame lies with the patient. Tell it true and straight and we can help. This is a partnership. We don't always have to agree to get good results. But the give-and-take of direct communication is essential.

—J. F.

SURGERY

Surgery is one of the things you might want to talk over with your doctor. The greatest single advances in treatment of rheumatoid arthritis and osteoarthritis over the past twenty years have been surgical: the development of joint replacement surgery. We do not discuss surgery for arthritis in detail in this book, since every decision is individual and requires a great deal of discussion between you and your doctor. When considering surgery, think it over. Talk it over. Decide. Here are ten general considerations to keep in mind if the question of surgery comes up.

1. Arthritis surgery is seldom urgent. These are "elective" operations, and should be undertaken when the disability and pain from a joint have failed medical management and justify the pain, risk, and expense of the operation. You don't have to decide in a hurry. Think it over. Get multiple opinions. Take your time.

2. Arthritis surgery does not replace medical management and self-management. Instead, it means that you must pay particular care to the other parts of your treatment program.

3. Surgery is most likely to be productive when you are in good shape. Your exercise program is critical to getting you ready for surgery and for recovering from it.

4. Surgery works best when one joint (or a few joints) is causing most of your problems. If many joints are severely affected, surgery on just a few will have limited benefit.

5. Surgery works better on large joints than on small ones. The intricacies of operation and recovery are such that the postoperative scarring in small joints may reduce the benefit.

6. Total joint replacement usually provides better results than lesser operations. The most dramatic surgical advances have been made in replacement operations for the joints. In particular, pain relief is greatest with these operations.

7. Total joint replacement is most predictably beneficial in the hip, then in the knee. Procedures for other joints are newer and less established, but getting better.

8. Total joint replacements don't last forever. A good average for hip replacement, for example, is fifteen years. Procedures for replacement of the replacement are good and getting better, and the current models of prosthetic joints look like they will last longer than the older ones.

9. Hand operations, with or without artificial joints, are better at restoring appearance than at restoring function. Best results tend to be when a deformity, such as subluxation, is itself interfering with function.

10. Relatively simple operations, such as bunionectomy or removal of a Morton's neuroma, can sometimes be dramatically effective.

References

Fries, James. F. *Aging Well*. Reading, MA: Addison-Wesley, 1989.

Pantell, Robert H., James F. Fries, and Donald M. Vickery. *Taking Care of Your Child*. 3rd ed. Reading, MA: Addison-Wesley, 1990.

Vickery, Donald M., and James F. Fries. *Take Care of Yourself*. 4th ed. Reading, MA: Addison-Wesley, 1989.

The Arthritis Foundation and the Arthritis Society

The Arthritis Foundation in the United States, New Zealand, and Australia and the Arthritis Society in Canada are truly marvelous institutions. They sponsor programs in public education and professional education, support young professionals establishing research careers in arthritis, and provide direct support for research activities. They lead the fight for increased government programs of research and service.

The Arthritis Foundation or Society consists of a national office and local chapters or branches around the country. You will usually want to contact the local chapter, which can advise you of doctors and clinics in your area, provide instructional materials, and occasionally help with financial problems. There may be a schedule of activities you could attend. Or you might want to volunteer your efforts.

In the United States look in the telephone directory under Arthritis Foundation or call 1-800-283-7800 for toll-free information. The address of the national office is:

The Arthritis Foundation
1314 Spring St., N.W.
Atlanta, GA 30309

For addresses in New Zealand, Australia, and Canada, look at the following list:

Arthritis Foundation of New
  Zealand
National Office
P.O. Box 10-020
Wellington
Telephone: (04) 721-427

ARTHRITIS FOUNDATION OF
VICTORIA
Yarra Boulevard
Kew, Victoria 3101
Telephone: (61) 3-862-2555
            3-862-2022

Arthritis Foundation of Australia
National Office
P.O. Box 121
Sydney NSW 2001
Telephone: (02) 221-2456

AFA Tasmania
84 Hampden Road
Battery Point Hobart 7000
Telephone: (002) 34-6489
            23-7318

AFA New South Wales
P.O. Box 370
Darlinghurst NSW 2010
Telephone: (02) 281-1611

AFA Australian Capital Territory
P.O. Box 352
Woden ACT 2606
Telephone: (062) 81-6814

AFA Queensland
P.O. Box 901
Toowong QLD 4066
Telephone: (07) 371-9755

Western Australia Arthritis &
  Rheumatism Foundation
  (WAARF)
P.O. Box 34
Wembeley WA 6014
Telephone: (09) 387-7066

AFA South Australia
99 Anzac Highway
Ashford SA 5035
Telephone: (08) 297-2488

AFA Northern Territory
P.O. Box 2045
Darwin NT 0821

Arthritis Society of Canada
National Office
250 Bloor Street East, Suite 401
Toronto, Ontario M4W 3P2
Telephone: (416) 967-1414

Newfoundland Division
Box 522, Station C
St. John's, Newfoundland A1C 5K4

Prince Edward Island Division
P.O. Box 1537
Charlottetown, P.E.I. C1A 7N3

Nova Scotia Division
5516 Spring Garden Road
Halifax, Nova Scotia B3J 1G6
Telephone: (902) 429-7025

New Brunswick Division
65 Brunswick Street
Fredericton, New Brunswick
E3B 1G5
Telephone: (506) 454-6114

Quebec Division
2075 University Street, Suite 1206
Montreal, Quebec H3A 2L1
Telephone: (514) 842-4026/4848

Ontario Division
250 Bloor Street East, Suite 401
Toronto, Ontario M4W 3P2
Telephone: (416) 967-1414

Manitoba Division
386 Broadway Avenue, Suite 105
Winnipeg, Manitoba R3C 3R6
Telephone: (204) 942-4892

Saskatchewan Division
864 Victoria Avenue East
Regina, Saskatchewan S4N 0P2
Telephone: (306) 352-3312

Alberta Division
301, 1301–8th Street S.W.
Calgary, Alberta T2R 1B7
Telephone: (403) 228-2571/2572

British Columbia and Yukon
  Division
895 West 10th Avenue
Vancouver, British Columbia
V5Z 1L7
Telephone: (604) 879-7511

Index

247

ARTHRITIS: A Comprehensive Guide to Understanding Your Arthritis

Third Edition

James F. Fries, M.D.

The Companion Volume to THE ARTHRITIS HELPBOOK
The Book that Answers All Your Questions About Arthritis

You can have much more control over your arthritis than you think. In this enormously helpful book, arthritis expert Dr. James Fries has created a program that will help you take an active role in understanding and defeating your arthritis. Fully revised to include the most up-to-date medical information, Dr. Fries' 3-step program shows you how to:

- Identify the kind of arthritis you have
- Work with a doctor to choose the best treatment and medication program
- Cope with the daily problems of pain

Thirty-one easy-to-read decision charts illustrate when to use home treatment and when to consult a doctor. There's also sensitive advice on dealing with emotional and sexual difficulties and a section that answers common questions about employment. With a wealth of information on all aspects of arthritis, no one who has arthritis can afford to be without this book. Ask for ARTHRITIS by James Fries at your bookstore, or send the coupon below to:

Addison-Wesley Publishing Company
General Books Division
Retail Sales
Reading, MA 01867
